ESSAY

ON THE TRUE ART

OF PLAYING

KEYBOARD
INSTRUMENTS

An engraving by F. C. Kruger, Sons, Berlin, which appeared in *Allgemeine Deutsche Bibliothek*, Vol. 34, Berlin and Stettin, 1778

ESSAY

ON THE TRUE ART

OF PLAYING

KEYBOARD

INSTRUMENTS

By

Carl Philipp Emanuel Bach

Translated and Edited by

WILLIAM J. MITCHELL

ASSOCIATE PROFESSOR OF MUSIC, COLUMBIA UNIVERSITY

W · W · NORTON & COMPANY · INC · *New York*

PRINTED IN THE UNITED STATES OF AMERICA

To Heidi, in grateful appreciation of her active interest in the manuscript and willingness to assume many of its burdens, and to Judy and Tommy for their forbearing good behavior during its preparation.

PREFACE

THE PRESENT edition of Bach's *Versuch über die wahre Art das Clavier zu spielen* is the first complete English translation, having been preceded only by excerpts and sections which appear principally in books by Dannreuther, Dolmetsch, and Arnold. It is also the eleventh in the complete series of printings, reissues, and editions going back to the publication in 1753 of the original edition of Part One. Published privately by Bach, it was set up by the court printer to Frederick the Great, Christian Friedrich Henning. A second printing was made in 1759 at Berlin by George Ludewig Winter, again with the author as publisher. The same pair produced the first edition of Part Two in 1762. Remaining copies of both parts along with manuscript supplements were sold to Engelhardt Benjamin Schwickert of Leipzig, who reissued the work in 1780, the year of the transaction. The nature of this edition will be discussed in the Introduction that follows. The first and only revision of Part One was published in 1787 along with an unaltered Part Two by Schwickert, who also issued Part Two, revised, in 1797. Thus, on the face of it, the Essay appeared four times during the eighteenth century.

In 1852 Gustav Schilling edited the Essay "in the raiment and after the needs of our time." But raiment and needs combined to produce only a curious distortion of the original. It was published in Herzberg by Franz Mohr, and reappeared in 1856, published by Franz Stage of Berlin.

In our own century, Walter Niemann prepared an abridged edition, disrespectfully ignoring Bach's stern reproof of all "compendium writers." This publication, based on the editions of 1759 and 1762, first appeared in 1906, published by C. F. Kahnt of Leipzig. It was reprinted in 1917, 1920, and 1925. It has not been possible to secure additional information about a projected new German edition "with manuscript supplements," which was announced several times during the last decade. It is to be published by Gustav Bosse of Regensburg.

The present translation combines the original and revised editions of the eighteenth century. All of Bach's alterations, additions, and footnotes have been incorporated into the main text, but are identified in the editor's notes. For the rest, the organization of material in Part One follows the German text in all details. Part Two, however, has been slightly altered in order to make it more accessible to the reader. The original edition and all subsequent ones consisted of forty-one separate chapters, some hardly a page in length. The sequence of these suggested a larger organization. Thus, without altering the order of these chapters, but simply by demoting many of them to the rank of sections, the total has been reduced to four. The first and last alone retain their original status. But twenty successive chapters, following the first, have been grouped under the heading Thorough Bass, and the next nineteen under the heading Accompaniment, this being the subject matter of these originally separate chapters.

The musical examples for Part One were originally engraved and published under separate cover. These have been placed in the text and numbered serially throughout. The examples for Part Two were originally printed in with the text, but were unnumbered. For purposes of easy reference and maintenance of order these also have been numbered in continuation of the examples to Part One. In preparing them for the present edition, the C-clef which Bach used for the right-hand staff, after the dying fashion of his time, was discarded in favor of the more familiar G-clef.

As part of the illustrative material for Part One, Bach wrote *Achtzehn Probestücke in sechs Sonaten.* Bound originally with the examples, they are an integral part of the entire work. With respect to technical and interpretative problems contained in them, they range from fairly easy to quite difficult. At least one of the pieces, the free fantasia of the last Sonata, is among the finest of Bach's works. It achieved immediate and lasting fame in the eighteenth century. To the revision of 1787 Bach added *VI Sonatine Nuove.* Written in his broad, later style, they seem to have been designed to form an introduction to the more challenging earlier pieces. The relatively large format that would be required for a practicable edition of all of these made it impossible to include them here. However, they are available in modern editions, the *Probestücke* having been published by Schott, and the *Sonatine Nuove* by Nagel. Also, all but the first sonata of the *Probestücke* appear in volume 11 of *Le Trésor des pianistes*, Paris, 1861–72.

Translation and editing of the *Versuch* would have been a far more difficult, if not an impossible, task had it not been for the generous assistance of my colleagues, members of our library staff, and my students. I am particularly indebted to Professor Erich Hertzmann for much wise counsel, to Mrs. Susanne Morse, who edited the manuscript with great care, to Miss Jane Paul, who patiently trailed and captured many elusive details of information, and to Mr. Wolf Franck of the Music Division of the New York Public Library, who brought to my attention several choice items that would otherwise have escaped me.

W.J.M.

CONTENTS

ILLUSTRATIONS

INTRODUCTION

SOON AFTER Emanuel Bach's death on December 14, 1788, plans were formed to erect a commemorative monument in the *Michaeliskirche* in Hamburg. To this project, which did not mature, the renowned poet and Bach admirer, Friedrich Gottlieb Klopstock, contributed an epitaph:

> Tarry not, imitators,
> For you must blush if you remain.
> Carl Philipp Emanuel Bach,
> Profoundest harmonist,
> United novelty and beauty;
> Was great
> In text-led strains
> But greater yet
> In bold, wordless music;
> Surpassed the inventor of keyed instruments,
> For he raised the art of performance
> Through teaching
> And practice
> To its perfection.

Something less than inspired, it has value as a catalogue of Bach's principal activities, and as a summary of the basis of his fame in the minds of his contemporaries. Our chief concern here is with the Bach who "raised the art of performance, through teaching and practice, to its perfection."

The most famous pupil of Bach was his youngest brother, Johann Christian, who studied with him during the four years he spent in Berlin after his father's death. Another was the widely known Czech pianist, Jan Ladislav Dussek, who spent about a year at Hamburg in 1783 with Bach, after having already come into prominence. Dussek was praised by both Haydn and Mendelssohn, and described

1

in W. J. Tomaschek's Autobiography as being "the first pianist who placed his instrument sideways on the platform, in which our pianoforte heroes now all follow him, though they have no very interesting profile to exhibit." It is doubtful that he learned this as any essential part of his study with Bach.

Other pupils were less well known, such as Nikolaus Joseph Hüllmandel, the Königsberg organist Carl Gottlieb Richter, Friedrich Wilhelm Rust, and Carl Fasch, who alternated with and later succeeded Bach as accompanist to Frederick the Great, after being coached in the musical idiosyncrasies of the flute-playing monarch. For the rest, a good deal of Bach's teaching was directed to the amateurs in whom he had an enduring interest.

But it would be a gross injustice to both him and his pupils to limit Bach's influence solely to those who studied directly with him. His fame as the founder of a school was achieved much more significantly through the agency of his music and the *Essay*. The latter was called by Haydn "the school of all schools." And Mozart, Beethoven, and Clementi added their endorsements, speaking uniformly of Bach as one whose music must be studied, not simply played. Beethoven, after hearing the young Czerny perform in 1801, turned to the father and said, "The boy has talent; I shall take him as my own student and teach him. Send him to me once a week. Be sure to procure Emanuel Bach's instruction book on the *True Art of Playing Keyboard Instruments,* so that he may bring it to his next lesson." Czerny goes on to relate that Beethoven's method followed the *Essay* closely and included the playing of the *Probestücke*. All of these men, especially Haydn, who discovered Bach early in life and never forgot him, can be called his pupils in this broader sense of the term.

The *Essay* became famous as an instruction book almost immediately and reached many students throughout the latter half of the 18th century. No record is available of the number of copies that were printed, but an idea of the rate of its distribution can be gained by consulting a letter that Bach wrote to Engelhardt Benjamin Schwickert, April 10, 1780. In it he expressed his willingness to turn over control of the work to this Leipzig publisher. He wrote in part: "I can now say with certainty that I still possess 260 copies of Part One and 564 of Part Two." For these 824 copies, with the examples to Part One and manuscript revisions to the entire book, Bach asked and evidently received 180 louis d'or. To dispel any false notion that the matter was urgent, Bach added shrewdly, "I am no more obliged to sell than you are to buy." The transaction was completed.

The 824 copies, some going back 21 years, others 18, must represent only the lesser part of the total printed in 1753, 1759, and 1762. But more information is provided by the fact that Schwickert, who most certainly was not inclined to destroy merchandise on which Bach placed a retail price of 3 thalers an item, reissued the *Essay* in 1780 by simply altering the title page of the acquired copies to make room for the name of the new publisher. The title page of this so-called "Third Edition" retained the revealing *"Zweite Auflage"* of the edition of 1759.

The 260 copies of Part One must have been largely sold by 1787, when Schwickert issued the revised edition, and the 564 copies of Part Two had been exhausted by 1797, when it reappeared in revision. This represents a yearly average sale of between 30 and 40 copies for each part, which, if extended backward to the original years of publication, would suggest that up to the appearance of the revisions between 1000 and 1500 copies of each part had been printed and sold. A modern publisher would sniff disdainfully at such paltry figures, but it should be kept in mind that the reading public in the 18th century was far smaller than it is today. Also, methods of printing and distribution were extremely modest. The publisher Göschen later (1787–90) printed 2000 copies of Goethe's *Werke*, but could find no more than 602 subscribers to the series. And sales of the individual volumes were even smaller. The Jena *Litteratur Zeitung*, a very popular and widely read journal of the time, achieved its success on issues of 2000 copies, according to a letter written by Göschen to Wieland. For a work like the *Essay*, designed for a very limited public, to reach our suggested, conservatively estimated number of copies, is indeed impressive, when compared with these other figures. It must also be remembered that the copying and borrowing of books were widespread practices at this time. Hence 1000 to 1500 copies served many more than the equivalent number of readers.

Other indications of the spread of Bach's *Essay*, but with totally unsatisfactory results, are found in an open letter of protest that the author published in the *Hamburger unpartheiischer Correspondent,* 1773, No. 7. Dated January 11, 1773, it runs in part:

I have observed with greatest satisfaction the change that has come over the world of keyboard playing since the publication of my Essay. I can assert without boasting that since its appearance, teaching and playing have improved. And yet I must regret that my high motives have innocently given rise to old and even worse barbarisms. Vain and selfish addlepates are no longer satisfied with playing their own fabrications creditably and forcing them on their students. No! They must seek immortality through authorship. As a result so many school and text books have appeared since my Essay that no end of them can be seen. I have been injured most by those that contain stolen passages both with and without acknowledgment. Plagiarizing is free to all and I have nothing to say against it. But it is most harmful to strip plagiarizations of their proper contexts, and explain or apply them incorrectly. Everyone knows the damage that can be done by an incorrect fingering, a wrong explanation and application of embellishments, a thoroughly bad chord. I can assert without anger, and in truth, that every instruction book that I have seen since the publication of my Essay (and I believe I have seen them all) is filled with errors. What I say can be proved if necessary.

However, the *Essay* in its uncorrupted form reached all parts of the Continent. "Sale of my works is chiefly in the North, in Russia, Livonia, Courland, Sweden, Denmark, Holstein, Hanover, Mecklenburg, in Lauenburg, and Lübeck . . . ," wrote Bach in the letter to Schwickert. But it also made its way southward. Czerny, for one, procured his copy in Vienna. Thus the seed of the Bach influence was widely scattered. Some concept of the impact of his music and *Essay* on the 18th century can be gained from Mozart's famous sweeping statement, as quoted by Rochlitz: "He is the father, we are the children. Those of us who do anything right, learned it from him. Whoever does not own to this is a scoundrel."

The evidence that is provided by such testimony from many sources, and by the sale and spread of the *Essay,* makes it clear that Emanuel Bach's contributions were no small part of the forces that directed the leading musical activities of the time. It should not be necessary to seek for superficial thematic similarities between his works and others' in order to prove this. Mozart gave succinct expression to the relationship of the music of his generation to Bach's: "We can no longer do as he did; but the way in which he did it places him beyond all others." It takes a true student to make so profound an observation. Rochlitz, the source of this as well as the preceding statement, is not always dependable; but in this case he can be trusted, simply because he lacked the insight necessary for the formulation of so penetrating an observation.

It is not pointless to inquire after the teachers of this teacher. Dr. Charles Burney in his *Present State of Music* wrote of Bach: "How he formed his style, where he acquired all his taste and refinement, would be difficult to trace; he certainly neither inherited nor adopted them from his father . . ." But in his *History*, he asserts, "It appears from Hasse's operas, where Emanuel Bach acquired his fine vocal taste in composing lessons, so different from the dry and laboured style of his father." Philipp Emanuel was indeed a great admirer of *Il caro Sassone*, as the Italians called that favored composer of operas, but it is certain that the *Essay* owes much to Johann Sebastian. "In composition and keyboard performance, I have never had any teacher but my father," we are told in the Autobiography. Repeatedly in the *Essay* he mentions his indebtedness to his father.

But a large part of the practical wisdom contained in it must have been gathered during the years that he spent at the court in Berlin. Engaged informally in 1738 by Frederick, the crown prince, he was appointed to his position as chamber cembalist on the new king's accession in 1740. We read in Emanuel's Autobiography: "I . . . had the honor to accompany alone at the harpsichord the first flute solo that he played as king at Charlottenburg."

Bach absorbed much through his duties at the court. His presence was required almost daily, for he played the accompaniments at the king's private concerts. These chamber concerts were held from 7 to 9 P.M. except on Mondays and Fridays, when Frederick the Great attended the opera. Punctuality was the king's rule in all affairs, hence the musicians found it advisable to be assembled before the required time. Precisely at 7 he would appear and sound the pitch. Earlier, the waiting musicians could hear him rehearsing the more challenging passages of the evening.

There was not much variety over the years. Usually the main fare consisted of about six concertos played by the monarch. Later this number was reduced to three or four. Most of these were composed by Johann Joachim Quantz, flute virtuoso, whose playing had aroused the young Frederick's interest in that instrument. Frederick had received flute lessons from Quantz regularly since 1727, and the teacher wrote approximately 300 concertos for the exclusive use of the king. Occasionally, Frederick played one of his own works. Quantz and other instrumentalists played too, their performances being varied with arias sung by the court singers.

Emanuel Bach's music was not popular at the court. Burney, after his visit of 1773, made no mention of the performances of Bach's music, but wrote: "The compositions of the two Grauns and of Quantz, have been in favour with his Prussian majesty for more than forty years . . ." And later: "It must be owned that many of the passages, in these pieces of M. Quantz are now become old and common; but this does not prove their deficiency in novelty, when they were first composed, as some of them have been made more than forty years."

Burney give us an intimate picture of one of the private concerts:

M. Quantz bore no other part in the performance of the concertos tonight, than to give the time with the motion of his hand, at the beginning of each move-ment, except now and then to cry out *bravo!* to his royal scholar, at the end of solo parts and closes; which seems to be a privilege allowed no other musician of the band. The cadences which his majesty made were good, but very long and studied. It is easy to discover that these concertos were composed at a time when he did not so frequently require an opportunity of breathing as at present; for in some of the divisions, which were very long and difficult, as well as in the closes, he was obliged to take his breath, contrary to rule, before the passages were finished.

There is no strong reason to believe that this concert which Burney attended after Bach's departure for Hamburg was very different, except in unimportant details, from earlier ones.

From other contemporaries, chiefly Johann Friedrich Reichardt and Carl Fasch, Bach's alternate at the harpsichord and later *Kapell-meister,* we win more information. Fasch asserted that the king, along with Bach and Franz Benda, was a great artist in adagio play-ing, but that his rhythmic sense was not always dependable, espe-cially in rapid passages. As monarch he retained and exercised the right to bring the ensemble into agreement with his wayward tempos by beating time forcefully. A story goes that a royal admirer on one such occasion exulted, "What rhythm!" To which Bach replied dryly, "What rhythms!" The fruits of these daily experiences appear throughout the *Essay.* They can be found in the many details of practical advice that Bach gives to his reader.

These two sources of Bach's artistic education, his father's instruction and the execution of his duties in the service of the king, were supplemented by a third, his association with many of the leading musical figures of his day. At the court were two of the brothers Graun: Carl Heinrich, music director and celebrated composer of *The Death of Jesus,* and Johann Gottlieb, conductor of the royal orchestra, composer, and eminent violinist. Quantz, already mentioned, was present as chamber musician. His *Versuch einer Anweisung die Flöte traversiere zu spielen* (Berlin, 1752) was a spur to Bach. Five members of the Benda family played at the court, including Franz and, for a shorter time, Georg. Johann Friedrich Agricola, too, was there as court composer, "more corpulent than Jomelli, or than his relation Handel," according to Burney, who visited him later.

In Berlin was also the quarrelsome Johann Philipp Kirnberger, like Agricola a student of Johann Sebastian Bach. Engaged as violinist in the court from 1751, he left to become musical director to the Princess Amalie in 1758. He wrote several important theoretical works and contributed many of the musical articles to J. G. Sulzer's *Allgemeine Theorie der schönen Künste* (Berlin, first edition 1771–74), the remainder being written by his pupil Johann Abraham Peter Schulz. On adding the name of Friedrich Wilhelm Marpurg to this roster we have reassembled the group of writers who made Berlin the hub of musical theory. Burney in *The Present State of Music* writes of Berlin:

I was impatient to begin my musical inquiries in a place . . . where both the theory and practise of music had been more profoundly treated than elsewhere, by professors of great and acknowledged abilities, who are still living; and who have published the result of their long experience and superior skill in treatises which are regarded throughout Germany as classical.

He proceeds to enumerate, not without errors, writings by Quantz, Bach, Agricola, Marpurg, Kirnberger, and Sulzer.

With the exception of Quantz's *Versuch* and two publications by Marpurg, all of the writings of these men appeared after Bach's *Essay.* Its influence is apparent in many of them, just as it is in still later works such as Türk's *Clavierschule* (1789) or Milchmeyer's *Die wahre Art das Pianoforte zu spielen* (1797). But traffic in ideas ran in two directions; Bach met his associates frequently and exchanged opinions with them. In his Autobiography he wrote: "My Prussian duties never left me enough time to travel in foreign countries. . . . This lack . . . would have been harmful to anyone in my profession, had I not had the good fortune from my youth on to hear at close range the finest of all kinds of music and to meet masters of the first rank, many of whom became my friends." Bach absorbed much from these friendships, the results of which, carefully evaluated and recast, appear throughout the *Essay*. Most easy to discover are those points on which he and his contemporaries disagreed. Although he rarely mentions anyone by name, it is clear that he and Quantz were divided on several matters.

In order to complete our sketch of the *Essay*'s background we must direct our attention to Bach's abiding interest in the proper instruction of the musical novice. A great deal of his music was written for teaching purposes. The title of his best-known keyboard works, the collections for Connoisseurs and Amateurs, indicates the spread of his interests. In addition, the Sonatas with varied reprises and the pieces published in Marpurg's and others' collections were designed for the non-professional musician. It is true that the *Essay* was written for the student whose aim was complete mastery of the keyboard. But the Introductions to both parts show clearly that Bach was well aware of the general state of musical instruction, indeed that he wrote with it in mind. Especially is this true of the Introduction to Part One, where he writes caustically of the pretentiousness of the average teacher, his abysmal ignorance and unmusicality.

A few contemporary documents give us information on keyboard instruction at the time. The first, a continuation of the open letter that has already been quoted, states Bach's views on teaching the serious and the casual student:

Those who assert that my Essay is too long, say nothing and at the same time reveal their gross ignorance. I divide all keyboard performers into two groups. In the first are those for whom music is a goal, and in the second, all amateurs who seek thorough instruction. My Essay is intended for the first group; no paragraph is superfluous. In fact it will be seen from the supplements soon to appear that far from having said too much, I have not yet said enough. Teachers must know everything that appears in my Essay and be clever enough to select the manner and order of instruction best adapted to the students that they teach. Niceties come last, as expressed in one of my Introductions.

Nothing fundamental can be learned without time and patience. Study of keyboard performance is not a compendious affair, and dare not be if it is to be learned thoroughly. What is there to say about those false instruction books which in their alleged brevity are almost as long as mine?

For the second group, the amateurs, there is indeed no instruction book, if this could once be impressed upon their teachers. Instead, one should proceed as I used to, unwillingly but out of necessity. Before each period, I wrote out the lesson that I intended to give and concerned myself only with the most essential principles. Niceties of, and proper contexts for, embellishments, refinements of accompaniment, the divided accompaniment, etc. had to be omitted; they were not needed. Throughout, the student was not allowed to commit a single error like those that are accepted as postulates in many books. If the student was prepared, it turned out that the entire transcribed lesson (without examples and the rudiments, which were presupposed since they can be taught as well by a village schoolmaster as by the greatest artist) filled about a half sheet of paper.

Hence, for purposes of thorough instruction the abridging of a keyboard handbook, even when it is done without errors, clearly does more harm than good. All of the compendium writers that I know have written, in certain respects, too little, in others, too much, but in all respects, masses of errors. What miserable nonsense can be found in some! And this is the reason: to judge from their books, the authors have never studied composition, which they must by all means know in order to construct an accompaniment. This study is not merely of the rules of composition; it bears directly on an understanding of composition. In a word, no one can put his trust in a keyboard instruction book, if the author has not previously made himself known and proved himself worthy to be considered an accomplished composer through his good compositions.

In *Der critische Musicus an der Spree*, the weekly that Marpurg published in 1749, there are two more letters, satiric in nature and probably written by the publisher, that refer to keyboard playing and instruction. These give us more information than is revealed in many textbooks of the time. The first, attributed to an anonymous young lady, appeared in the issue of March 11, 1749. It runs, in part:

My dear Papa acquired an excellent instrument at an auction for 15 groschen and 6 pfennige. I am instructed on it by a very clever country organist from a near-by town. We let him visit us at his convenience every two weeks, and on each trip he gives me a half-hour lesson. He is not expensive; we pay him roughly 2 or 3 ducats a month, and each year my dear Mama gives him a bushel of oats. Even if I had no interest in music, this man would be the one to create it. He is quite unassuming, but for a man of common blood he knows very well how to get along with people. He always sits on my left when I play and never forgets to bow with a few light steps after each lesson. In order to relieve my mind of unnecessary bother he marks all notes with letters, although I am already beginning to recognize the c-clef on the first and other lines. He cannot bear the g-clef. It was introduced abortively, he says, by musical freethinkers, and his teacher's grandfather was their sworn enemy. He considers fingering a small matter which he leaves to my discretion, although he insists on banishing the thumb, and often expresses annoyance at those who make so much use of it.

Because he has no interest in ornaments and does not want to delay my progress for two or three years, he disregards all of them, asserting that they hamper rapid playing. Also, he assures me that I shall soon begin to play the latest arias, since I already have under my fingers about a half dozen chorales, in addition to the Smithy's Courante, some popular songs, and two Polish dances. So I am prepared for more difficult pieces. I must not forget to tell you that my resourceful master carries with him a Jew's harp or a pipe with which he often accompanies me so that, as he expresses it, he can give me a few ideas about concertos.

The second letter appeared in the issue of May 13, 1749, and is signed Musenhold. The body of it describes a projected method of financing an orchestra in a small town by means of contributions and the novel imposition of fines for such transgressions as a lady's premature wearing of a new coiffure or a husband's withholding of a small service from his spouse. The correspondent proceeds to describe the sorry personnel of the incumbent orchestra and concludes as follows:

Bamboozler, our keyboardist, has fine hands. But he is unable to put them to good use except when the governess, hired by the mother, excuses herself for a moment, leaving him alone with his young lady students. The mechanics of fingering are completely unknown to him. In right-hand trills, he uses only the second and third fingers, refusing to allow the third and fourth to play on any account. In playing three-part chords in the right hand in which the lowest tones lie a fourth apart and the upper a third (par ex. *d*, *g*, *b*) he uses the second, third, and fifth fingers, even though the middle tone must be played by the fourth. And so, from the beginning, he ruins his students' hands. Also, he is so bad at thorough-bass that he knows neither the tones nor the tonality of the chord of the augmented second. In accompanying he is like the lowliest chorale player; he leaps all over the keyboard from one octave to another with his right hand, as if the identity of chords were known to him only here and there. And another proof that he knows nothing about harmony: not only does he play all mistakes from poor copies of arias, he transcribes them note for note in his students' copy books.

If Bach was unacquainted with these two letters, published in Berlin by a musician who was well known to him, it made little difference, for this famous son and pupil of "old Bach of Leipzig," as Marpurg called him, this celebrated keyboard player who knew and practiced at its best the music of Berlin, who knew many of the coregnant musicians of his time, was also conversant with the common day-to-day practices. The content of the *Essay* provides us with direct evidence, for the discussions that it contains run from the finest and subtlest topics to the broadest and most basic. If it disagrees with Quantz, or echoes Couperin, it also lashes the local pedantic music masters.

The *Essay* is first and foremost a practical book that was designed less for discussion than for instruction. Its ancestry runs back through works like Mattheson's *General-Bass Schule,* Heinichen's *General Bass,* to Niedt's *Musicalische Handleitung,* the text on which his father's teaching was based. Also in the background is François Couperin's *L'Art de toucher le clavecin.* There is no trace of the speculative temper of the Age of Reason that brought forth Lessing's *Laokoon,* Sulzer's *Allgemeine Theorie . . . ,* or earlier, Charles Batteux's *Les Beaux-Arts reduits a une même principe.* For works that pronounced first principles and the governing laws of esthetics, Bach had only the practitioner's scorn. "They dispense their alms with a completely unhappy arbitrariness," he writes in the *Essay.*

Primarily the book seeks clarification and improvement of the keyboardist's lot through a painstaking ordering and exposition of the several factors that relate to the practice of his art. The author's qualifications were eminently suited to the requirements. Of his practical experience and wisdom we already know. His contemporaries set the highest store on his expressive playing. As a composer he was the leading exponent of the *Empfindsamkeit,* the German counterpart of the *style galant.* Beyond this he had an enduring interest in all music, as well as highly developed critical faculties. In his Autobiography he wrote:

It is because I have never liked excessive uniformity in composition or taste, because I have heard many different kinds of good things, because it has always been my opinion that the good should be accepted regardless of where it may be found, even when it appears in small details of a piece; it is because of these considerations and the assistance provided by a God-given natural ability that the variety which is attributed to my compositions has arisen.

Another important qualification: he was a collector by nature. In his estate were over 300 portraits of famous men, mostly musicians, which he had gathered together over the years. Many of these hung in his home in Hamburg, where Burney saw and remarked on them. And without his careful preservation of many of his father's scores, our knowledge of the Leipzig Bach's music would be far poorer. Wide musical experience, catholic tastes and interests, discrimination, the collector's habits of acquisitiveness, all of these factors contribute to the value of the *Essay* and lend to it a unique quality. But, finally, there can be found on more than one page a sly, sometimes a caustic, wit. Johann Friedrich Doles, a school companion and one of Johann Sebastian's successors at the Thomasschule, once said, "Like many boys of active mind and body, he was afflicted from childhood on with the malady of the roguish tease." Symptomatic are his remarks on local teachers, Italian accompanists, the performance of incompletely marked scores.

Nowhere is Philipp Emanuel's indebtedness to his father more clearly expressed than in the chapter on fingering. The son worked out the details, but the father fixed the basic principles. However, it is clear from the reference to fingering as "a secret art, known and practiced by very few," that the Bach family did not discover it, but rather organized and elaborated its technique. Other facts can be adduced to support this view.

Of the older fingering, it can be said that it lacked systematization. It was conditioned by earlier musical styles and was characterized in general by a sparing use of the thumb and fifth finger with a consequent favoring of the middle fingers. For example, in running passages the right hand often ascended and the left hand descended by repeatedly crossing the third finger over the fourth. As the right hand descended the third finger repeatedly crossed the second. The thumb came into repeated use only in wide stretches and as the left hand ascended, a common fingering being 4,3,2,1,2,1,2,1. The differences from one school to another lay essentially in the amount of use allotted to the extreme fingers. In Girolamo Diruta's *Il Transilvano* (1593?, 1597) these hapless members are almost completely banished. More kindly disposed toward them were the English virginalists and Germans such as Elias Nicolaus Ammerbach, in whose *Ein New Kunstlich Tabulaturbuch* (1575) the fourth finger of the left hand crosses the thumb in stepwise ascent. In François Couperin's *L'Art de toucher le clavecin* (1716, 1717) the thumb is employed frequently in wide stretches, and in running passages for the left hand, but in the right no more frequently than others had used it. Characteristic for the French school at this time is the replacement of one finger by another on an unrepeated, held tone, along with direct repetitions of a single finger in running passages. A palpable misprint accounts for the claim that *L'Art de toucher* . . . foreshadows the newer fingering.

A very important innovation of the new method was the turning under of the thumb in running and arpeggiated passages. The older fingering made use of the thumb in large stretches and runs, but in the latter its sole function was to strike the key and remain inactive while the second or rarely the third and fourth vaulted it. Yet the turned thumb in the Bach fingering must have been known and employed by Domenico Scarlatti, for one, for the virtuoso passages in his sonatas could hardly have been delivered satisfactorily without it. For corroborative evidence we can call on Franz Anton Maichelbeck, in whose *Die auf dem Clavier lehrende Caecilia* (Augsburg, 1738) the turned thumb is called for repeatedly. This fact is of special interest here, for Maichelbeck's own keyboard works incorporate many of the bravura elements of the Scarlatti sonatas.

Further, Marpurg's *Die Kunst das Clavier zu spielen* (1750/51) employs the turned thumb as a basic technique in the performance of scales. It is quite possible, however, that Emanuel Bach had a part in the working out of this feature of Marpurg's short treatise. Certainly Marpurg did not hesitate to pick plums from the *Essay* once it had appeared.

If, then, the new fingering was known to some, it remained a closed book to the rank and file of teachers and students until Bach's systematic exposition appeared in 1753. Marpurg's satiric letters, quoted earlier, are clear enough proof of this, and also of the fact that the old fingering had outlasted its function. "Who does not know when a new epoch began for music in general, and for its most accurate and finest performance in particular . . . ," wrote Bach in his Autobiography. The new style demanded a new delivery.

Bach's fingering is the foundation of modern technique. Of the older methods but few details remain in his exhaustive exposition, such as the crossing of 3 over 4 in the ascending right hand, but this only as an alternative to the new method of turning the thumb. As keyboard style developed, as the pianoforte with its different action came into its own, certain extensions of technique were required. These were provided by Clementi, Czerny, J. B. Cramer, and many others. If Muzio Clementi is sometimes credited with introducing modern finger technique, we need only read his own acknowledgment of indebtedness to the *Essay* in order to restore the proper sequence: "Whatever I know about fingering and the new style, in short, whatever I understand of the pianoforte, I have learned from this book."

The most extended contemporary review of the *Essay* appeared in the *Bibliothek der schönen Wissenschaften und der freyen Künste* (Vol. 10, Pts. 1, 2, 1763/4). In it Bach's work is ranked as the equal of Quantz's *Versuch*, Leopold Mozart's *Violinschule*, and Agricola's translation with additions of Tosi's *Opinioni*. The review is laudatory on all counts save those that refer to the chapter on embellishments, where several exceptions are taken to Bach's treatment and organization of material. Whether these differences of opinion are entirely justified is less significant than the fact that they indicate that Bach did not, as indeed he could not, represent all practices of the eighteenth century. Taste and style are important factors in his treatment. Further, although Bach's ordering of his material is clear and logical, it is obvious that a somewhat different organization might have been undertaken. All in all, the chapter on embellishments contains a large but discerning selection of ornaments from all styles.

Ornamentation at the time of the *Essay* was of two kinds. There were first the optional elaborations which performers were expected to interpolate into the pieces they played. Ornamentation in this sense was a dying practice. Johann Sebasian Bach had already subscribed to the writing out of every note that was to be performed. Philipp Emanuel, following his father's practice, treats free elaboration only briefly, in connection with the performance of fermatas and cadenzas.

The second kind was the stereotyped short embellishments, the appoggiaturas, trills, turns, etc. To these, Bach directed his full attention. The task that he set for himself was a twofold one. First he classified each type and designated a distinctive sign, notation, or position for each subtype. For example, the section on the turn includes the turn over a note, after a note, over a tie, over a dot, the trilled turn, the snapped turn, and the ascending turn. In all, he cites seven types and twenty-four subtypes of ornaments exclusive of slight variants. While the ends at which Bach arrived are, in certain instances, peculiar to his own judgment in these matters, the idea of sorting and classifying embellishments was not at all new, for this was the subject matter of many books and prefatory notes of the time and earlier. Much more original and provocative was the specifying of the exact musical context that was suited to each ornament. Here Bach attempted to assist the performer who must know where to insert unspecified ornaments. For, if the practice of providing free elaborations was approaching its end, the more modest one of inserting short embellishments was still a vigorous art. Certainly it met with Bach's approval, where the other did not.

The chapter on embellishments is a difficult, but an inescapable and rewarding assignment for the musician who would discharge creditably his responsibilities to 18th-century music. Generally speaking, Bach's contemporaries and later composers did not accept his advocacy of a separate designation for each ornament. Instead, they followed the practice of using a few signs to cover all cases, when they did not write out the ornament completely. Today we have come to believe that each of these signs represents a single, pat formula. The often gruesome results of this misapprehension can be heard from conservatory to concert hall. Bach's chapter is a primary, corrective source work. In it we are provided with an opportunity to study in detail the exact manner in which these ornaments were performed by one of the most precise and sensitive artists of his period.

In the third chapter of the *Essay,* Bach writes of performance. On the evidence presented by his own keyboard music, it is doubtful that he possessed or sought the technical wizardry of Domenico Scarlatti. His fame derived from other sources. It was the heightened expressiveness of his playing, the daring originality of his music that impressed his listeners. Among those who heard him and remarked on his performance were the poet Klopstock, the musicians and musicographers Marpurg, Reichardt, and Burney. The last-named wrote in his *Present State of Music:* "His performance today convinced me of what I had suggested before from his works; that he is not only one of the greatest composers that ever existed, for keyed instruments, but the best player in point of expression; for others, perhaps, have had as rapid execution: however, he possesses every style; though he confines himself chiefly to the expressive." And the author, possibly Reichardt, of *Musikalischer Almanach, Alethinopel* (1782) writes similarly: "To know Bach completely one must hear the wealth of his imagination, the profound sentiment of his heart, his constant enthusiasm as he improvises on his Silbermann clavichord."

As the principal practitioner of the *Empfindsamkeit,* with its emphasis on the feelings, the "affections," with the clavichord as its best-loved instrument, Bach made technical mastery of the keyboard only a contributory factor to the expressive end that he sought. Music here was far removed from a decorative art, from abstract patterns of sound; it was, above all else, a vehicle for the expression of the emotions. Music must languish, it must startle, it must be gay, it must move boldly from one sentiment to another; these were the requirements that had to be met by the composer. And the performer must understand the true content of each piece that he played. He must transmit accurately and faithfully its expressive nuances to an audience whose heart must be stirred. This was the core of the aesthetic doctrine of the Berlin school. Its artistic parallels were the English sentimental novels and the romantic Germans of the literary movement that became known later as the *Sturm und Drang.*

Throughout the *Essay* Bach distinguishes between the learned and galant styles in music. He set no high store on the former, although he wrote his share of polyphonic pieces and had a deep admiration for his father's works. His predilection was for the galant style, French in derivation. Yet his own music and manner of performance were far different from the patterned forms, the restrained elegance and grace of the rococo. His manner of delivery, like his music, was replete with personal expressiveness, with song. This view is clearly expressed in his Autobiography: "My principal aim, especially of late, has been directed toward playing and composing as vocally as possible for the keyboard, despite its defective sustaining powers. This is no easy matter if the sound is not to be too thin or the noble simplicity of melody ruined by excessive noise. . . . I believe that music must, first and foremost, stir the heart. This cannot be achieved through mere rattling, drumming, or arpeggiation, at least not by me."

Thus in the chapter on performance the points stressed are those concerned with expressive playing, with correct interpretation. It is only after attention has been directed to these matters that Bach turns to such technical details as the notation and performance of detached and joined notes, the execution of the vibrato and portato, dotted notes, sustained and arpeggiated tones. And like the tempo rubato and dynamic shading, all of these matters are of importance only as they advance the first aim of the performer, to seek and interpret correctly the true expressive content of each piece that he performs.

To many it must seem strange that Philipp Emanuel, modernist and eclectic of the eighteenth century, did not employ the theories of Rameau, in writing the chapters on intervals and thorough bass. He was not ignorant of the writings of the Clermont organist whose *Traité* had appeared forty years before Part Two of the *Essay*. Indeed, the *Essay* was written after the publication of all of Rameau's theoretical works.

Bach and his father were acquainted with Rameau's theory, which has become the basis of most of the modern writings on harmony, but they disagreed with it. This was made known in a letter to Kirnberger, cited in his *Kunst des reinen Satzes* (Pt. II, Sect. 3, p. 188): "You may proclaim that my and my deceased father's basic principles are contrary to Rameau's." Extended consideration had been given by the members of the Bach school to the new theories of the fundamental bass, the suppositional root, the triad as the mother of all chords, and the seventh as the origin of all dissonances. This is apparent from the analyses in the Rameau manner which can be found, according to Spitta, in the definitive autographs of the Sarabande and two Menuets from Johann Sebastian Bach's D minor French Suite, and in Fischoff's autograph of the C minor Fugue and D minor Prelude of the *Well-Tempered Clavier*. Later, Kirnberger analyzed the B minor Fugue of Book One and part of the A minor Prelude of Book Two with the avowed purpose of proving the superiority of his own analytic procedure over Rameau's. In only one respect can it be said that Philipp Emanuel made use of any of the new principles. He speaks several times of chord inversion. But this principle was known before the *Traité* was published, having made its appearance in Andreas Werckmeister's *Hodegus curiosus* (1687) and Godfrey Keller's *Rules . . .* (before 1700).

Bach's rejection of Rameau can be traced largely to the fact that the latter had pronounced a *theory*, whereas thorough bass was essentially a practice. Certainly, as Bach presents his material, it is apparent that the pervasive problems were first tactile and then

artistic, but never speculative. Thus in organizing the chords of
thorough bass, Bach follows an older principle. Chords, regardless
of their origin, are grouped according to the definitive interval that
they contain. For example, all chords that contain sevenths are
treated successively. They are the chord of the seventh, the seven-
six, the seven-four, and the seven-four-two chords. Although only
the first of these is a chord in the Rameau sense, all are chords in
Bach's sense. Each of them must be recognized from its signature
and played instantaneously. The student's task was to locate at the
keyboard the definitive interval and then to bring under his fingers
the various accompanying intervals. Identification of the root, real
or supposed, did not aid him in his direct gauging of intervals above
a given bass tone. Moreover, in thorough bass some chords were
closely associated, even though their roots were not identical. For
example, above certain bass tones the six-three and six-four-three
chords were regarded as interchangeable. Knowledge of the fact that
these chords had different roots would have deterred rather than
aided the student.

The greatest difficulty with the older system was caused by the
great increase in the number and variety of chords that made
their appearance in the course of the eighteenth century. Mattheson
referred scornfully to the thirty-two posted by Heinichen, and listed
seventy, but overlooked six of the latter's chords. Bach has twenty,
but includes many others as subtypes, chromatic variants, and alternates. It was this unwieldy bulk of chords that aided the spread of
Rameau's system, but it is not pointless to note that the theory
gained unquestioned acceptance only after the period of the basso
continuo had passed. Bach's method, the one he inherited from his
father, was the only effective introduction to the musical practices
of his time.

The crucial difference between Rameau and Bach is most evident
in those places where Philipp Emanuel explains the nature of
chords. Where Rameau's emphasis rests on the vertical origins of a
chord, Bach's rests on its behavior. Repeatedly he cites context,
voice leading, rhythmic and melodic manipulation as the critical
chord-shaping factors. Thus there are two kinds of six-four chords,
those that retard a following five-three, and those that retard a
following six-three. Where Rameau calls the two identical because
their roots are identical, Bach differentiates between them because

their behavior is different. The first attempt to reconcile these two points of view, harmonic function and behavior, was made by Kirnberger, whose works, despite certain obvious shortcomings, should be examined by all. He distinguishes between essential and inessential chords, and makes the root a determinative factor of a succession of chords rather than a single chord.

In general, the chapters on intervals and thorough bass are concerned solely with the rudiments of accompaniment. Attention is directed to chord construction, doubling, and spacing. This was the groundwork that must be covered by every student accompanist. But it was hardly enough to make a skilled practitioner of the keyboardist. So, after treating the raw material, Bach turns in the chapter on accompaniment to refinements, stylistic matters, and special problems of settings, such as the treatment of appoggiaturas, passing tones, etc. He writes of the liberties that may be taken, of the amount of freedom from four-part accompaniment that may be indulged, of the ways in which a realization might be made into an active, essential part of a composition.

On only one final point is his thorough, detailed exposition less than adequate—he did not include a complete piece with a fully realized accompaniment. The examples themselves are highly informative and shed light on many particulars of construction, but they are, by nature, isolated fragments. While it would have been impossible to construct an accompaniment in which all problematic matters would find illustration, nevertheless a single complete movement would have clarified our concept of the total shape of an accompaniment, of its balances and parallelisms.

The extemporaneous realization of a figured bass is a dead art. We have left behind us the period of the basso continuo and with it all the unwritten law, the axioms, the things that were taken for granted; in a word, the spirit of the time. To become convinced of this one need merely play through the effulgent nineteenth-century tone poems that were added as accompaniments to eighteenth-century works; or the shy, halting harmony exercises that are prevalent in our own day. These latter reveal their timidity all the more clearly through their small notation. Both types, it should be remembered, were painfully and studiously wrought, but they fail completely to enter the creative milieu of the eighteenth century. To be sure there were bad, faltering accompaniments in the eighteenth century too. We can read about them here and elsewhere.

But it is illuminating to read first-hand accounts of the accompaniments fashioned by one of the greatest improvisers of all time. Writing of Johann Sebastian Bach, Johann Friedrich Daube expressed himself as follows in 1756:

> For the complete practice of thorough bass it is necessary to know three species: the simple or common; the natural, or that which comes closest to the character of a melody or a piece; the intricate or compound.
>
> The excellent Bach possessed this third species in the highest degree; when he played, the principal part had to shine. By his exceedingly adroit accompaniment he gave it life when it had none. He knew how to imitate it so cleverly with either the right hand or the left, and how to introduce an unexpected counter-theme against it, that the listener would have sworn that everything had been conscientiously written out. At the same time, the regular accompaniment was very little curtailed. In general his accompanying was like a *concertante* part most carefully constructed and added as a companion to the principal part so that at the appropriate time the upper voice would shine. This right was given at times even to the bass, without slighting the principal part. Suffice it to say that anyone who missed hearing him missed a great deal.

Lorenz Mizler also listened to Bach's accompaniments. He wrote in 1738:

> Whoever wishes truly to observe what delicacy in thorough bass and very good accompanying mean need only take the trouble to hear our Capellmeister Bach here, who accompanies every thorough bass to a solo so that one thinks it is a piece of concerted music and as if the melody he plays in the right hand were written beforehand. I can give a living testimony of this since I have heard it myself.

Because thorough-bass realizations were created extemporaneously and served only an immediate purpose, there was no need to write them out. Nevertheless, a few have come down to us, some avowed realizations, others that partake so much of the nature of an accompaniment that they can be used to supplement Emanuel Bach's discussion. As listed here they range from the simple, through the natural, to the intricate, as classified by Daube:

Philipp Spitta's *J. S. Bach* (Novello, 1899, III, 388 ff.) contains a realization by H. N. Gerber with corrections by Bach of a Sonata for Violin and Bass by T. Albinoni.

Georg Philip Telemann, *Singe- Spiel- und General Bass Uebungen,* ed. by Max Seiffert, Bärenreiter, 1935. This volume contains several songs with fully realized accompaniments. It was designed as an instruction book.

Musical Offering by J. S. Bach, prepared by H. T. David, G. Schirmer, 1944.

pp. 47 ff. This carefully edited work contains a realization by Kirnberger of the Andante from the Trio. The remaining movements of the Trio and mirror canon (pp. 59 ff.) have accompaniments by an unknown student of the eighteenth century. These accompaniments have in the past been incorrectly attributed to Kirnberger (*cf.* H. T. David, *J. S. Bach's Musical Offering,* G. Schirmer, 1945, pp. 99 ff.).

G. F. Handel, *Werke,* Vol. 48, p. 115, Adagio. The keyboard part is superscribed *cembalo concertato,* but is in the nature of an arpeggiated realization.

J. S. Bach, *Werke,* II, 2, pp. 97 ff., Aria, *Chi in amore.* This is the most complex of the accompaniments listed here, but even in its elaborated qualities it suggests an extemporaneous realization of the "intricate" kind. The keyboard part is superscribed *cembalo obligato.*

F. T. Arnold, *The Art of Accompaniment from a Thorough Bass,* London, 1931, Ch. IV. This chapter contains suggestive, short, but complete examples from textbooks by Heinichen, Mattheson, and Geminiani.

An accompaniment from a thorough bass demands more than a carefully gathered knowledge of eighteenth-century idioms. It requires in addition a highly creative imagination. When these two factors are present much of the elusive spirit of a good setting can be recaptured. As an example, Brahms' accompaniments to Handel's *Duetti e Terzetti* may be cited. They appear in Handel's *Werke,* Vol. 32, 2nd ed. Nos. Ib and X to the end of the volume. Nos. XV-XX were published in Handel's *Duette,* Peters, No. 2070.

It is a rare privilege to be invited into a composer's workshop to look on as he fashions a model for us, as in the chapter on improvisation. Partial glimpses of the creator at work are provided in letters scattered through the centuries; and many rare vistas are opened up to the careful student of Beethoven's notebooks. But aside from these and the final chapter of the *Essay,* our only recourse is a vast desert of textbooks on the proper writing of inventions, academic fugues, sonatas, songs, etc. Their authors' compositions being at best of only minor significance, such books represent but secondary sources for those who wish to know intimately of the problems and processes of creation.

Burney in his *Present State of Music* describes Philipp Emanuel's improvising as follows: "After dinner, which was elegantly served, and cheerfully eaten, I prevailed upon him to sit down again to a clavichord, and he played with little intermission, till nearly eleven o'clock at night. During this time, he grew so animated and possessed, that he looked like one inspired. His eyes were fixed, his under lip fell, and drops of effervescence distilled from his countenance." Reichardt was bewitched by Bach's communicative improvisations.

Significant in Bach's exposition is the omnipresence of a ground plan, regardless of whether the subject of discussion is the short preliminary exercise, modulation, or the complete fantasia. The improvisatory character of this type of composition is achieved not by a meaningless wandering from key to key, but by an imaginative manipulation of details that fit persuasively into a unified whole. But the relation between execution and plan is bold and free. Nowhere does the plan obtrude. Its function is to direct the general course of the work, and this it accomplishes by remaining quietly where it belongs, in the background. And when necessary it yields to a free twist of the foreground. Under the conditions set by Bach the sample piece could scarcely turn out to be one of his best works. His avowed purpose is to show the student how to construct a free fantasia. Limitations imposed by this aim were severe. Yet for all its circumscribed, unassuming modesty, it breathes the same atmosphere as the famous final piece of the *Probestücke,* also a free fantasia.

In this chapter, as in many parts of the chapter on thorough bass, Bach presents himself as an analyst. His procedure is to discuss each inflection with relation to its normal behavior. It is instructive to compare such a method with the present practice of chord-naming which is passed off almost everywhere as analysis. Where the latter is mechanical and visual, Bach's approach is aural and artistic. The requirements of such an approach are keen perceptive powers, the ability to evaluate musical processes, and a long experience in the art. Bach had all of these qualities, and having them, he could never have regarded analysis as a search for chord roots and identification tags.

The *Essay* was Bach's only extended theoretical work. Aside from it and certain illustrations that appeared in Marpurg's *Abhandlung von der Fuge,* there was only one paper that came to print, a Suggestion for the Constructing of Six Bars of Double Counterpoint in the Octave (*Einfall* . . .) which appeared in Marpurg's *Historisch-Critische Beyträge* (Vol. III, Pt. 2, pp. 167 ff.). It is a work more ingenious than useful. Other writings, some of which were planned as supplements to the *Essay,* were concerned with thorough bass, fingering, embellishments, modulation, and the free fantasia. They

remained in manuscript (Wotquenne, Nos. 121, 256, 258). Whatever merits can be found in these other works, they contributed
little to their author's renown. None worked as did the *Essay* to
establish him as one who "raised the art of performance through
teaching and practice to its perfection."

PART ONE

Carl Philipp Emanuel Bachs

Versuch

über die wahre Art

das Clavier zu spielen

mit Exempeln

und achtzehn Probe=Stücken in sechs Sonaten

erläutert.

Erster Theil.

Zweyte Auflage.

In Verlegung des Auctoris.

Berlin, 1759.
Gedruckt bey George Ludewig Winter.

Title page of the first edition of *Essay on the True Art of Playing Keyboard Instruments*, Part I

FOREWORD TO PART ONE

EYBOARD INSTRUMENTS[1] have many merits, but are
beset by just as many difficulties. Were it necessary, their
excellence would be easy to prove, for in them are combined
all the individual features of many other instruments. Full harmony, which requires three, four, or more other instruments, can
be expressed by the keyboard alone. And there are many similar
advantages. At the same time, who is not aware of the many demands that are made upon it; how it is considered insufficient for
the keyboardist merely to discharge the normal task of every executant, namely, to play in accordance with the rules of good performance compositions written for his instrument? How, beyond
this, he must be able to improvise fantasias in all styles, to work out
extemporaneously any requested setting after the strictest rules of
harmony and melody; how he must be at home in all keys and transpose instantly and faultlessly; and play everything at sight whether
designed for his instrument or not; how he must have at his command a comprehensive knowledge of thorough bass which he must
play with discrimination, often departing from the notation, sometimes in many voices, again in few, strictly as well as in the galant
manner, from both excessive and insufficient symbols, or unfigured
and incorrectly figured basses; how he must often extract this

[1] *Clavier*. The meaning of the term "clavier" has suffered so many ramifications
that it seemed wise to avoid it entirely and use instead the more stable "keyboard
instruments." In J. S. Bach's time, *Clavier* referred to all keyboard instruments. Hence
Das Wohltemperirte Clavier should read *The Well-Tempered Clavier* rather than
Clavichord. But in the generation of C. P. E. Bach and later, Clavier often meant
only clavichord. However, there can be no doubt of the inclusive meaning of the term
in the title of this Essay, despite the further confusion added by Burney when he
calls it (*The Present State of Music*, Vol. II, p. 263) "An Essay on the Art of Playing
the Harpsichord." Translation of *Clavier* as "keyboard instruments" or simply "keyboard" led inescapably to "keyboardist" as the translation of *Clavierist*.

thorough bass from large scores with unfigured or even pausing basses (when other voices serve as harmonic fundament) and with it reinforce the ensemble; and who knows how many other things? All this must be done competently, often on an unfamiliar instrument which has not been tested to determine whether it is good or bad, whether it is playable or not, in which latter case extenuation is but rarely granted. On the contrary, it can be expected that, normally, improvisations will be solicited without anyone's being concerned whether the performer is in the proper mood, and if he is not, without any effort being made to create or maintain the proper disposition by providing a good instrument.

Notwithstanding these demands, the keyboard has always found its admirers, as well it might. Its difficulties are not enough to discourage the study of an instrument whose superior charms are ample compensation for attendant time and trouble. Moreover, not all amateurs feel obliged to fulfill all of the requirements. They satisfy as many of them as they care to or as their innate talents permit.

However, keyboard instruction could be improved in certain respects to the end that the truly good which is lacking in so much music, but particularly keyboard music, might thereby become more widespread. The most accomplished performers, those whose playing might prove instructive, are not to be found in such numbers as might perhaps be imagined. And yet, study by listening, a kind of tolerated larceny, is the more necessary in music because, even if ill-will were not so great in mankind, many matters would still present themselves which cannot be easily demonstrated, much less written down, and would have to be acquired by ear alone.

In presenting an introduction to keyboard playing it has not in the least been my intention to treat systematically all of the previously mentioned tasks and to show how they may be satisfactorily discharged. Neither the art of improvising nor thorough bass is discussed here. These have long since been dealt with in part in many excellent books. It is my aim to show the performer how he may play solos [2] correctly and thereby gain the approbation of connoisseurs. He who has done his part in this respect will already have

[2] *Handsachen*. Mattheson (*Der vollkommene Capellmeister*) writes: ". . . Everything that is played on keyboard instruments falls into two classes, solos (*Handsachen*) and general bass." However, cf. Pt. II, *Introduction*, ¶¶ 12–15, where Bach's description of *Handsachen* would seem to limit the term to certain types of keyboard solos.

accomplished much, for his facility will help him to succeed far more easily in his remaining studies. The demands made of the keyboard as compared with other instruments testify to its comprehensiveness and many capabilities; and it can be observed from the history of music that those who have achieved renown in the world of music have usually excelled on our instrument.

In all matters, I have had in mind chiefly those teachers who have failed to instruct their students in the true foundations of the art. Amateurs who have been misled through false precepts can remedy matters by themselves from my teachings, provided they have already played a great deal of music. Beginners, by the same means, will easily attain a proficiency that they could hardly have believed possible.

Those who expected a voluminous work from me are in error. I believe I deserve more gratitude if through brief precepts I have made practicable, easy, and agreeable many things that are quite difficult in the study of the keyboard.

I ask the forbearance of my readers for repeated mention of divers truths, made necessary partly because matters on hand demanded it, partly to avoid frequent cross references, and finally, because I feel that certain principles cannot be stated too often. And perhaps some will find themselves embarrassed by these truths, although I wrote them without the slightest intention of malice.

Should the present work meet with the approval of connoisseurs, I might find therein the encouragement to continue with a few supplements. The acclaim [3] accorded this work by the musical public has given me the incentive to enlarge the present third edition with textual additions and six new keyboard compositions [4] in fulfillment of the promise made in the Forewords to the first and second editions.

[3] This sentence was added to the ed. of 1787.
[4] See Note 17, Introduction to Pt. I.

INTRODUCTION TO PART ONE

1

THE TRUE ART of playing keyboard instruments depends on three factors so closely related that no one of them can, nor indeed dare, exist without the others. They are: correct fingering, good embellishments, and good performance.

2. Owing to ignorance of these factors and their consequent absence from performance, keyboardists can be heard who after torturous trouble have finally learned how to make their instrument sound loathsome to an enlightened listener. Their playing lacks roundness, clarity, forthrightness, and in their stead one hears only hacking, thumping, and stumbling. All other instruments have learned how to sing. The keyboard alone has been left behind, its sustained style obliged to make way for countless elaborate figures. The truth of this is attested by the growing beliefs that to play slowly or legato is wearisome, that tones can be neither slurred nor detached, that our instrument should be tolerated only as a necessary evil in accompaniment. As ungrounded and contradictory as these charges are, they are, nevertheless, positive reactions to the false art of playing the keyboard. In view of the opinion that the keyboard is unsuited to present styles, and the consequent discouragement of many from studying it, I fear that the skill, already waning, which has been brought to us chiefly by great performers, will suffer an even worse decline.

3. In addition to the neglect of the three factors mentioned above, students are taught the wrong position of the hand. At least their errors remain uncorrected. Thus, the last possibility of their playing competently is removed, for it is easy to imagine the kind of sounds produced by stiff, wire-strung fingers.

4. Most students are required to play their teacher's own works,

for nowadays it seems to be scandalous not to compose. Good pieces by others which might be studied profitably are withheld under the pretext that they are obsolete or too difficult. Worst of all, there is a malicious prejudice against French keyboard pieces. These have always been good schooling, for this country is sharply distinguished from others by its flowing and correct style. All necessary embellishments are clearly indicated, the left hand is not neglected, nor is there any lack of held notes; and these are basic elements in the study of coherent performance. Our pedants can often play nothing but their own fabrications; their abused, awkward fingers deliver these stiffly; they can compose only what their hands can subdue. Many are held in high esteem who hardly know how to perform tied notes. Consequently there arise great quantities of miserable works and abominable students.

5.   To begin their studies, pupils are racked with vapid *Murkys* [1] and *Gassenhauer* [2] in which the left hand, its role reduced to a mere thumping, is rendered useless for its true employment. Actually the left hand should be preferentially and intelligently exercised in order to attain a facility equal to that of the right, which by the very nature of things is constantly active.

6.   Should the student in listening to other music acquire a more discriminating taste, he is thenceforth revolted by the pieces he must practice; and, convinced that all keyboard music is poor, he seeks refuge in arias which, when well set, and sung by reputable voices, are suitable for the development of good taste and the study of good performance but not for the development of the fingers. [3]

7.   Teachers feel that they must do violence to these arias and transcribe them for the keyboard. Along with other disparities, the left hand as usual is badly treated. A sluggish or even a drum bass [4] is assigned to it which, even when it is suited to the character of the piece, is more harmful than beneficial to the left hand.

8.   As a result of all this the keyboardist loses the special asset,

---

[1] An accompaniment consisting of broken octaves.

[2] A *Gassenhauer* was a popular song or vaudeville in Bach's time and later. Cf. Moser, *Musiklexikon*.

[3] A similar protest was raised by F. W. Marpurg in *Die Kunst das Clavier zu spielen:* "The arias which students are given serve to form their taste, but not to create facility and dexterity, above all in the left hand."

[4] *Trommel-Bass;* a scornful reference to basses fashioned out of repeated tones. They were an intermediate step between the older linear bass and the somewhat later harmonic, catapulting bass.

possessed by no other instrumentalist, of keeping time easily and enunciating its smallest fraction with exactness, an ability which he acquires in playing idiomatic keyboard music, for this comprises more syncopations, short rests, and rapid dotted rhythms than any other type of composition. On our instrument such difficult elements are quite easy to master because one hand assists the other to hold the beat, and this brings in its train the spontaneous sharpening of the rhythmic sense. I [5] know from experience that rapid syncopations and, above all, short rests cause great ado among the most rhythmically sure and accomplished of other instrumentalists. All enter too late, even though other parts that enter just ahead of them provide the same assistance as the keyboardist has in his hands. To the latter these things are easy even when he omits the left hand or accompanies with other instruments. Provided that he is certain of the tempo, his entrance will always be exactly right. Quantz [6] in his Flute Method, page 113, even advocates a delayed entrance (which goes to prove that a correct entrance is nearly impossible) and thus takes the lesser of two evils.

9. The student in playing the basses described above develops a stiff left hand, for the amount of harm done by performing quick repeated notes without a change of fingers is nearly incredible. Many have suffered this injury as a result of industrious and prolonged study of thorough bass, wherein they have had to play such notes with either hand but particularly with the left in octaves.

9a.[7] I take this opportunity to express my thoughts on the per-

[5] Remainder of paragraph from ed. of 1787.

[6] The reference is to Johann Joachim Quantz (1697–1773), engaged as flute teacher to Frederick the Great, and later as his *Kammermusicus* and court composer. His encyclopedic work, *Versuch einer Anweisung die Flöte traversiere zu spielen* (Berlin, 1752), reads, in the passage that Bach mentions, "At short rests which occur on downbeats in place of principal notes, caution must be taken to avoid coming in too soon with the note that follows. For example, when the first of four sixteenths is a rest, the performer must wait half again as long as the value of the rest, for the following notes must be shorter than the first. This applies as well to thirty-seconds." (Ch. 12, ¶ 12). An abridged modern edition, prepared by Dr. Arnold Schering, was published at Leipzig in 1906.

[7] This long paragraph appeared originally as a footnote and was retained as such in all editions. At first glance it is puzzling in both its length and somewhat heated style, for the practice advocated here of omitting certain repeated notes from the left hand was not new. For example, Heinichen (*General Bass*, 1728) recommends not only the expedient suggested, but also the changing of repeated notes into broken octaves or into a right-hand Alberti figure against simple chords in the left (cf. Arnold, *Art of Accompaniment from a Thorough-Bass*, p. 774 ff.). Saint Lambert makes similar suggestions (p. 196, *l.c.*). However, the entire matter clears up on turn-

formance of quick repetitions in the left hand for the benefit of those who are charged with the task of playing thorough bass. The device, an everyday occurrence in the present style, offers great risk of stiffening and ruining the best of hands. This remark can stand as a good argument against those who ask expressly that all notes written for the left hand be performed. Certainly the *right* hand is not required to accompany all notes, particularly when the bass contains so common a device as the passing tone.[8] The quick repetitions of whose hazards I speak are eighth notes in rapid, and sixteenths in more moderate tempos.[9] Further, I assume that another instrument is playing the bass with the keyboard. When it plays alone, these notes, like the tremolo,[10] must be performed with alternating fingers. Although the consequent omission of the octave will detract from the sonority of the bass, this small defect is to be preferred to other greater evils. With an accompanying bass instrument it is best to omit one, three, or five notes according to the tempo and meter and strike the others in octaves (or double octaves with both hands in a fortissimo), employing a heavy attack, somewhat sustained so that the strings will vibrate sufficiently and the tones blend with each other. In order not to confuse the ensemble, the first bar may be played as written and notes left out from there on. Another means that may be employed when every note must be played is to strike the key alternately with each hand. However, it has been my experience that, because the right hand usually comes in late, this expedient may upset the ensemble, a fact that has strengthened my conviction that the keyboard is and must always remain the guardian of the beat. It is considered correct and indeed

---

ing to Quantz's *Versuch,* where we find the following statement (Ch. XVII, Sect. IV, "Of the Keyboard Accompanist," ¶ 32): "With regard to allegro movements it is important that the accompanist . . . . possess the facility in his left hand to play everything clearly and purely, . . . that when many eighth notes occur on a single tone he play every one with his left hand, and avoid the practice of some who for untimely reasons of convenience, strike one note and omit the following three or even seven, especially in vocal works." When all factors are considered, i.e., the publication dates of both Essays (Quantz 1752, Bach 1753), the close association of both men as fellow court musicians, etc., it becomes clear that Quantz is referring to Bach and that Bach's paragraph is an elaborate rejoinder and defense of his own practice.

[8] See Ch. IV, ¶¶ 68–78, and Ch. VI, especially ¶ 3, for a description of passing tones in the eighteenth-century sense.

[9] Cf. Ch. VI, "Passing Tones," ¶¶ 4, 7–12.

[10] . . . *Wie die Schwärmer.* The term was used chiefly with reference to the string tremolo, although Marpurg applies it to repeated notes at the keyboard. The Italian word was *Bombo.* Arnold translates literally, "resembling crackers' (Arnold, *op. cit.,* p. 776).

advisable for the accompanist to repeat chords which are sustained by the rest of the ensemble in order to maintain a clear indication of the meter; [11] the correctness and advisability of omitting notes should be conceded for the same reason; the more so when such omissions are compared with the hazards and impracticability of literal performance. And this latter is really hazardous, for on other instruments such notes are played with the tongue or the wrist; but the keyboardist must express these rumblings with a rigid arm when, due to octave doubling, he is unable to employ alternating fingers. In doing this the left hand grows stiff and incapable of performing the passage satisfactorily for two related reasons: The first, because in a prolonged contraction all muscles are employed; the second, because most of the fingers are inactive. It can be established through experiment that the left hand and entire arm grow so tired, twisted, and taut from thumping away at a drum bass that it is impossible to play anything active afterwards. This clinking noise is impossible for another reason: Many of the drum basses that are encountered today cannot be survived because of their sheer length. In all styles the other musicians have occasional rests; the keyboard, however, is constantly at work often for as many as three, four, or even more hours without respite. Assuming that one were hardened to such labor, even the most dependable musician would begin eventually to waver drowsily and unwittingly through fatigue. The drum bass, in most cases devoid of expression and calling for little mental effort, can only annoy and weary a performer who, as a consequence, loses the inclination and ability to perform stirring passages fittingly. Further, this injurious clinking is contrary to the nature of the harpsichord as well as the piano-forte, for both instruments are thereby robbed of their natural tone and clarity; the tangent of the harpsichord seldom reacts quickly enough. The French, who understand the keyboard and know that it is capable of more than mere strumming, take pains even today to inform the keyboardist that in such passages not all notes are to be played. Further, broad accented tones contribute to the expression of basses that carry dots or dashes over the first of a group of notes. Many cases arise where a clear, strong attack with both hands is not only advisable but mandatory. The keyboard, entrusted by our fathers with full command, is in the best position

[11] Cf. Ch. VI, "Performance," ¶ 18.

to assist not only the other bass instruments but the entire ensemble in maintaining a uniform pace. And yet the best musician, fatigued, may find it difficult to guide even his own pace at times, even though he might be the master of his powers under normal conditions. Such being the case with one performer, how much more important it is that our expedient be employed in an ensemble; the more so because time is beaten today only in larger compositions. The tone of the keyboard which, correctly placed, stands in the center of the ensemble, can be heard clearly by all.[12] And I know that even diffuse, elaborate compositions played by impromptu, average performers can be held together simply by its tone. If the first violinist stands nears the keyboard as he should, disorder cannot easily spread. In arias, the singer's burden is lightened by our means when the tempo changes precipitately, or when all parts scramble while the voice alone has long notes or triplets which because of their division demand a clear beat. The less the bass is preoccupied with difficult, involved runs, the more easily will it be able to maintain a steady pace; the more it is, the more frequent will be the spectacle of compositions starting more vigorously than they end. Should someone hasten or drag, he can be most readily corrected by the keyboardist, for the others will be too much concerned with their own figures and syncopations to be of any assistance. Especially those parts that employ the tempo rubato will find herein a welcome, emphatic beat. Finally, it is easy (and often necessary) to make minor changes of tempo by this means because exact perception will not be hindered by the keyboard's excessive noise, and, in addition, those performers located in front of or beside the keyboard will find in the simultaneous motion of both hands an inescapable, visual portrayal of the beat.

10.   Teachers try to make amends for a stiff left hand by teaching their students to favor the right and garnish adagio or expressive passages with a wealth of pretty little trills to the revulsion of good taste. These are often interchanged with senile, pedantic embellishments and fumbling, inept runs in the playing of which the fingers seem to grow choleric.

11.   Before we proceed to remedy these faults with well-grounded instruction, something remains to be said about keyboard instruments. Of the many kinds, some of which remain little

12 Cf. Plate IV.

known because of defects, others because they are not yet in general use, there are two which have been most widely acclaimed, the harpsichord and the clavichord. The former is used in ensembles, the latter alone. The more recent pianoforte, when it is sturdy and well built, has many fine qualities, although its touch must be carefully worked out, a task which is not without difficulties. It sounds well by itself and in small ensembles. Yet, I hold that a good clavichord, except for its weaker tone, shares equally in the attractiveness of the pianoforte and in addition features the vibrato and *portato* [13] which I produce by means of added pressure after each stroke. It is at the clavichord that a keyboardist may be most exactly evaluated.[14]

12. A good clavichord must have in addition to a lasting, caressing tone, the proper number of keys, extending at the very least from the great octave C to the three-lined *e*. The upper limit is needed for the playing of scores written for other instruments. Composers like to venture into this high register because many instruments can reach it quite easily. The keys must be properly weighted to help raise the fingers after each stroke. In order that the strings may be attacked as well as caressed and be capable of expressing purely and clearly all degrees of forte and piano, they must be resilient. Taut [15] strings keep the tone of a vibrato pure; yet they should not be too taut or they will sound strained and the performer will be unable to achieve any volume; on the other hand, if they are too loose, they will sound impure and unclear if they sound at all. The [16] keys must not fall too deep, and the pegs must be tightly fitted so that the strings will be capable of withstanding the full force of an attack and remain in tune.

13. A good harpsichord must have uniform quilling in addition

---

[13] *Die Bebung und das Tragen der Töne.* Cf. Ch. III, ¶¶ 19–20, and the accompanying Note 17.

[14] J. F. Reichardt wrote: "Not only does Bach play a slow, singing adagio with the most touching expression (to the embarrassment of many instrumentalists who could imitate the voice with far less difficulty on their own instruments), he sustains, even in this tempo, a note six eighths long with all degrees of loudness, both in the bass and the treble. But this is perhaps possible only on his very fine Silbermann clavichord for which he has written sonatas in which long sustained notes occur.

"And it is the same with the extraordinary power which Bach can give to a passage: it is the utmost fortissimo. Another clavichord would go to pieces under it. Likewise, his most delicate pianissimo would not sound at all on another clavichord."

[15] This sentence, up to the semicolon, appears as a footnote in the ed. of 1787.

[16] This sentence appears as a footnote in the ed. of 1787.

to a good tone and the proper range. The tests of the quilling are neat, facile execution of embellishments, and an equal, quick reaction of each key as the thumbnail sweeps over the entire manual with a light, uniform pressure. The action of the harpsichord must not be too light and effeminate; the keys must not fall too deep; the fingers must meet resistance from them and be raised again by the jacks. On the other hand, they must not be too difficult to depress. For the benefit of those whose instruments have less than the desirable range, I have so constructed my Lessons [17] that they may be played on a four-octave keyboard.

14.   Both types of instrument must be tempered as follows: In tuning the fifths and fourths, testing minor and major thirds and chords, take away from most of the fifths a barely noticeable amount of their absolute purity. All twenty-four tonalities will thus become usable. The beats of fifths can be more easily heard by probing fourths, an advantage that stems from the fact that the tones of the latter lie closer together than fifths. In practice, a keyboard so tuned is the purest of all instruments, for others may be more purely tuned but they cannot be purely played. The keyboard plays equally in tune in all twenty-four tonalities and, mark well, with full chords, notwithstanding that these, because of their ratios, reveal a very slight impurity. The new method of tuning marks a great advance over the old, even though the latter was of such a nature that a few tonalities were purer than those of many present non-keyboard instruments, the impurity of which would be easier to detect (and without a monochord) by listening harmonically to each melodic tone. Their melodies often deceive us and do not expose their impurity until it is greater than that of a badly tuned keyboard.

15.   Every keyboardist should own a good harpsichord and a good clavichord to enable him to play all things interchangeably. A good clavichordist makes an accomplished harpsichordist, but not

---

[17] *Probestücke*. This refers to the pieces written by Bach to illustrate the Essay. They are available in the following modern editions:

(a) *Sechs Sonaten für Klavier*, ed. by Erich Doflein, Édition Schott, Nos. 2353–54 (1935). These are the "18 Lessons in 6 Sonatas" which appeared with the first ed. of the Essay. The Adagio of Sonata V appears in *Zeitschrift für Musik*, no. 103, 1936, *Notenbeilage*, and the Fantasia of Sonata VI can be found in *Vierteljahrschrift für Musikwissenschaft*, No. 7, 1891.

(b) *Kleine Stücke für Klavier*, ed. by Otto Vrieslander, Nagels Musik-Archiv, No. 65, Hannover, 1930. Includes (Nos. 19–24) the *VI Sonatine Nuove* which were published in connection with the third ed. of the Essay in 1787.

the reverse. The clavichord is needed for the study of good performance, and the harpsichord to develop proper finger strength. Those who play the clavichord exclusively encounter many difficulties when they turn to the harpsichord. In an ensemble where a harpsichord must be used rather than the soft-toned clavichord, they will play laboriously; and great exertion never produces the proper keyboard effect. The clavichordist grows too much accustomed to caressing the keys; consequently, his wonted touch being insufficient to operate the jacks, he fails to bring out details on the harpsichord. In fact, finger strength may be lost eventually, by playing only the clavichord. On the other hand, those who concentrate on the harpsichord grow accustomed to playing in only one color, and the varied touch which the competent clavichordist brings to the harpsichord remains hidden from them. This may sound strange, since one would think that all performers can express only one kind of tone on each harpsichord. To test its truth ask two people, one a good clavichordist, the other a harpsichordist, to play on the latter's instrument the same piece containing varied embellishments, and then decide whether both have produced the same effect.[18]

16.   After mastering the requisite knowledge of keys, notes, rests, rhythm, and so forth, students should be made to spend a good deal of time practicing only the examples of fingering, slowly at first and then more rapidly until in due time good fingering, as difficult and varied as it is at the keyboard, will become so much a matter of habit that it may be put out of mind.

17.   Above all, practice in unison those examples in which fingering is given for both hands, so that they will become equally dexterous.

18.   Then ply at the chapter on embellishments, practicing them until they can be performed skillfully with proper facility. Since this is an assignment on which a lifetime may well be spent

18 J. F. Reichardt wrote: "Bach's manner of playing would not have been devised at all without the clavichord, and he devised it only for the clavichord. But he who once masters this instrument plays the harpsichord quite differently from those who never touch a clavichord. For him harpsichord compositions may be written which under the hands of the mere harpsichordist become insipid, often unintelligible, and disconnected."

Also: "Soul, expression, feeling, these things Bach gave first to the clavichord, and the harpsichord could not receive the smallest degree of them save from the hand of him who knew how to animate the clavichord."

(embellishments demand in part more technique and dexterity than runs) the student should not be detained after his ability, depending on his aptness and age, is great enough to stand him in modest stead.

19.   After this, proceed directly to the Lessons; play them first without the ornaments, which should be practiced separately, and then with them, according to the rules treated in the chapter on performance. This must be done first at the clavichord and later interchangeably with the harpsichord.

20.   The whole approach to performance will be greatly aided and simplified by the supplementary study of voice wherever possible and by listening closely to good singers.

21.   In order to become oriented at the keyboard and thus make easier the acquisition of a necessary skill at sight reading, it is a good practice to play memorized pieces in the dark.

22.   In notating the Lessons, I have scored everything that seemed necessary; and I have played them many times with great care so that not even the smallest detail would escape me. Therefore I believe that if everything is given careful attention, finger dexterity as well as taste will be improved to the point where other, more difficult things may be studied.

23.   In order to avoid ambiguity I have written all triplets without the numeral three, and indicated the detached notes not with strokes, but with dots, and abbreviations such as *f., p.,* and so forth, without a period in most places.

24.   Because I wanted to publish a complete work illustrative of fingering in all keys, the use of embellishments, and all varieties of expression, I could not prevent an increase in the difficulty of the Lessons. I considered it better to serve everyone rather than append a collection of very easy pieces and leave many things untouched. I hope that after clear preliminary instruction, the fingerings and performing directions, painstakingly added, will make the more difficult pieces a great deal easier It is dangerous to delay the student with too many easy things, for no progress can be achieved in this manner. A few simple pieces at the beginning suffice, after which the wise teacher will do better to introduce his pupils gradually to more challenging works. It is in accord with the art of teaching and the reason asserted above that by this means the student will be unaware of the increasing difficulty of his tasks. My

deceased father made many successful experiments of a similar nature. He introduced his pupils directly to his moderately difficult pieces. Therefore, no one need fear my Lessons.

25.   Should some because of their facility be inclined to read the Lessons at sight, I urge them first to study every smallest detail with proper diligence.

CHAPTER ONE

FINGERING

1

TO A LARGE extent the shape of an instrument determines its fingering. It would appear to be most arbitrary in the case of keyboard instruments, for the arrangement of the keys is such that any one of them may be depressed by any finger.

2. For this and other reasons the study of fingering is a treacherous path along which many have erred. For one thing, there is only one good system of keyboard fingering, and very few passages permit alternative fingerings. Again, every figure calls for its own distinctive fingering, which may require modification simply through a change of context, and the comprehensiveness of the keyboard creates an inexhaustible wealth of figures. Finally, the true method, almost a secret art, has been known and practiced by very few.

3. This erring is the more considerable, the less one is aware of it, for at the keyboard almost anything can be expressed even with the wrong fingering, although with prodigious difficulty and awkwardness. In the case of other instruments the slightest incorrectness of fingering is usually betrayed by the downright impossibility of performing the notes. As a result, all manner of things have been ascribed to what is believed to be the difficulty of the instrument and the compositions written for it.

4. From these remarks it can be seen that correct employment of the fingers is inseparably related to the whole art of performance. More is lost through poor fingering than can be replaced by all conceivable artistry and good taste. Facility itself hinges on it, for experience will prove that an average performer with well-trained fingers will best the greatest musician who because of poor fingering is forced to play, against his better judgment.

5. Because almost every figure requires its own, distinctive fin-

gering, present-day musical thought, so radically different from that of the past, has devised a new method of execution.

6.   Our forefathers were more concerned with harmony than melody and played in several parts most of the time. We shall soon learn that in this style the position of each finger is immediately apparent since most passages can be expressed in only one way and are variable to only a limited degree. Consequently, they are not so treacherous as melodic passages with their far more capricious fingering. Furthermore, in earlier times the keyboard was tuned differently and not all twenty-four keys were available as they are now. Consequently, the variety of passages was not great.

7.   Hence, today, much more than in the past, no one can hope to play well who does not use his fingers correctly. My deceased father told me that in his youth he used to hear great men who employed their thumbs only when large stretches made it necessary. Because he lived at a time when a gradual but striking change in musical taste was taking place, he was obliged to devise a far more comprehensive fingering and especially to enlarge the role of the thumbs and use them as nature intended; [1] for, among their other good services, they must be employed chiefly in the·difficult tonalities. Hereby, they rose from their former uselessness to the rank of principal finger.

8.   Because this new fingering is such that everything can be played easily with it at the proper time, I shall expound it here.

9.   However, before proceeding to the actual use of the fingers, I must mention certain points, some of which must be known in advance of our study, others of which are so important that without them even the best rules are futile.

10.   The performer must sit at the middle of the keyboard so that he may strike the highest as well as the lowest tones with equal ease.

11.   When the performer is in the correct position with respect to height his forearms are suspended slightly above the fingerboard.

12.   In playing, the fingers should be arched and the muscles relaxed. The less these two conditions are satisfied, the more atten-

---

[1] The few extant, notated fingerings attributed to J. S. Bach are largely in the older style. They may be found in his *Werke,* 36.4, pp. 126, 224, 237. However, cf. Spitta, *Bach,* Vol. II, pp. 34–41; *The Bach Reader* (Norton, New York, 1945), pp. 223, 306–312; and Dolmetsch, *The Interpretation of the Music of the XVIIth and XVIIIth Centuries,* pp. 412 ff.

tion must be given to them. Stiffness hampers all movement, above all the constantly required rapid extension and contraction of the hands. All stretches, the omission of certain fingers, even the indispensable crossing of the fingers and turning of the thumb demand this elastic ability. Those who play with flat, extended fingers suffer from one principal disadvantage in addition to awkwardness; the fingers, because of their length, are too far removed from the thumb, which should always remain as close as possible to the hand. As we shall see later, the principal finger is thereby robbed of all possibility of performing its services, whence it comes about that those who seldom use the thumb play stiffly, something that those who use it correctly can not do even willfully. For the latter, everything is easy. This can be observed immediately in a performer: If he understands the correct principles of fingering and has not acquired the habit of making unnecessary gestures, he will play the most difficult things in such a manner that the motion of his hands will be barely noticeable; moreover, everything will sound as if it presented no obstacles to him. Conversely, those who do not understand these principles will often play the easiest things with great snorting, grimacing, and uncommon awkwardness.

13.   Those who do not use the thumb let it hang to keep it out of the way. Such a position makes even the most moderate span uncomfortable, for the fingers must stretch and stiffen in order to encompass it. Can anything be well executed this way? The thumbs give the hand not only another digit, but the key to all fingering. This principal finger performs another service in that it keeps the others supple, for they must remain arched as it makes its entry after one or another of them. Those passages which, without the thumb, must be pounced upon with stiff, tensed muscles, can be played roundly, clearly, with a natural extension, and a consequent facility when it lends its assistance.

14.   It is evident that the muscles cannot remain relaxed nor the fingers arched in leaping or stretching; and even the snap [2] calls for a momentary tension. These are, however, the rarest cases and take care of themselves by their very nature. All others follow the precepts of Paragraph 12. Especially children's hands, not yet fully

---

[2] *Das Schnellen.* The nature and execution of this technical element of clavichord playing are described in Ch. I, ¶ 90; Ch. II, "The Trill," ¶¶ 8, 36, and "The Snap," ¶ 11.

grown, should be trained to stretch as far as possible, rather than leap everywhere with the fingers bunched, as so often happens. In this manner it will be easy to strike the keys accurately, and the hands will not readily depart from their proper position of swinging horizontally over the keyboard, which they tend to lose in leaps by inclining to one or another side.

15. Pupils need not be alarmed when a passage must be tested by their teachers in order to ascertain its best fingering. Occasionally, doubtful cases arise which, even when they are played correctly at the first reading, might require reflection before the fingering can be recited to another person. Teachers are rarely provided with a second instrument at which they might settle such issues while accompanying their pupils. From all this it can be seen, first, that in spite of the endless variety of fingerings, a few good principles are sufficient to solve all problems; and second, that through diligent practice, execution becomes so mechanical that, eventually, a stage is reached where, without further concern, full attention may be directed to the expression of more important matters.

16. While playing, always think ahead to the approaching notes, for these often necessitate modification of a normal fingering.

17. The form of one hand being the reverse of the other, I have found it advisable to illustrate the exceptional cases [3] in contrary motion in order to make them identically applicable to both hands. Most of the examples that did not call for inversion have been fingered for both hands so that they might be practiced in unison. Every opportunity to practice in this manner must be seized, as recommended in the Introduction. The clef signatures [4] of each example indicate the hand for which the fingering numerals are intended. When numerals appear both above and below the notes, those above refer to the right hand and those below to the left, regardless of the clef.

18. Having disposed of these preliminary points, all grounded in Nature, let us now proceed to the school of fingering. Here, too,

[3] As described in ¶¶ 86–92.

[4] The examples for the right hand appeared in the customary descant clef in the original. In order to make them more accessible to modern readers, out of touch with C-clefs, they have been transcribed in the familiar G-clef.

I shall build upon Nature, for a natural fingering devoid of unnecessary strain and extension is clearly the best.

19.   The shapes of our hand and the keyboard teach us how to use our fingers. The former tells us that the three interior fingers are longer than the little finger and the thumb. From the latter we learn that certain keys are longer and lie lower than the others.

20.   I shall follow the usual designations by indicating the thumb with the numeral 1, the little finger with 5, the middle finger with 3, that next to the thumb with 2, and that next to the little finger with 4.

21.   I shall call the raised and recessed keys by the more usual than correct name of half tones.[5]

22.   It follows directly from the statements of Paragraph 19 that the black keys belong essentially to the three longest fingers. Hence, the first principal rule: Black keys are seldom taken by the little finger and only out of necessity by the thumb.

23.   I have found it advisable because of the great variety of passages to construct all types of examples; some in one voice, others in several, some in conjunct motion, and others in disjunct.

24.   The scales have been arranged according to keys in the first examples, which will illustrate all twenty-four, ascending and descending. Thereafter, the order of illustrations will be as follows: Progressions in several parts; spans and leaps, because these can be more readily gauged after the study of progressions, or even traced back to chords; and, finally, tied or held notes, a few licenses, exceptional cases, and certain expedients. The Lessons will account for the remainder. In appending these with their continuous passages of all types, I believe I have served a greater purpose and stimulated more interest in the difficult study of fingering than I could have hoped for had I amassed quantities of fragmentary examples, for these would have made the work overlong and unendurable.

25.   Change of fingers [6] is the most important element in our study. Our five fingers can strike only five successive tones, but

[5] *Halbentöne*. The "raised and recessed keys" of Bach's day were not universally black, hence he could not use the convenient "black keys," which appears from this point on as the translation of the term that he adopted with easily understandable misgivings.

[6] *Die Abwechselung der Finger.*

there are two principal means whereby we can extend their range as much as required, both above and below. They are the turning of the thumb [7] and the crossing of the fingers.[8]

26. Of the five fingers, the thumb alone is naturally adept at turning under. Flexible and propitiously short, it is the only one to be concerned with this technique, which is employed when the fingers, playing in their normal order, cannot encompass the range of a passage.

27. Crossing over is a technique limited to the remaining fingers. It occurs when a longer one vaults a shorter, including the thumb, in order to strike a tone that lies beyond the natural range of the fingers. This device must be practiced until it is brought to the point where the fingers will not interlock.

28. These are to be avoided: Turning the thumb under the little finger, crossing the second finger over the third, the third over the second, the fourth over the fifth, and the fifth over the thumb.[9]

29. The correct application of these two techniques can be learned most readily from the patterns of scales. In playing these and runs based on them our precepts find their principal employment. It is understood that in the performance of scalewise runs which begin or end differently from those illustrated here the performer must allocate his fingers so that they will come out correctly without his feeling obliged always to use the assigned finger on a given tone.

30. Figure 1 represents the ascending scale of C major with three fingerings for each hand. None of them is impracticable, although those in which the third finger of the right hand crosses the fourth, the second of the left hand crosses the thumb, and the

Figure 1   Figure 2

---

[7] *Das Untersetzen.*   [8] *Das Überschlagen.*

[9] Observe that one important technique of the older fingering is not ruled out, the crossing of 3 over 4. It appears more than once in the fingerings of scales, and in ¶ 30 is among those that Bach expressly prefers.

thumbs strike *f* are perhaps more usual than the others. Applications of each are shown in Figure 2.

31.   Figure 3 illustrates the descending scale of C major. Here, too, there are three fingerings, all of which are good in various situations, as indicated in the examples of Figure 4, although aside from these cases which require the specified fingerings, one may turn up more often than the others.

Figure 3   Figure 4

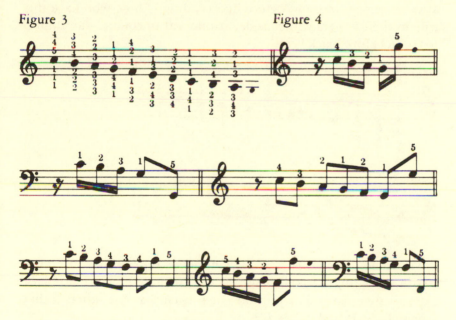

32.   It can be seen in Figures 2 and 4 that owing to the necessity of paying heed to the approching notes, the little finger is held in reserve in stepwise passages and is used only at the beginning or when a run happens to terminate exactly with it. This is illustrated in the examples of scales where its use is specified. Elsewhere its place is usually taken by the thumb. In order to avoid confusion with regard to the little finger and to illustrate a more ex-

tended change of fingers, I have led the scales beyond the octave.

33.   In Figure 5 we find A minor, ascending, with two fingerings for each hand. The best are those directly above and below the notes. Nevertheless, the others may be applied to good ends, as illustrated in Figure 6. However, since many more might be devised were I inclined to construct the examples, and since those in Figure 6 are not as natural as those that I have recommended, I include them here more as a warning than as an endorsement, the more so, because I know that they enjoy scattered popularity. Their defect is the assignment of *d* to the thumb despite the succeeding *e* and two black keys, for the thumb is best used immediately before black keys. In any event, this fundamental rule should be observed: The thumb of the right hand is brought in after one or more black keys in ascending, before them in descending, and the left thumb after in descending, and before in ascending. Those who have this rule in their fingers will consider it unusual to commit the thumb too soon before black keys.

Figure 5

Figure 6

34.   The descending scale of A minor is represented in Figure 7 with three fingerings. Because, as in C major, there are no black keys, all are good and practicable. Less usual than the others is that in which the thumb takes *d*.[10]

35.   The ascending G major scale and its three fingerings appear in Figure 8. Those marked with an asterisk are the least usual. The middle one in the G-clef and the lowest in the bass present an opportunity to state a new rule: Crossing the fingers, that is, passing

---

[10] This turns out to be the most usual modern fingering, at least for the right hand. Perhaps Bach's reservations are concerned with the use of the fifth finger, which does not appear in the alternative fingerings.

Figure 7

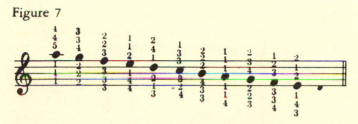

the second finger over the thumb or the third finger over the fourth, is applied primarily to passages with no accidentals, where, if necessary, it may occur several times in succession. Occasionally, it may be used in connection with a single black key in this manner: The thumb or the fourth finger plays the tone immediately preceding the black key, which is then struck by the second or the third finger, an action easily performed by either, owing to their convenient length. Thereupon, and in accordance with the rule stated in Paragraph 33, the thumb takes its assigned place as a matter of course. Example *a* of Figure 9 might stand for an exception to our rule were it not more usual to execute the passage by turning the thumb as in Example *b*. It is better in such cases to cross the second finger over the thumb than the third finger over the fourth. In order to illustrate the crossing of fingers in connection with black keys I have written two octaves of this scale.

Figure 8

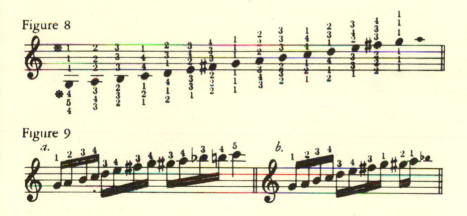

Figure 9

36. G major, descending, also with three fingerings, is illustrated in Figure 10. That in which the thumb takes *c* is clearly the least frequent; the farthest from the notes are the most dangerous; but all may be used.

Figure 10

37. E minor, ascending, has only one good fingering (Figure 11). It is inadvisable to take the fourth step, *a,* instead of the fifth, *b,* with the thumb unless the succession demands it. Contrary to the rule of Paragraph 33, the thumb must avoid *g* when the ascending scale ends on the octave, or there will be too few fingers to complete it. As we shall see later, this rule suffers a few exceptions, which, however, do not in the least reduce its value in the complete school of fingering.

Figure 11

38. E minor, descending, is illustrated in Figure 12 with two fingerings for each hand, of which those directly above and below the notes are the best.

Figure 12

39. F major, ascending, has only one good fingering for the right hand, as in Figure 13, but three for the left, all of which are useful in certain situations and should therefore be practiced.

Figure 13

40. F major, descending, appears in Figure 14 with two fingerings in the G-clef and three in the bass, of which those directly above and below the notes are the most usual. There is nothing irregular about the others. They are to be noted because there may be need for them at times.

Figure 14

41. D minor, ascending, as shown in Figure 15 has three fingerings for each hand, all of which are good and should be practiced, although those farthest removed from the notes are somewhat less usual than the others.

Figure 15

42. D minor, descending, appears in Figure 16 with two fingerings for each hand. Those that lie farthest from the notes are poorer because the black key, *b*-flat, calls for the thumb on *a*.

Figure 16

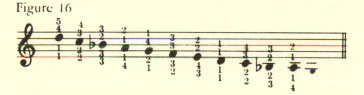

43. Only one fingering is possible for B-flat major, ascending and descending, as illustrated in Figure 17.

Figure 17

44. G minor, ascending, in Figure 18 has two fingerings for the right hand and three for the left. Those directly above the notes and farthest below follow the rule of Paragraph 33. However, the others will prove serviceable on occasion.

Figure 18

45. G minor, descending, in Figure 19 has only one fingering. It is understood that when a passage does not begin exactly as illustrated here, the appropriate finger must take the initial tone.

Figure 19

46. D major, ascending, in Figure 20 has only one fingering for the right hand, but three for the left. According to the rule covering the use of the thumb, and in all passages that begin or end differently from the illustration, the fingering immediately below the notes should be employed. However, the others are good, particularly in the illustrated case, and should be practiced. The second fingering in the bass demonstrates the merits of crossing the fingers as discussed in Paragraph 35.

Figure 20

47. D major, descending, in Figure 21 has three fingerings for the right hand and two for the left, all of which are useful.

Figure 21

48. B minor, ascending, appears in Figure 22 with one fingering for each hand. When a passage for the left hand begins below the first step of the scale, the thumb replaces the fourth finger on *b*. In this connection note that the fingering for the higher octave should be used to play all variants of the beginnings of scales. There is an unavoidable departure in the right hand from the rule of Paragraph 33. Those who have this rule in their fingers must be careful not to assign the thumb to *d* instead of *e*—a difficulty that makes the scale rather treacherous.

Figure 22

49. B minor, descending, with one fingering is shown in Figure 23. To construct an alternate setting for the right hand, begin with the little finger, place the thumb on *e*, and the third finger on *d* in order to bring in the thumb again on *b*. This setting, while it is not incorrect and may be used, is good for only one octave. Extension of it might easily prove confusing.

Figure 23

50. A major, ascending, is illustrated in Figure 24 with one fingering for the right hand and two for the left. That which stands just below the notes agrees with the frequently cited rule and in most cases is more useful than the one below it, which, nevertheless, is required at times.

Figure 24

51. A major, descending, in Figure 25 has only one fingering. It is understood, as previously noted, that when the scale begins above

the initial tone of the illustration the right hand takes *a* with the thumb rather than the little finger. Also, when a passage for the left hand in this key begins on the tonic degree, 1–2–3 should be substituted for 2–3–4.

Figure 25

52.   F-sharp minor, ascending, with one fingering appears in Figure 26. The value of the rule cited in Paragraph 33 will become apparent in the forthcoming scales, for as they increase in accidentals or black keys, they grow simpler, less treacherous, and easier to learn.

Figure 26

53.   F-sharp minor, descending, has, according to Figure 27, one fingering in common with A major. We learned in Paragraph 50 that the additional setting for the latter in the ascending left hand is used only occasionally. As we proceed, note that descending minor scales employ the same fingerings as major scales with the same key signature or, in the case of enharmonically equivalent signatures, the same fingering as major scales whose tonic degrees lie a minor third above those of minor scales.[11]

Figure 27

54.   E major in Figure 28 has a simple fingering for both hands, ascending as well as descending. C-sharp minor, descending, is the same. Because anyone can determine the steps of descending minor scales from the statement in Paragraph 53, I shall omit their illustration as superfluous unless they have an exceptional fingering.

[11] I.e. a minor third, not as notated, but at the keyboard.

Figure 28

55. C-sharp minor, ascending, has only one good fingering, as illustrated in Figure 29.

Figure 29

56. B major, ascending ·and descending, and G-sharp minor, descending, take only one fingering, which is shown in Figure 30. The latter, ascending, is different in the size of its intervals but not in the fingering, as we can see in Figure 31.

Figure 30

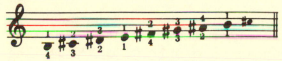

Figure 31

57. F-sharp major, ascending and descending, has one fingering in common with E-flat minor, descending, as illustrated in Figure 32. The same is true of E-flat minor, ascending, except for the difference in the size of its intervals and the notation (Figure 33). In the left hand there is an exception to the rule of Paragraph 33, according to which the thumb should take *d* rather than *c*.

Figure 32

Figure 33

58. D-flat or C-sharp major, its fingering applicable to ascending as well as descending scales, appears in Figure 34. B-flat minor, descending, takes the same. B-flat minor, ascending, and its fingerings, of which there are two good ones for the left hand, appear in Figure 35.

Figure 34

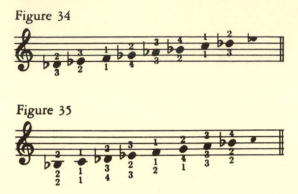

Figure 35

59. A-flat major in Figure 36, ascending and descending, has one fingering in common with F minor, descending. The latter with its ascending execution is shown in Figure 37. The left hand has two good fingerings, of which the one directly below the notes is the better, although the other demonstrates anew the remarks of Paragraphs 35 and 46.

Figure 36

Figure 37

60. E-flat major is illustrated in Figure 38. The fingering applies to ascending and descending scales, as well as to C minor, descending. This latter scale, ascending, in Figure 39 has two good settings for each hand, of which the more removed from the notes apply

only to progressions within an octave. Note that as scales lose accidentals (which occurs in the ascending minor before other scales) the number of fingerings increases.

Figure 38

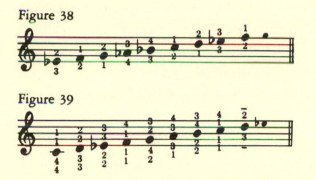

Figure 39

61. From the study of these scales we learn that the thumb is never placed on a black key, that it may be used after the second finger, after the second and third fingers, or the second, third, and fourth, but never after the fifth. Note that in order to maintain a uniform fingering in playing through two or more octaves of a scale with its seven degrees, the thumb is usually employed once after the second and third finger, and again after the second, third, and fourth. In ascending with the right hand and descending with the left this action of the thumb is called turning, a technique which must be practiced until the principal finger has learned to turn and take its note automatically. The performer who has reached this point has gained the summit of fingering.

62. We learn, further, that a crossing occurs when the second finger, the second and third fingers, or the second, third, and fourth pass over the thumb or when the third passes over the fourth. Later, we shall find an exception, allowed under certain conditions, in which the fourth crosses the fifth.[12] Also, a case will arise in the study of embellishments in which the third finger *strikes* a key after the second.[13] However, this striking must not be confused with a crossing, which refers only to those cases where one finger crosses another which is still depressing the key that it has struck; in the former the initial finger leaves the key and the hand is shifted.

63. Finally, we learn that scales with few or no accidentals per-

[12] See, in the present chapter, ¶ 93.
[13] See Ch. II, "The Turn," ¶ 30.

mit the greatest variation with respect to fingering and the techniques of turning and crossing. The others have only one execution. Hence, because the former have many fingerings, because both techniques must be correctly applied to them without confusing one with the other, and because a fingering, once it has been chosen, must be retained in all registers, particularly with regard to the thumb, the so-called easy keys are, in fact, much more challenging and elusive than the so-called difficult ones. These have only one execution, in which the thumb soon learns through practice to take its tones effortlessly. These keys are called difficult because they are never or, at best, rarely played or employed in their own right. As a result, their notation as well as the location of their tones remains unfamiliar. Once forbidding, when they were played without the thumb or the correct use of it, the difficult keys have become inviting, thanks to the true study and employment of the fingers. Thus, in earlier times one of the great advantages of the keyboard, the facility with which it can express all twenty-four tonalities, lay hidden behind ignorance. While [14] speaking of accidentals, I must state my opinion concerning their employment. Our forerunners followed the correct practice of placing an accidental before each altered note which did not succeed itself directly. Today, one accidental is considered sufficient for several such notes. Accidental signs must be used generously to clarify unexpected modulatory shifts and their occasional resultant ambiguities.

64.   Crossing and turning, the principal means of changing the fingers, must be applied in such a manner that the tones involved in the change flow smoothly. In keys with few or no accidentals the crossing of the third finger over the fourth and the second over the thumb is in certain cases more practicable and better suited for the attainment of unbroken continuity than other crossings or the turn. With regard to the latter, when a black key acts as the pivot the thumb is conveniently provided with more room in which to turn than in a succession of white keys. In keys without accidentals crossing should cause no stumbling, but in the others care must be exercised because of the black keys.

65.   All runs must be approached in the light of these scales and the two techniques derived from them. Certain exceptional

14 Remainder of paragraph from ed. of 1787.

cases and licenses will be reserved for discussion at the end of this chapter.

66. We shall now treat progressions in parts. Leaps will be included in this discussion because under normal circumstances they must be devised with a view to an unforced execution by fingers of average length and are therefore fingered in the same manner as part progressions. Should some find it more comfortable, because of their longer fingers, to take chords, arpeggios, or stretches with a fingering different from that recommended here, they may do so, provided that the comfort is not imaginary. I have stressed leaps and stretches in a slow movement, the B-flat adagio,[15] in order to make them easier. Those who wish to practice them rapidly by themselves may do so.

67. Adjacent tones, struck simultaneously, are taken by adjacent fingers. The preceding and following tones determine which pair of fingers is to be used. Examples of such seconds are contained in Figure 40. Observe that the thumb avoids black keys. In the examples, notes without fingering numerals are to be played by the finger assigned to the preceding note. Each clef appears only once and remains in force until replaced by another.

Figure 40

---

15 The middle movement of Sonata II. Cf. Pt. I, Introduction, Note 17.

68.   Broken seconds are played by alternate fingers as illustrated in Figure 41. Alternation [16] is better for this kind of passage, usually slurred, than a repeated finger [17] which causes an excessive detaching of the notes. It should be noted here and more frequently as we proceed that the thumb and second finger of the left hand are used, generally, in those places where the right hand employs the second and third fingers.

Figure 41

69.   Thirds are played by the fingers which are indicated in the several examples under Figure 42. Here, too, attention must be directed to preceding and succeeding notes. The thumb and the little finger do not play black notes, except when a contextual leap makes it necessary. Because successive thirds are often encountered, I have introduced several examples in order clearly to indicate the necessary finger changes. The little finger may also strike a black note when the accompanying finger does likewise. Viewed in this light, the fingering for the right hand in Example *a* is not as good as that in Example *b* nor that for the left hand in Example *c*. The little finger is neither repeated directly nor succeeded by another (*d*). Normally, it is employed but once and then only on the extreme notes of a succession of thirds (*e*) unless single tones intervene, as in Example *f*. Note that repeated thirds are played by repeated fingers, as in the third and following examples. The same applies to successive thirds in fast tempos, like those in Example *g*, for a change of fingers is more difficult. In conclusion, observe that many fingerings are used on thirds, although some are more frequent than others. 1, $\overset{5}{2}$, $\overset{5}{3}$, $\overset{4}{}$, being unnatural, are to be avoided.

Figure 42

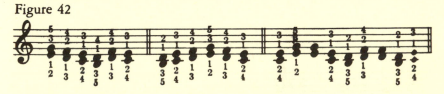

[16] *Das Abwechseln.*   [17] *Das Fortsetzen eines Fingers.*

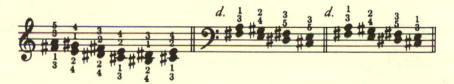

70.   In slower tempos, broken thirds, singly or in succession, are played in the same manner as the thirds described in the preceding paragraph. Several successive broken thirds in rapid tempos are played with a pair of repeated fingers, $\frac{1}{3}$ or $\frac{2}{4}$, so long as black keys do not intervene (Figure 43, Example *a*). When they do, the fingering is changed, the thumb being withheld from them (*b*). $\frac{5}{3}$ or $\frac{2}{1}$ are employed in passages containing a sustained or an interpolated tone (*c*). When necessary, the thumb may play black keys in such spans.

Figure 43

71.   Fourths are taken in the manner of Figure 44. In the examples written in the G-clef the lowest notes are to be played by the left hand, and in the bass clef the uppermost notes by the right. Broken fourths in a slow tempo have the same fingering. A succession of these without black keys is executed by a pair of repeated fingers, $\frac{1}{4}$ or $\frac{5}{2}$ (*a*). With black keys, $\frac{2}{4}$ may be used, but only once at a time (*b*). Broken fourths may also be played $\frac{1}{2}, \frac{1}{3}, \frac{2}{4},$ or $\frac{5}{3}$, provided that the succeeding notes call for it, as shown in example *c* and further.

Figure 44

72.   Fifths and sixths may be taken in three ways, as illustrated in Figure 45. Figure 46 indicates the execution of a series of sixths. Broken sixths are played in the manner discussed previously in the cases of thirds and fourths. In stretches such as these the little finger may be repeated directly; in other words, it may be played before the extremity of a passage has been reached.

Figure 45   Figure 46

73.   Sevenths and octaves are played $\frac{5}{1}$. Those who have long fingers and find it easy to take a seventh containing a black key with $\frac{5}{2}$ or $\frac{4}{1}$ may do so. Beyond this, it is permissible in playing these large intervals to use the thumb as well as the little finger on black keys without further ado.

74.   Octaves that leap, particularly in the left hand, where they appear most frequently, call for the repeated thumb and little finger. Those who are not sufficiently trained to execute the octave doublings of thorough bass can practice by playing any given bass first with the thumb and then with the little finger. In doing this, progress will be made not only in a fundamental kind of finger repetition, but also in becoming familiar with the keyboard.

75.   In leaps of an octave, preceding or succeeding notes may require the second finger to take the place of the thumb, or the fourth finger to take the place of the fifth, as shown in the examples

of Figure 47. When the thumb occupies a black key it cannot be crossed by other fingers in the manner of Figure 48.

Figure 47

Figure 48

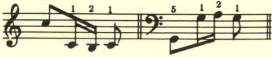

76.   We shall now discuss the execution of three-toned chords. Their fingering within the interval of a fourth is shown in Figure 49. The additional tones of examples *a* and *b* call for a special fingering.

Figure 49

77.   Figure 50 illustrates the execution of three-toned chords within the interval of a fifth. With respect to example *a*, note that

in addition to the minor triad built from *f,* the same fingering applies to those from *c, c*-sharp, *f*-sharp, *g, g*-sharp, *b*-flat, and *b.* And with respect to Example *b,* the fingering of the major triad built from *d* applies equally to those built from *c*-sharp, *d*-sharp, *e, g*-sharp, *a, b*-flat, and *b.* The longer third finger rather than the fourth takes the third of major and minor triads, particularly when it falls on a black key.

Figure 50

78.   Three-toned chords within the interval of a sixth are taken in the manner of Figure 51. Figure 52 illustrates the same chords in the interval of a seventh, and Figure 53 in the interval of an octave. Any finger may play black keys in wide stretches, as stated in Paragraph 73, for a measure such as this is always better than an avoid-

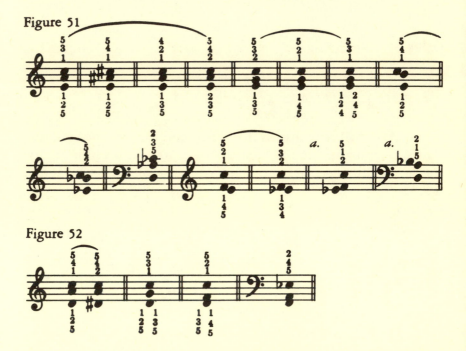

Figure 51

Figure 52

Figure 53

able strain. The [18] execution of Figure 51, Example *a*, is comfortable for some hands.

79. The fingering of four-toned chords appears in the examples of Figure 54. Example *a* represents such a chord within the interval of a fifth; Example *b*, within the interval of a sixth. Chords built from the first degrees of the major keys listed in Paragraph 77 may be taken in the manner of the illustration in the bass clef under Example *b*. The chords of Example *c* lie within the interval of a seventh, and those of Example *d* within the interval of an octave. The illustrations marked with double asterisks in Example *c* are for long fingers. The examples marked 1, 2, 3, 4 refer to the triads of Figure 50, Examples *a* and *b*, now become four-toned chords; all

Figure 54

18 This sentence and Figure 51, Example *a*, are from the ed. of 1787.

of the triads ·discussed in Paragraph 77 are to be taken similarly when a fourth tone has been added to them.

80.   When either of the outer parts of four-toned chords falls on a black key, it is best to take a fingering in which, if possible, either the thumb or the little finger is not used. However, since it is not always comfortable to omit the little finger, whence it plays black keys more often than the thumb, the performer should be guided by contexts and, not all fingers being alike, seek after an unforced and natural setting, especially in spans. A slight discomfort being preferable to a greater one, it is better to commit the little finger or the thumb to a black key than to omit them and cause an excessive, hazardous stretch. Performance of a succession of full chords is facilitated by changing the fingers whenever possible.

81.   When both outer parts of four-toned chords fall on black keys the two shortest fingers may be employed without further ado, for when both play such keys the entire hand moves to the rear of the keyboard, thereby removing the objections to their use.

82.   Since arpeggiated and leaping passages are largely reducible to chords, they should be played according to corresponding rules of fingering and examined in the light of particulars already discussed. The examples fashioned out of the chords in Figure 55 will make my meaning clearer to the reader.

Figure 55

83. Good performance, as well as preceding tones, calls for an occasional slight change in the fingering of broken chords. The third finger is sometimes better than the fourth in descending arpeggios, although the latter is to be preferred when the tones are struck simultaneously (Figure 55, Example 1). With regard to good performance, the keyboardist cannot always expect the degree of clarity from a weaker finger that a stronger finger achieves quite readily, for clarity is won principally through uniform pressure. In this respect, those who are left-handed possess no small advantage on our instrument.[19] In Example 2, Figure 55, the third of the arpeggio has been taken by the third finger because of the preceding *f*.

84. Having learned the prime importance of correct use of the thumb in conjunct as well as disjunct, one-part as well as fully set passages, we can understand more clearly the amount of harm done by methods of keyboard instruction appearing even in this day which, wrong in many of their teachings, are particularly in error on this point. One author dispenses entirely with the thumb; another is even more antagonistic toward his students—not only must they make all of their fingers clamber indiscriminately and out of sequence over the entire keyboard, they must be able to do this on any one key alone. The first develops pupils whose fingers stumble, miss, and interlock; the other's tire needlessly and unseasonably, for their hands must be continually twisted and distorted in order to allow the thumb to take black keys without rhyme or reason, even in tonalities with many accidentals. Because of this distortion the remaining fingers lose their natural position and must be forced into use. There is, consequently, no chance to loosen or relax the muscles, and the fingers stiffen.[20]

19 Bach enjoyed this advantage, according to Reichardt (*Selbst Biographie, Allgemeine Musikzeitung, Jhr. 16, 1814*, No. 2).

20 This paragraph indicates that the inadequacy of the older fingering was far from common knowledge. For example, as eminent a musicographer as Johann Mattheson, who prided himself on his keyboard ability, describes a fingering in his *Kleine General-Bass-Schule* (1735) in which the ascending right hand employs principally 3 over 4, and the descending, 3 over 2, the thumb being unemployed. (Cf. Spitta, *Bach*, II, p. 38). Couperin's fingering (Cf. Vol. I of his *Oeuvres*, Paris, 1933) is discussed later in ¶ 88.

85. As we have already learned, leaps and progressions in parts are easier to execute than scales. Sustained tones will prove even simpler, for, it being mandatory to hold them strictly for their assigned length, there is rarely more than one way to perform them. Greater latitude is allowed here than would be otherwise advisable; the repeated finger, the thumb on black keys, and other expedients which will be discussed later are all freely employed. Since it is not easy to err under such conditions, the few examples of Figure 56 should suffice.

Figure 56

86. Figure 57 is the first of a few exceptional examples. In it leaps appear in which the second finger (*a*), the third finger (*b*), and the fourth (*c*), cross the thumb. In Figure 58 we see the thumb used in broken passages. Note that this finger is uniformly followed by the fourth, and the second by the fifth.

Figure 57

Figure 58

87. One of the most important licenses is the omission of certain fingers from stepwise successions. This technique is shown in Figure 59, where, in preparation for the approaching leaps, the omissions in the asterisked example are clearly better than the settings marked with double asterisks. Omissions are frequently called for in the bass. The natural flexibility of the thumb makes Example 1, where three fingers are omitted, easier than Example 2, where only two are omitted.

Figure 59

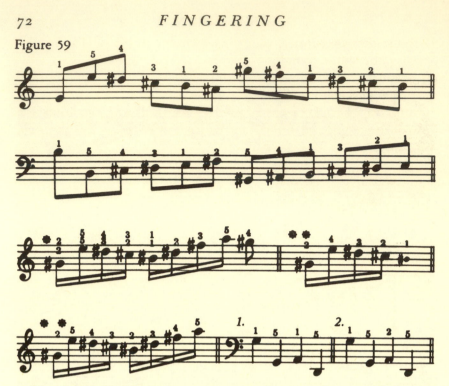

88.   In the Lessons, when two numerals appear in succession over a single note, the first of the assigned fingers is not released until the second has arrived, for such notes are to be sounded only once unless an embellishment intervenes. The successions of Figure 60, Example *a,* as well as the performance of certain embellishments call for this replacing of a finger. Occasionally it is needed in order to sustain the tones of an arpeggio (*b*). The flexibility of the thumb makes it well suited for replacement. Because it is not easy to employ this device skillfully it is correctly restricted to relatively long notes and cases of necessity. This precaution should be heeded in the use of all expedients which, partly by their nature, partly by their unusualness, are and remain difficult. Pupils should not be permitted to employ them except as a last resort or to avoid an even greater difficulty. Couperin,[21] who is otherwise so sound, calls for replacement too frequently and casually. Undoubtedly, the thumb's correct use was not fully known in his time, as suggested by some of his fingered examples in which he replaces fingers instead of using the thumb or the repeated finger, both of which are easier.

[21] François Couperin in *L'Art de toucher le clavecin,* Paris, 1717.

Because our forerunners rarely used the thumb, it got in the way. Hence, they often found that they had too many fingers. Gradually, it began to play a more active rôle, but traces of the old method survived and many were not enterprising enough always to set the thumb on appropriate tones. Today, despite improvements in the use of the fingers, we find, at times, that we have too few of them.

Figure 60

89. Because of this, it is permissible, on occasion, to use a finger twice in succession even when the notes change. This occurs most frequently and happily in moving from a black key to an adjacent white one. Slurred notes can be well expressed in this manner. (Figure 61). A simple device, it may be employed for other purposes, too, and in faster tempos than those suitable for replacements and finger repetitions on a single tone. Observe that it may be used to perform detached as well as slurred notes. The first of these uses appears near the beginning of the F-sharp minor Lesson [22] and the second in Figure 56. Beyond this, we have already learned from Paragraph 88 that the repeated finger is more natural, even on successive tied notes (where there might be a choice of expedients), than the replaced finger.

Figure 61

90. Tones repeated at a moderate speed are played by a single finger, but alternating fingers are employed in fast repetitions.[23]

[22] Sonata IV, third movement, bars 6–7. Cf. Pt. I, Introduction, Note 17.
[23] *Die Wiederholungen.* Marpurg's term is *"die Schwärmer."*

Only two fingers should be used at a time. The little finger is the poorest because its weakness retards the snap, a quick retraction which occurs when a finger leaves a key as rapidly as possible so that the succeeding finger may play its tone distinctly. This kind of passage is most easily performed on the clavichord.

91.   Alternating fingers may be employed to advantage in slower repetitions by playing the final note of the series with the finger that leads best to the following notes, as illustrated in Figure 62. Such situations occur often in the left hand.

Figure 62

92.   When, in keys with many accidentals, there appear passages not so extended as to require the normal succession of fingers after the thumb has turned, it is possible to take, instead, the finger that has preceded the thumb. In so doing, the hand maintains a single position, thereby avoiding the awkward shift caused by a normal,

Figure 63

but in this case rapid, crossing. This rule applies solely to those cases in which a single tone follows that taken by the thumb. Should two tones follow, the fingers are to be played in their usual order. Both types appear in Figure 63. Some employ this device in passages with two succeeding tones, as indicated by the uppermost numerals of the two final examples. While this is not incorrect, I maintain that it is mandatory to hold to the normal order except in those few cases where a modification helps to eliminate awkwardness.

93.   In the Lessons there are two places [24] where, contrary to the stated rule, the little finger is used in a one-part passage before the limit of the range has been reached. Both are quoted in Figure 64. The first is justified by the moderate speed of the notes. A crossing such as this is to be employed only when the fourth, a longer finger, takes a black key by a slight twist of the hand while the little finger plays one of the adjacent white keys. It should be employed only once at a time. The second illustrates an unavoidable contraction of the hand, facilitated by the long note; otherwise the fingering would be incorrect. Because of the rapid tempo a replacement on *f* would probably be more difficult than a contraction. In execution the hand should be turned slightly to the right. In the same piece replacements must be employed on short notes preceding an embellishment in order to avoid a precarious leap.[25] This will be more clearly understood after the discussion of embellishments.

Figure 64

94.   In three or more part compositions where each voice expresses an individual line there arise situations in which the hands must be interchanged in order to perform the notes correctly, even though only one hand should play them according to the notation.

95.   Finally, in order to provide an opportunity for both hands to practice simultaneously, I have appended in Figure 66 two exercises in treacherous keys with one accidental, consisting, in the first, of a stepwise figure and, in the second, of a mixture of leaps and

[24] Sonata I, first movement, bars 18–19, and Sonata II, third movement, bars 22–23. Cf. Pt. I, Introduction, Note 17.
[25] Sonata II, third movement, bars 12, 14, 30, 32. Cf. Note 24.

Figure 65

steps. Both call for turning and crossing as well as the use of the little finger.

Figure 66

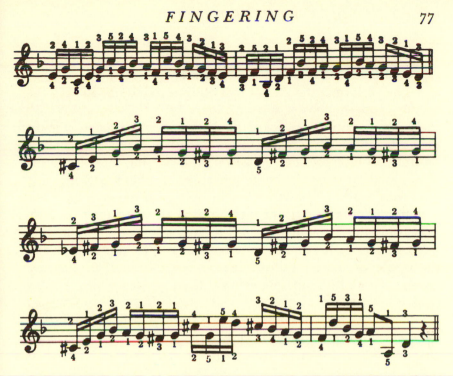

96.   At those places in the Lessons where the performer might be in doubt or even err in choosing the hand assigned to the notes, I have turned the stems upward to indicate the right hand and downward to indicate the left. When, owing to limitations of space, a few notes in the inner parts lack tails, their nature and length must be ascertained from the notes struck with them in other inner parts or the bass. Since I have tried throughout to lighten the beginner's tasks and have seized every opportunity to indicate through the notes the hand assigned to them, no one should be dismayed to find the values of certain tones and the conduct of parts notated unconventionally at times. Despite this, the trained performer will have no difficulty in following the path of each voice and determining the note lengths. The occasions for these remarks can be found in the D major and A-flat Lessons.[26]

97.   Among the Lessons there is one in which the hands cross.[27] I thought it wise to illustrate a natural use of this kind of juggling, even though it has not been very much employed of late. I have

[26] Sonata IV, second movement, and Sonata VI, second movement. Cf. Note 24.
[27] *Sonata VI,* first movement. Cf. Note 24.

indicated the notes that belong to each hand by means of clef signs. It is also possible to do this with written directions. Compositions can be found in which the composer calls for needless crossing. The performer should not feel obliged to indulge in such imposturing but should seek instead a more natural execution. Nevertheless, the technique is not to be discarded for it helps to make the keyboard a more comprehensive instrument and opens up new possibilities of expression. However, the crossing must be so devised that the passage is either unplayable any other way or playable only with a difficulty that causes an ugly garbling or even a dismembering of the parts. For the rest, it is a vain tempest that can blind only the ignorant, for the initiated know clearly that, considered by itself, there is no challenge in it save its unusualness, and this is soon overcome. And yet, it is everyone's experience that excellent and also difficult pieces have been written which employ crossed hands.[28]

98.   Comments on the fingering of embellishments must be withheld until the symbols have been explained in the following chapter. When the fingering of fully written embellishments is omitted it must be ascertained from the finger assigned to the principal tone.

99.   Finally, I refer my reader to the Lessons, where continuous examples of all types of fingering will be found.

[28] In *Bibliothek der Schönen Wissenschaften,* Vol. 10 (1763), Pt. I, p. 58, there appears the following comment on this paragraph: "About forty or fifty years have passed since such sorcery became known in Germany. A keyboardist by the name of Sandoni is said to have started it in a little piece, and a great host of lesser keyboardists tried to achieve eminence by way of the same kind of fraud."

Today, Pietro Giuseppe Sandoni (ca. 1680–1750) is remembered chiefly as the husband of the famous singer, Francesca Cuzzoni. He reached London about 1726, after a highly successful European career at the keyboard. Domenico Scarlatti, whose use of this technique needs no extended comment, seems to have preceded him in London by some six years.

As for Bach, he had excellent models in at least two works of his father; the Gigue of the B-flat major Partita, and the C minor Fantasia. Indeed, Carl Philipp's first composition (1731, Wotquenne No. 111) made use of the device. In his autobiography, mention of the work, which he engraved himself, is joined with the following remark: ". . . a natural and at that time much exploited form of magic." To this Nohl *(Musikerbriefe,* 1873) adds, parenthetically, "introduced chiefly by Domenico Scarlatti."

CHAPTER TWO
EMBELLISHMENTS

GENERAL

1

NO ONE disputes the need for embellishments. This is evident from the great numbers of them everywhere to be found. They are, in fact, indispensable. Consider their many uses: They connect and enliven tones and impart stress and accent; they make music pleasing and awaken our close attention. Expression is heightened by them; let a piece be sad, joyful, or otherwise, and they will lend a fitting assistance. Embellishments provide opportunities for fine performance as well as much of its subject matter. They improve mediocre compositions. Without them the best melody is empty and ineffective, the clearest content clouded.

2. In view of their many commendable services, it is unfortunate that there are also poor embellishments and that good ones are sometimes used too frequently and ineptly.

3. Because of this, it has always been better for composers to specify the proper embellishments unmistakably, instead of leaving their selection to the whims of tasteless performers.

4. In justice to the French it must be said that they notate their ornaments with painstaking accuracy. And so do the masters of the keyboard in Germany, but without embellishing to excess. Who knows but that our moderation with respect to both the number and kinds of ornaments is the influence which has led the French to abandon their earlier practice of decorating almost every note, to the detriment of clarity and noble simplicity?

5. In summary: Good embellishments must be distinguished from bad, the good must be correctly performed, and introduced moderately and fittingly.

6.   Embellishments may be divided into two groups: in the first are those which are indicated by conventional signs or a few small notes; in the second are those which lack signs and consist of many short notes.

7.   I shall treat the latter group only briefly in connection with the performance of *fermate*. There are several reasons for this. For one thing, their use is governed chiefly by taste; as a result, they are too variable to classify. Further, in keyboard music they are usually written out.[1] In any event, there is no real need for them,[2] thanks to the adequacy of the others. I shall discuss in detail only those in the first group, for most of them have a long and close association with the keyboard and will undoubtedly always remain in favor. To the accepted embellishments I have added a few new ones. All will be explained and their proper contexts specified insofar as it is possible to do so. I shall fix their best fingering when necessary and indicate their correct execution. Illustrations will elucidate those points that cannot be completely put into words. I shall point out certain incorrect or, at least, unclear signs so that they may be differentiated from the correct, and at the same time I shall criticize poor ornaments. Finally I shall refer my readers to the Lessons and hope throughout to remove the false assumption, occasionally encountered, of the need for profuse keyboard ornamentation.

8.   Nevertheless, those who are adept at it may combine the more elaborate embellishments with ours. However, care must be taken to use them sparingly, at the correct places, and without disturbing the affect[3] of a piece. It is understood, for example, that

---

[1] It was customary for the performer in earlier times to add his own embellishments and elaborations freely. The practice was changing about 1750 to the modern method, whereby the composer specifies every last detail and the performer, hopefully speaking, follows orders. Indicative of the widespread nature of the earlier practice is Bach's Foreword to Two Trios (Wotquenne No. 161), the first of which is programmatic. He was anxious to have the first Trio performed as written and in order to attain this end (which would be taken for granted today) wrote: "It would be best to play the first Trio as notated, without the addition of free ornaments." (Cf. Hans Mersmann in *Bach Jahrbuch*, 1917.) J. S. Bach won the censure of J. A. Scheibe because of his practice of writing out all detail (Cf. *The Bach Reader*, Norton, New York, 1945, pp. 237 ff.). It should be added that Bach was a master at introducing ornaments of all kinds into other composers' works. Philipp Emanuel's position here is undoubtedly influenced by his father's stand. The opening sentence of § 8 suggests indirectly a defensive reason for the stand taken by both. Evidently, not enough performers were "adept at it."

[2] That is, there is no real need for them as free embellishments interpolated by the performer.

[3] The premise of the theory of the affects was that music is capable of being more

the portrayal of simplicity or sadness suffers fewer ornaments than other emotions. He who observes such principles will be judged perfect, for he will know how to pass skillfully from the singing style to the startling and fiery (in which instruments surpass the voice) and with his constant changing rouse and hold the listener's attention. With these ornaments, the difference between voice and instrument can be unhesitatingly exploited. For the rest, as long as embellishments are applied with discretion no one need pause to decide whether a played passage can or cannot be sung.

9. Above all things, a prodigal use of embellishments must be avoided.[4] Regard them as spices which may ruin the best dish or gewgaws which may deface the most perfect building. Notes of no great moment and those sufficiently brilliant by themselves should remain free of them, for embellishments serve only to increase the weight and import of notes and to differentiate them from others. Otherwise, I would commit the same error as orators who try to place an impressive accent on every word; everything would be alike and consequently unclear.

---

than a mere pattern of sounds but is, rather, expressive of many passions. It was therefore considered insufficient for a performer to play a piece solely in a technically correct manner. He must "rouse and still the passions" by portraying the proper affect. All writers of the Berlin School, Quantz, Marpurg, Sulzer, and Bach, were preoccupied with the theory of the affects. The term and discussion of its meaning recur throughout the Essay. Cf. Paul Lang, *Music in Western Civilization* (Norton, New York, 1941, pp. 434 ff.). For the rest, the following excerpt from Marpurg (*Der Critischer Musicus an der Spree*, Sept. 2, 1749) will serve for general purposes of orientation: "The rapidity with which the emotions change is common knowledge, for they are nothing but motion and restlessness. All musical expression has as its basis an affect or feeling. A philosopher who explains or demonstrates seeks to bring light to our understanding, to bring clarity and order to it. But the orator, poet, musician seek more to inflame than enlighten. With the philosopher there are combustible materials which merely glow or give off a modest restrained warmth. Here, however, there is but the distilled essence of this material, the finest of it, which gives off thousands of the most beautiful flames, but always with great speed, often with violence. The musician must therefore play a thousand different roles; he must assume a thousand characters as dictated by the composer. To what unusual undertakings the passions lead us! He who is fortunate, in any respect, to capture the enthusiasm that makes great people of poets, orators, artists will know how precipitately and variously our soul reacts when it is abandoned to the emotions. A musician must therefore possess the greatest sensitivity and the happiest powers of divination to execute correctly every piece that is placed before him."

4 Marpurg wrote in *Der Critischer Musicus an der Spree* (1750–51): "A special distinction of Berlin music is that it makes very sparing use of manners and embellishments; but those that are used are the more select and the more finely and clearly performed. The performances of the Grauns, Quantz, Benda, Bach, etc., are never characterized by masses of embellishments. Impressive, rhetorical, and moving qualities spring from entirely different things, which do not create as much stir, but touch the heart the more directly."

10.   We shall see presently that many passages allow for more than one kind of embellishment. In such cases, the art of variation may be used to advantage; introduce first a caressing ornament, then a brilliant one, or for a change, if the passage permits, play the notes directly as written but always in furtherance of the true affect and in accordance with the rules of good performance which will be treated later.

11.   It is difficult to prescribe the correct context for every embellishment, for all composers are free to introduce their favorites where they will, so long as good taste is not thereby assailed. Suffice it if we instruct our reader through a few well-established precepts and examples. At least he will learn that the nature of a passage can narrow his choice of ornaments. Thus, while the performer will have no need for concern in those compositions where all embellishments are specified, where few or none are indicated he will know how and where to insert them in the customary manner.

12.   Because I have yet to find a forerunner who might have broken a path for me,[5] no one should criticize me for holding that, despite certain established cases, it is conceivable that exceptions can arise.[6]

13.   In order to master this material with its many minutiae and apply it intelligently, the ear must be trained through constant listening to good music. Above all, to understand many things more clearly, the performer must possess a knowledge of thorough bass. It is a matter of experience that those who are not well grounded in the study of harmony fumble in darkness when they use embellishments and must thank their good fortune rather than insight when they are successful. With this in mind I shall add a bass to the illustrations whenever it is necessary.

14.   Singers and instrumentalists other than keyboardists who wish to perform well need most of our short embellishments just as much as we do. However, our ways are much more orderly than theirs, for keyboardists have given embellishments specific signs the more exactly to indicate the detailed performance of their compositions.

15.   Because others have not shown such commendable fore-

---

[5] This statement refers only to the problem of defining the contexts suited to each ornament at the keyboard and not, as Dannreuther (*Musical Ornamentation*, Part II, p. 5, footnote) believed, to the general description of ornaments and their signs.

[6] See, for example, Ch. II, "The Appoggiatura," ¶ 16.

sight, but have tried, rather, to indicate everything through only a few signs, the study of ornamentation is much more taxing for them than it is for the keyboardist. Their signs have grown ambiguous or, indeed, incorrect, a condition which even today causes many improprieties in performance. For example, the mordent, one of the most essential and widely used embellishments, is known by its sign to few outside of keyboardists. I know of one place in a certain piece which as a consequence is often ruined. The passage, if it is not to sound insipid, requires a long mordent which, because of the nature of the passage, no one could presume, unless it were specified by its symbol. And yet, even in the presence of its indication (known only to keyboardists), a trill is performed, owing to the ambiguity caused by a general lack of signs. We shall realize later in studying the great difference between the two ornaments how awkward it is to substitute one for the other.

16.   The French are especially careful in setting the signs of their embellishments. But unfortunately we have so far removed ourselves from their music and their fine style of playing that the exact meaning of their embellishments is vanishing to the point where signs once well known are becoming unrecognizable even to keyboardists.

17.   The tones of an embellishment adjust themselves to the accidentals of the key signature. Beyond this, we shall soon learn that at times, preceding and succeeding tones or, more frequently, modulations require additional alterations. The trained ear recognizes such contexts immediately.

18.   However, I have found it advisable to follow the practice of adding accidental signs to the symbols of ornaments in order to assist the performer. In the Lessons, they will be met singly and in pairs wherever they are required.

19.   All ornaments stand in proportioned relationship to the length of the principal note, the tempo, and the affect of a piece. In those cases where a variety of embellishments is used and the performer is not too restricted by the affect, note that the more tones contained in an ornament, the longer the principal note must be, regardless of whether the source of this length is the note itself or the tempo. The brilliance of an embellishment must not be dulled by excessive space following its execution. On the contrary, the performer must avoid a too hurried performance, which blurs certain

ornaments. This is caused mostly by the introduction of embellishments containing many tones and the excessive embellishment of rapid notes.

Figure 67[7]

20.   Nevertheless, we shall soon learn that it is permissible to introduce an embellishment which does not completely fill out the written length of a long note. However, the last tone of the embellishment must not be released until the following note arrives, for the primary aim of all embellishments is to connect notes.

21.   Hence, embellishments are better suited to slow or moderate than to rapid tempos, and to long rather than short notes. Observe [8] especially that embellishments are best applied to those places where a melody is taking shape, as it were, or where its partial, if not complete, meaning or sense has been revealed. Hence, with regard to the latter case, they are found chiefly at half or full closes, caesurae, and *fermate*.

22.   In explaining symbols and small notes, I shall write out the correct lengths of the notes expressed by them. Small notes have been notated in their real values in the Lessons.

23.   All embellishments notated in small notes pertain to the following tone. Therefore, while the preceding tone is never shortened, the following tone loses as much of its length as the small notes take from it. This observation grows in importance the more it is neglected and the less I was able to avoid a separation of such notes from their principal tones in the Lessons, owing to the space taken up by the mass of fingering numerals, symbols of ornaments, and expression marks.

24.   According to this rule the small notes rather than the principal tone are struck with the bass and the other parts. The performer should make them glide into the following tone. It is wrong

7 From the ed. of 1787.
8 Remainder of paragraph from ed. of 1787.

to jump roughly on the principal tone, for this causes further awkwardness in the introduction as well as the execution of embellishments. It [9] might seem superfluous to repeat that the other voices including the bass must be struck with the initial tone of an embellishment. Yet as often as this rule is cited, so often is it violated.

Figure 68[10]

25. Because our present taste, to which Italian *bel canto* has contributed greatly, demands more than French ornaments alone, I have had to accumulate the embellishments of several countries. To these I have added a few new ones. I believe that that style of performance is the best, regardless of the instrument, which artfully combines the correctness and brilliance of French ornaments with the suavity of Italian singing. Germans are in a good position to effect such a union so long as they remain free of prejudices.

26. Therefore it may well be that some, predisposed to only one taste, will not be satisfied with my choice of ornaments. However, it is my belief that in music no one can offer reasonable criticism who has not listened to all styles and cannot select the best from each. I agree with a certain great man's opinion [11] that, although one taste may be better than another, each contains something good and none is so perfect that it will not endure additions. It is through such additions and refinements that we have progressed this far and will advance even further, but, certainly, not through addiction and restriction to only one style. Everything good must be put to use regardless of its origins.

27. Embellishments and their execution form a large part of good taste. Therefore the performer must not be inconstant and ac-

[9] Remainder of paragraph from ed. of 1787.
[10] From the ed. of 1787.
[11] His father's. Marpurg wrote in *Der Critische Musicus an der Spree*, Sept. 2, 1749, "In every type of music, in the music of every country there are bad and also good things. This is the opinion of old Bach of Leipzig who certainly counts for something in music."

cept uncritically every new random ornament. Nor should he be so predisposed toward himself and his own taste that he is obstinately unwilling to accept anything strange. Certainly severe tests should precede the acceptance of the new, for it is possible that unnatural novelties might in time make good taste as rare as skill. However, while it is wise not to be the first, one should also not be the last to acknowledge new ornaments in order not to fall out of style. Do not turn against them because they sound unattractive at first. The new, as engaging as it may be at times, very often repels us. This may indicate the presence of merits that will prove more long-lived than those qualities which at first are entirely too pleasant. As a rule we soon tire of such charms and they end by revolting us.

28. Just because most of the illustrations of embellishments are written for the right hand, it must not be assumed that I forbid these adornments to the left. In fact I advise strongly that all ornaments be practiced by both hands, the more so because this develops a general facility and dexterity. We shall see later that certain ornaments are frequently assigned to the bass. Moreover, all imitations must be exact to the smallest detail. Hence, the left hand should practice ornaments until it can imitate skillfully, for ornaments that lose their charm through poor execution are better omitted entirely.

29. It will be gathered from the following pages that the explanations of ornaments which have been added to the second part of my Sonatas [12] are wrong. The publisher presumed to print these under my name without my consent or knowledge. I am as guiltless here as I was in the case of the publication of *VI Sonates nouveaux per Cembalo, 1751,* listed under my first and family names on page 8 of this year's edition of Lotter's *Catalogus aller musicalischen Bücher.*[13] I have not yet examined these Sonatas, but I am quite certain that either they are not mine at all or, at the most, are old, badly copied things, stolen and then published, a very usual occurrence.

[12] The Württemberg Sonatas (Nagels Archiv Nos. 21, 22) as published by J. Huffner in Nuremberg, 1744.

[13] An old firm of music printers founded about 1726 in Augsburg by Johann Jakob Lotter. The works mentioned may be the six Sonatinas listed by Wotquenne (No. 64) as composed in Leipzig in 1734 and revised in Berlin in 1744. Or, as suggested by Bach, they may be works falsely ascribed to him. Johann Christian Bach, along with many other well-known composers of the time, was a victim of this practice.

THE APPOGGIATURA [1]

1. Appoggiaturas are among the most essential embellishments. They enhance harmony as well as melody. They heighten the attractiveness of the latter by joining notes smoothly together and, in the case of notes which might prove disagreeable because of their length, by shortening them while filling the ear with sound. At the same time they prolong others by occasionally repeating a preceding tone, and musical experience attests to the agreeableness of well-contrived repetitions. Appoggiaturas modify chords which would be too simple without them. All syncopations and dissonances can be traced back to them. What would harmony be without these elements?

2. Appoggiaturas are sometimes written in large notation and given a specified length in a bar. At other times they appear in small notation, and the large notes before which they stand retain their length visually although in performance they always lose some of it to the ornament.

3. The little that is noteworthy about the former will be reserved for the conclusion of this section. Both types ascend as well as descend to the principal note.

4. In execution some appoggiaturas vary in length; others are always rapid.

5. Because of their variability, such appoggiaturas have been notated of late in their real length [2] (Figure 69). Prior to this all were written as eighths. At that time, appoggiaturas as diverse as ours were not yet in use. Today, we could not do without the notation of their real values, for the rules covering their length in performance are insufficient to cover all cases, since all types appear before every kind of note.

6. We can readily see in the examples of Figure 69 that at times appoggiaturas repeat the preceding note (a), at times they do not (b), and that the following note may lie a step above or below, or it may be separated from the ornament by a leap.

---

[1] *Der Vorschlag.*

[2] This practice was generally adopted in the latter half of the eighteenth century. The alternative (cf., par ex., Haydn) was to write the ornament in large notation, as described in ¶ 2. Hence the rules of length as discussed later in ¶ 11 refer to a dying practice, not always applicable even to the music of J. S. Bach. Cf. H. Schenker, *Ein Beitrag zur Ornamentik,* pp. 26 ff.

Figure 69

7.   With regard to execution we learn from this figure that appoggiaturas are louder than the following tone, including any additional embellishment, and that they are joined to it in the absence as well as the presence of a slur. Both of these points are in accord with the purpose of appoggiaturas, which is to connect notes. They must be held until released by the following tone so that both are smoothly joined. An undecorated, light tone which follows an appoggiatura is called the release.

8.   Because the sign of the appoggiatura is universally known (like that of the trill) it is one of the few ornaments whose introduction is usually notated. Nevertheless, since one cannot always depend on this, it is necessary to fix the proper contexts of the variable appoggiatura, insofar as it is possible to do so.

9.   In addition to the observations of Paragraph 6, the variable appoggiatura in duple time appears commonly on either the down beat (Figure 70, Example *a*) or the upbeat (*b*); but in triple time only on the downbeat (Figure 71) and always before a relatively long note. Further, it is found before cadential trills (Figure 72, Example *a*); before half cadences (*b*), caesurae (*c*), *fermate* (*d*), and final tones with (*e*) or without (*f*) a preceding trill. We learn from Example *e* that the ascending appoggiatura after a trill is better than the descending; hence, the illustration under *g* is poor. Slow dotted notes also take the variable appoggiatura (*h*). When such notes have tails, the tempo must be a suitable one.

Figure 70

Figure 71

Figure 72

10.   The ascending variable appoggiatura is difficult to use except when it repeats the preceding tone; but the descending kind is met in all contexts.

11.   The usual rule of duration for appoggiaturas is that they take from a following tone of duple length one-half of its value (Figure 73, Example *a*), and two-thirds from one of triple length [3] (*b*). In addition the examples of Figure 74 and their executions should be carefully studied. Appoggiaturas [4] which depart from this rule of duration should be written as large notes. Errors in execution, which distort melodies and often create false chords, are caused by inattentiveness and occasionally by distrust of the copyist's accuracy, for in earlier times all appoggiaturas were notated invariably as eighths.

Figure 73

Figure 74

12.   The examples under Figure 75 are frequent occurrences. Their notation is not the most correct, since in performance the rests are filled in. Dotted or longer notes should be written instead.

[3] In Chapter VI, "Appoggiaturas," ¶ 4, Bach adds, "The shortest of these is never more rapid than an eighth note in an allegretto."

[4] Remainder of paragraph from ed. of 1787.

Figure 75

13.   It is wholly natural that the unvariable short appoggiatura should appear most frequently before quick notes (Figure 76, Example *a*). It carries one, two, three, or more tails and is played so rapidly that the following note loses scarcely any of its length.[5] It also appears before repeated (*b*) as well as unrepeated (*c*) long notes. Further, it is found in caesurae before a rapid note (*d*), and in syncopated (*e*), tied (*f*), and slurred passages (*g*). In all such cases, the character of the notes remains unchanged. Example *h* with an ascending appoggiatura is better when the ornament is played as an eighth. For the rest, the short appoggiatura remains short even when the examples are played slowly.

Figure 76

[5] The notation of the short appoggiatura as a small eighth note with a diagonal stroke through the tail was not used by Bach, nor indeed by the Viennese Classical School. However, it did make its appearance in early nineteenth-century editions of their works, notably those of Mozart published by André. While the older notation gave rise to ambiguities (where variable and short appoggiaturas have the same notation) the later notation, apart from those cases where editors used it indiscriminately for both the long and the short ornament, has the disadvantage of dulling the performer's sensitivity to subtle variations of length in the short appoggiatura, as described in the following ¶ 14. A few short appoggiaturas, notated in the later manner, appear in J. S. Bach's *Werke*, 36.4, pp. 10–11, 14. They are not authentic.

14.   When these appoggiaturas fill in the interval of a third, they also are played quickly. However, in an Adagio their expression is more tender when (Example *a,* Figure 77) they are played as the first eighth of a triplet rather than as sixteenths. The accurate division of triplets can be learned from Example *b.* For various reasons the resolving tone of a melody must often be quitted abruptly. When such a tone is an appoggiatura, it too must be played rapidly (Example *c*). In [6] this example, the appoggiatura, which is present only to complete the run, must be very short so that the principal tone, *c,* which is the cause of the free execution and is therefore always especially important, loses little or nothing of its value.[7] Appoggiaturas before triplets must also be played quickly so that the rhythm remains clear (*d*) and distinguishable from that of Example *e.* When the appoggiatura forms an octave with the bass it is played rapidly because of the emptiness of the interval (*f*). On the other hand, it is often prolonged when it forms a diminished octave (*g*). It [8] remains short when it is substituted for a cadential trill (*h*).

15.   When a melody ascends a second and then returns to either a large note (Figure 78) or another appoggiatura (*a*), the middle tone may be readily decorated with a short appoggiatura. In Figure 79 there are many such passages containing notes of various lengths in duple and triple rhythms. We learn from Example *a* that a long appoggiatura may also be used here. It is taken for granted that the phrasing is normally legato in such a context, since detached notes must always be more simply performed and also because appoggiaturas are invariably joined to the following tone. Further, as

---

[6] This sentence appears as a footnote in the ed. of 1787.

[7] Or, as Bach explains manipulated progressions in Part II, the underlying progression is from the opening *d″* to the quarter note *c″*, and the outline of the upper voice is the two-part progression: d″—c″

g′-f′-e′.

[8] This sentence from the ed. of 1787.

with all ornaments, the tempo must be a suitable one, for an excessive speed does not allow for embellishment. The asterisked example is intended to show us that an appoggiatura does not sound well before a long note preceded by a much shorter one. Later, we shall learn that an ornament which is better at filling out may be introduced here.[10]

Figure 77 [9]

Figure 78

Figure 79

[9] Example *h* from the ed. of 1787.
[10] See Figure 153, Example *c*.

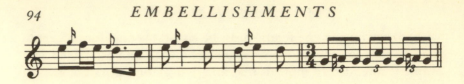

16. With regard to the rule covering the length of appoggiaturas, there are a few situations in which the ornament must be extended beyond its normal length because of the affect. Thus it may take up more than half the value of the following tone (Figure

80, Example *a*). At times the length is determined by the accompaniment, as in Example *b,* where, if the appoggiaturas are played as full quarter notes, the fifths struck against the bass will sound ugly. In Example *c,* if the appoggiatura is held beyond its written length, it will create open fifths. Again, in Figure 69, the appoggiatura in the asterisked example must not be prolonged or the seventh will sound too harsh.

Figure 80

17. Hence, as with all embellishments, the introduction of an appoggiatura must not corrupt the purity of voice leading. For this reason the examples of Figure 81 had better not be put into practice. Thus it is best to notate all appoggiaturas in their real length.

Figure 81

18. A profusion of appoggiaturas with their releases is particularly good in affettuoso passages since the releases usually expire pianissimo [11] (Figure 82). In other cases, however, they make a

Figure 82

[11] Cf. J. S. Bach, F minor Prelude, Bk II, WTC., and the Toccata of the E minor Partita.

melody insipid unless they are followed by livelier embellishments
or are themselves supplemented by additional ornaments

19.　When an appoggiatura is decorated, the following tone is
best performed plainly. Its simplicity will be happily complemented
by its usual piano execution. An undecorated appoggiatura, however, leads well to a succeeding embellishment. This latter is illustrated in Figure 83, Example *a,* and the former in Example *b.*

20.　The decorating of appoggiaturas leads us to other embellishments which will be explained later. Because these are often
written as small notes, it is better to write the appoggiatura in such
cases as a large note with its length clearly notated (Figure 83, Example *c*). In slow pieces the appoggiatura as well as the following
tone may be embellished on occasion (*d*).

21.　However, appoggiaturas are often written in large notation as a means of indicating that neither they nor the following
tones are to be decorated (*e*).

Figure 83

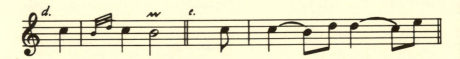

22.　Although the note following an appoggiatura relinquishes
part of its length, it does not lose any of its own embellishments
(Figure 84). On the other hand, embellishments which belong to
the appoggiatura should not be placed over the following tone.
They must always be written directly above the note to which they
pertain. If they are to be performed between the appoggiatura and
the following tone the symbol must be placed between the two
notes (Figure 85).

Figure 84　　　　　**Figure 85**

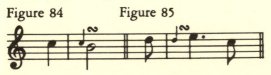

23.   Descending appoggiaturas written in large notation may be decorated by another appoggiatura, long or short, when they repeat the preceding tone [12] (Figure 86, Example *a*), or when they do not lead into closing tones (Example *b* is therefore wrong). Ascending appoggiaturas in large notation do not take another appoggiatura either from above or from below. (*c*). They may, however, be followed by one (*d*).

Figure 86

24.   A few additional incorrect uses of the appoggiatura remain to be considered. It is wrong to place a descending appoggiatura before the final tone of a cadence when the final tone is preceded by a trill without an appoggiatura (Figure 72, Example *g*). However, a trill which is graced by this ornament may be followed by a similarly graced final tone regardless of whether the final tone stands lower (Figure 87, Example *a*) or higher (*b*) than the trill. Another error is the separation of an appoggiatura from its following tone either because the ornament is prematurely quitted or because it has usurped a portion of the preceding note's value (Figure 88, Example *a*).

Figure 87

[12] Quantz and Bach are in complete disagreement over the performance of this appoggiatura. The former writes (*Versuch einer Anweisung die Flöte traversiere zu spielen*), "Two appoggiaturas are often found before a note, the first written as a small note and the second as a large, measured one. They appear at caesurae. The small note is short and placed on the preceding divided beat." Bach, of course, wanted the small note to be played on the beat of the large appoggiatura. This difference

25: This latter dislocation is the origin of the repulsive unaccented appoggiatura,[13] so extraordinarily popular, which is reserved, unfortunately, for the most legato passages, such as those in Figure 88, Example *b*. If appoggiaturas should or must be used in such cases, the asterisked executions are more tolerable. Hence, the remedy for unaccented appoggiaturas is to shift them ahead to the next accent. Yet a good and frequent use of the unaccented appoggiatura is illustrated in Figure 89, Example *a*. However, the last bar is more fashionable than harmonious. Figure 89,[14] Example *b*, is to be avoided. It illustrates those cases in which a very short descending appoggiatura is inserted between an ascending one and its principal tone at a cadence or in a melody which does not descend immediately afterward.

----

flares up when Bach (¶ 25) calls the weak-beat appoggiatura the *"hässlicher Nachschlag."* Cf. note 13.

[13] *Nachschlag*. Bach's high-handed treatment of this ornament has brought censure from many sources. For example, the *Bibliothek der schönen Wissenschaften*, in reviewing the Essay in 1763, wrote: "Marpurg [*Anleitung zum Klavierspielen*] gives us better information on the *Accent*, dividing it into *Vorschlag* and *Nachschlag*, which latter, Bach has actually neglected, treating it only superficially here and there." Later, Dannreuther and especially Dolmetsch grew exercised over Bach's feelings and pointed out, not without indignation, that this ornament had an honorable past (cf. Dolmetsch, *The Interpretation of the Music of the XVIIth and XVIIIth Centuries*, pp. 148 ff.). Quantz (*op. cit.*) gives consideration to the *Nachschlag* or, as he calls it, the *durchgehende Vorschlag*, an unaccented appoggiatura that fills in the interval of a third in the manner of Figure 87, Example *a*, here. In France, where it had wide use, it was known as *"couler les tierces."* Concerning its performance as a *Vorschlag* (cf. ¶ 14 here) Quantz writes: "This would be contrary to the French style from which the ornament springs and the intentions of its authors, who won almost universal acclaim for this device." Bach and Quantz are in obvious disagreement. The strong adjectives used by the former in describing it here and in the sections on *The Trill* (¶ 21), "The Turn" (¶ 29), also in Ch. III, ¶ 27, indicate that he must have winced more than once as court accompanist.

However, it must be pointed out in Bach's defense that he was not, as generally believed, unconditionally opposed to the ornament. See, for example, Figure 89, example *b*, and, in the Lessons, Sonata IV, second movement, and third movement, bars 14, 19, 46. A casual examination of the collections for Connoisseurs and Amateurs will reveal others. He always writes it in large notation except when it is incorporated into a larger ornament (cf. "The Slide"), because his basic rule for the performance of ornaments written in small notes is that they must be played on the beat of the following principal tone (cf. Ch. II, ¶¶ 23, 24). The essential reason for his disapproval becomes apparent upon reading his description of the functions of the appoggiatura in ¶ 1 of the present section, especially the last two sentences.

His immediate objections are directed to the excessive use of the ornament, its free insertion by performers, and above all its use where the appoggiatura proper is specified. All of us have suffered on this last score and hence should commiserate with Bach to a degree.

[14] Remainder of paragraph from ed. of 1787.

Figure 88

Figure 89[15]

26.   Other embellishments which are written as small notes will be explained in later sections.

THE TRILL

1.   Trills enliven melodies and are therefore indispensable. In earlier times they were introduced chiefly after an appoggiatura (Figure 90, Example *a*) or on the repetition of a tone (*b*). The first

[15] Figure 89, Example *b*, from ed. of 1787.

is called the enclosed trill. Today they are used in both stepwise and leaping passages, immediately at the beginning of a movement, in succession, at cadences, and, in addition, on held tones (*c*), *fermate* (*b*), and caesurae without (*e*) as well as with (*f*) an introductory appoggiatura. Thus, this embellishment has become versatile with the passing of time.

Figure 90

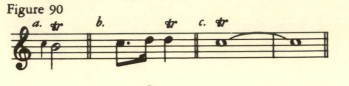

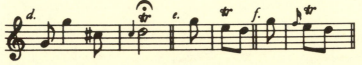

2.   However, it is strongly recommended that the trill be employed circumspectly in affettuóso passages.

3.   The accomplished keyboardist has four trills; the normal, ascending, descending, and half or short trill.

4.   Each has its distinctive sign in keyboard pieces, although all may be indicated by either the abbreviation *tr.* or a cross. The performer has no need to be unduly concerned about the proper location of the trill, for its acknowledged symbols are almost always notated.

5.   The normal trill has the sign of an *m* (Figure 91, Example *a*), which is extended when it appears over long notes (*b*). Its execution is illustrated in Example *c*. Since it always begins on the tone above the principal note,[1] it is superfluous to add a small note (*d*) unless this note stands for an appoggiatura.

Figure 91

---

[1] This is a rule of long standing. On the strength of Bach's inclusion of it and the numerous examples that follow, it is safe to conclude that there is no form of Bach trill that starts on the principal tone. The closest to one is the *ribattuta*, which is illustrated in passing (¶ 25 and Figure 105), although Bach does not give it its common name. Note, however, that when the trill proper enters in this example it is the ascending kind and does not commence on the principal tone. The trill-like long mordent starts on the principal tone, but it alternates with the lower neighbor

6. At times two short notes from below are appended. These are called the suffix,[2] and they serve to make a more rapid trill (Figure 92, Example *a*). The suffix is often written out (*b*) as well as indicated through an addition to the symbol (*c*). However, since the long mordent has almost the same symbol, I think it better to retain the *m* and avoid confusion.

Figure 92

7. Trills are the most difficult embellishments, and not all performers are successful with them. They must be practiced industriously from the start. Above all, the finger strokes must be uniform and rapid. A rapid trill is always preferable to a slow one. In sad pieces the trill may be broadened slightly, but elsewhere its rapidity contributes much to a melody. With regard to the amount of pressure, the performer must be guided by the nature of the passage, be it forte or piano, in which the trill appears.

8. In practicing the trill, raise the fingers to an equal but not an excessive height. Trill slowly at first and then more rapidly but always evenly. The muscles must remain relaxed or the trill will bleat [3] or grow ragged. Many try to force it. Never advance the speed of a trill beyond that pace at which it can be played evenly. This [4] precaution must be heeded in practicing rapid as well as difficult passages so that they may be performed with fitting lightness and clarity. Through intelligent practice it is easy to achieve that which can never be attained by excessive straining of the muscles. When the upper tone of a trill is given its final performance it is snapped; [5] after the stroke the upper joint of the finger is sharply doubled and drawn off and away from the key as quickly as possible.

9. The trill must be practiced diligently with all fingers so that

---

and hence has no bearing on the present point (cf. Figure 140, example *a*). However, see Schenker, *Ein Beitrag zur Ornamentik*, p. 34, ¶ 3, where a broader explanation is evolved.

[2] *Nachschlag*. Bach uses this term in a general rather than specific sense. It applies to ornaments, parts of ornaments, or other notes that fall on divided, or fractional, beats.

[3] From *meckern*. Marpurg calls it *chevroter*.

[4] This sentence and the following were footnotes in the ed. of 1787.

[5] Cf. Ch. I, Note 2.

they will become strong and dexterous. However, let no one believe that all of the fingers can be made to trill equally well. For one thing, there are natural differences among them, and for another, compositions usually offer more trills for certain fingers than for others; hence these are unwittingly given more practice. Yet prolonged trills appear at times in outer parts and preclude a choice of fingers, most of them being engaged in performing the inner parts. In addition certain passages are extremely difficult to perform unless the little finger has learned to trill rapidly, as illustrated in Figure 93.

Figure 93

10.   No one can succeed without a minimum of two good trills in each hand: The second and third, and the third and fourth fingers of the right hand; and the thumb and second, and second and third fingers of the left. It is because of this normal fingering of trills that the left thumb grows so agile and along with the second finger becomes about the most active of the left hand.[6]

11.   Some performers practice double trills in thirds with one hand. Various examples of these may be constructed from Figure 42. Such exercise, pursued as far as one wishes, is beneficial to the fingers, but aside from this it is better not to employ double trills unless they can be made to sound even and distinct, the two desiderata of good trills.

12.   When the upper tone falls on a black key and the lower on a white key it is not incorrect to perform a trill with the second finger of the left hand crossed over the thumb as illustrated in Figure 94. Also, some find it convenient to trill with the third and fifth or the second and fourth fingers of the right hand when the action of the keys is stiff.

---

[6] This is in complete agreement with Couperin (*L'Art de toucher le clavecin*). The thumb of the left hand played a more active role than that of the right in older systems of fingering. For example, a widely used ascending fingering for the left hand was: 4, 3, 2, 1, 2, 1, 2, 1, while the corresponding descent for the right hand was: 5, 4, 3, 2, 3, 2, 3, 2.

Figure 94

13.   Trills on long notes are played with a suffix regardless of a subsequent stepwise descent or ascent. The suffix may also be added to a trill followed by a leap (Figure 95, Example *a*). When the decorated notes are short, an ascent (*b*) is better after a suffix trill than a descent (*c*). Although in quite slow tempi the trills of Example *d* may be suffixed (despite the fact that the rapid notes following the dot may be used as substitutes), it can be seen that a descending second is the least favorable for such an addition. It is not unconditionally necessary to suffix the ornament, provided that the dotted notes are trilled for their full length. The manner of performing the endings in this example will be taken up in the following paragraph, which discusses dotted notes.

Figure 95

14.   Dotted notes followed by a short ascent also allow for suffixed trills (Figure 95, Example *e*). However, instead of the usual extremely rapid motion into the following note (*f*), when dotted notes are trilled a very short separation must be made between the last tone of the suffix and the following note (*g*). This separation need only be long enough to show that the suffix and the following note are two separate elements. Its length is dependent on the

tempo; hence the execution of Example *g* is only approximately suggested by the time value of the last tone of the suffix, for the note following a dot is always shorter in execution than its notated length (a point which will be treated in Chapter III).[7] The suffix running directly into the following note in Example *h* is, of course, incorrect. The composer who wishes such an execution must call for it expressly.

15. The suffix must be played as rapidly as the trill proper. A trill in the right hand for the thumb and second finger is not favorable for a suffix because it can be added only by crossing the fingers, which retards its pace. In this manner the best trill will be brought to a ruinous end.

16. The unsuffixed trill is best used in descending successions (Figure 96, Example *a*) and principally over short notes (*b*). The suffix is omitted from successive trills (*c*) and from trills followed by one or more short notes which are capable of replacing it (*d*). If this substitution is made, the asterisked example must not be played

Figure 96

in the slowest tempo. Further, the suffix is not employed over triplets (*e*). It is always omitted from the last of those in Example *e*, although it may be introduced into the first three, but only in very slow tempos.

17. The average ear can always tell whether the suffix should be used. I have discussed it here only for the benefit of beginners and because this is its proper place.

18. In very rapid tempos the effect of a trill can be achieved through the use of the appoggiatura (Figure 97). The last two short notes are not an unsatisfactory substitute for the suffix.

Figure 97

19. When accidental signs are not included with the symbols of trills and suffixes the correct alterations may be arrived at by considering the preceding tones (Figure 98, Example *a*) or the succeeding (*b*). Sometimes the ear alone or modulations will dictate the necessary changes (*c*). While we are on this subject, it should be observed that neither trills nor suffixes are allowed in the interval of an augmented second (d). Aside [8] from the keyboard there is a constant need for the notation of accidentals attendant on trills; especially in ripieno parts, for in these it is difficult to perceive modulations with their rapid alteration. For this reason many set the accidentals as appoggiaturas before the trill. This, however, is confusing in that it suggests a holding of the initial tone rather than an immediate trill.

Figure 98

[8] Remainder of paragraph from ed. of 1787.

20.   Among the errors unwittingly caused by trills we shall first mention the following: Many burden the first notes in the examples of Figure 99 with a trill despite the presence of a slur. No matter how enticing the appearance of such notes, they must not be trilled. Why must the finest legato passages be ruined so often by inept playing? Indeed, most errors are committed in just such places. Trills are introduced in an attempt to rescue these passages from oblivion. The pampered ear demands such treatment, being incapable of perceiving anything but a bustling noise. It is apparent that those guilty of these faults can neither think lyrically nor grant to each tone its proper weight and length. Tones will sing on the harpsichord as well as on the clavichord if they are not detached from each other, although one instrument may be better constructed for this purpose than another. The French are not well acquainted with the clavichord, most of their compositions being written for the harpsichord. Yet their works are replete with held and legato notes which are indicated copiously with slurs. Even when the tempo is too slow or the instrument not good enough to sustain tones properly, it is better to sacrifice a little of the clear flow of a legato passage than to disrupt it with trills, for a correct performance will be ample compensation for the lack of sonority. There are many things in music which, not fully heard, must be imagined. For example, in concertos with full accompaniment, the soloist always loses those passages that are accompanied fortissimo and those on which the tutti enters. Intelligent listeners replace such losses mentally, and it is primarily such listeners whom we should seek to please.

Figure 99

21.   There are other errors as ugly as they are frequent: The appending of a limp suffix to a trill as in Figure 100; the addition to the suffix of a short note, which can be justly included among the worthless unaccented appoggiaturas [9] (Figure 101); failure to give trills their full length, which (excepting the short trill) must always agree with the value of the note over which the symbol ap-

---

[9] Cf. Ch. II, "The Appoggiatura," Note 12.

pears; plunging directly into a trill without playing a preceding appoggiatura or properly joining both ornaments; performing such an impertinent trill loudly in a subdued, plaintive context; trilling excessively under the delusion that every moderately long note must bear a trill. These are the pretty little trills mentioned in Paragraph 10 of the Introduction.

Figure 100

Figure 101

22.   The ascending trill [10] with its symbol and execution appears in Figure 102. Because, aside from the keyboard, this symbol is not widely known, it is often notated in the manner of the asterisked examples; or the general abbreviation *tr.* is written, the choice of trill being left to the discretion of the performer.

Figure 102

23.   The ascending trill requires a long note, for it comprises many tones, including the normal suffix. A rapid suffix is written out. With regard to such details the performer should follow the precepts, previously discussed, of the normal trill.

24.   The examples of Figure 103 are noteworthy. Example *a* illustrates a suffix introduced after a tie; in Example *b* the suffix may be omitted because of the sixteenth; likewise in *c,* because of the thirty-seconds; however, in a sufficiently slow tempo, or at a cadence or before a *fermata* (it being permissible to broaden ad libitum in the latter two), the suffix is included and the succeeding short notes appended, the final one being played somewhat slower than the other (*d*). In my opinion, this widely used embellishment can be best applied to Example *c,* although the last notes must be played occasionally at other speeds. In passing, note that in minor mode cadences the trill is sometimes played on the sixth above the bass rather than the fifth.

[10] *Der Triller von unten.*

Figure 103

25.   Thus the ascending trill appears principally over long notes, especially at cadences, and before *fermate*. In addition, however, it is found over a repeated note as in Figure 104, Example *a*, in conconjunct motion (*b*), and after a leap followed by an ascending or descending progression (*c*). Over long notes of several bars, trills that threaten to lapse can be revived by means of the ascending prefix, but it must be interpolated without causing the slightest discontinuity. The ascending trill is well fitted to this purpose of resuscitation, for its insertion renews the fingers' strength. It is possible to move through an octave with such a trill, for its two short introductory notes facilitate the fingering. Figure 105 illustrates a manner of approaching it by means of a gradual acceleration,[11] a device frequently employed at cadences. The ascending trill may also be used in the course of modulatory changes, as in Figure 106. Figure 107 illustrates its application to caesurae.

Figure 104

Figure 105

11 Known generally as the *ribattuta*.

Figure 106   **Figure 107**

26. In successive leaps only the normal trill may be used (Figure 108). It is wrong to attempt to bring such a passage into bolder relief by means of ascending or descending [12] trills.

Figure 108

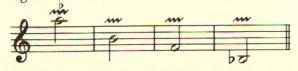

27. The descending trill is illustrated in Figure 109 with its correct symbol and execution. Apart from the keyboard it is occasionally notated in the manner of the asterisked example.

Figure 109

28. Because it contains more tones than any other trill it requires the longest notes. Hence both of the previously discussed trills are better suited for a cadence such as that of Figure 110 than the descending trill. In earlier times it was used widely, but today it is restriced largely to a repeated tone (Figure 111, Example *a*), descending successions (*b*), and downward leaps of a third (*c*).

Figure 110

[12] *Der Triller von oben.* Cf. ¶ 27.

29.   Because, as already mentioned, ornaments must not corrupt the purity of voice leading, it is better to employ either the
normal or the descending trill in Figure 112, for the ascending
trill creates forbidden fifths.

Figure 112

30.   The half or short trill,[13] which is distinguished from the
others by its acuteness and brevity, is notated for the keyboard in
the manner of Figure 113. Included in the figure is an illustration
of its execution. Despite the upper slur, which reaches from the
beginning to the end of the example, all notes are played except
the second *g* [14] and the last *f*, each of which is tied to its preceding
tone by another slur which indicates that it must not be struck.
The large slur merely specifies the attendant phrasing.

Figure 113

31.   The short trill joins the preceding note to the decorated
one and therefore never appears over detached notes. It represents
in miniature an enclosed, unsuffixed trill, introduced by either an
appoggiatura or a principal note.

32.   The half or short trill is the least dispensable, the most attractive, but at the same time the most difficult embellishment.
Played incorrectly, either it cannot be heard at all or else it sounds
limp and ugly, which are attributes far from its true ones. Unlike
other ornaments, it cannot be demonstrated slowly to students. It
must literally crackle. In order to be truly effective the upper tone
must be snapped on its final appearance in the manner described

[13] *Der halbe oder Prall-Triller*. The symbol is that of our inverted mordent, but
cf. Ch. II, "The Snap," ¶ 1 and note 1.

[14] In the original illustration (Figure 113 here) this "second *g*" was not tied to the
first, an oversight that has been perpetuated in most later (nineteenth- and twentieth-
century) reproductions.

in Paragraph 8, but with such exceeding speed that the individual tones will be heard only with difficulty. Herein lies its acuteness, which stands beyond comparison with the sharpest of other trills. Like the short appoggiatura, it may appear over rapid notes, but it must be played with such speed that the listener will not feel that the note to which it is applied has lost any of its length, but rather that it has entered precisely at the proper moment. It must not sound as frightening as it looks fully written out. The short trill adds life and brilliance to a performance. It is possible, when necessary, to omit any other ornament, even the other trills, and arrange matters so that easier ornaments may be substituted for them. But without the short trill no one can play successfully. Even if all other ornaments were correctly performed, no one could be happy in the absence of this one.

33.   Since the short trill demands great skill and speed in execution, it is best performed by those fingers that trill the best. Consequently, it is permissible, as illustrated in Figure 114, to take liberties with the fingering of a passage and adopt unusual expedients in order to execute the ornament. Of course, this must be done so skillfully that the performance as a whole does not suffer.

Figure 114

34.   The half or short trill appears only in a descending second regardless of whether the interval is formed by an appoggiatura or by large notes, as depicted in Figure 115. It is found over short notes (Example *a*) or over those made short by a preceding appoggiatura (*b*). In this latter respect, when it appears over a note extended by a *fermata*, the appoggiatura is held quite long and the trill is quickly snapped as the fingers withdraw from the keys (*c*).

Figure 115

35. In addition to its employment at cadences and *fermate* it is found in descending passages of three or more tones, as in Figure 116. In this use it resembles the unsuffixed trill in a descending succession and, like it, appears in passages where long notes are followed by short ones (Figure 117).

Figure 116

Figure 117

36. With regard to the execution of this trill, it must be pointed out that it is almost insuperably difficult to play it lightly at the pianoforte. Because the snap requires pressure, its performance on this instrument increases the volume. Yet it is impossible to perform our trill without this characteristic element. Hence the performer is faced with a dilemma, worsened by the fact that the short trill either by itself or combined with the turn often follows an appoggiatura and therefore, according to the rules governing the execution of appoggiaturas, must be played softly. The problem arises in all snaps, but particularly here, where it assumes its most radical form. I doubt that the most intensive practice can lead to complete control of the volume of the short trill at the pianoforte.

THE TURN [1]

1. The turn is an easy embellishment which makes melodies both attractive and brilliant. Its symbol and execution are shown in Figure 118. Leaps of an octave or other large intervals necessitate the use of four fingers in order to perform it. When such is the case it is customary to place two fingering numerals over the decorated note. Context [2] often requires the placing of one or two accidentals over the symbol. They appear on the right- or left-hand

---

[1] *Der Doppelschlag.*
[2] Remainder of paragraph from the ed. of 1787.

side according to whether they pertain to the first or the third tone, as illustrated in Example *a*.

Figure 118[3,4]

2. Because it is almost always performed rapidly I have had to illustrate the values of its notes in slow and rapid tempos. It is also indicated by the symbol that appears in the asterisked example. I have chosen the other in order to avoid an ambiguous placing of fingering numerals.

3. The turn is employed in slow as well as fast movements, and over slurred as well as detached notes. It does not appear to advantage over a very short note because the time demanded for the performance of its several tones may detract from the clarity of the melody.

4. The turn is sometimes found alone, sometimes in combination with the short trill, and also after one or two thirty-seconds in small notation which are placed before a large note and differ from the appoggiatura, as we shall see presently.

5. When the turn alone is used, its symbol may appear either directly over a note or after it, somewhat to the right.

6. In the first case it is employed, as illustrated in Figure 119, in stepwise successions (*a*), leaps (*b*), caesurae (*c*), cadences (*d*), *fermate* (*e*); immediately at the beginning (*f*), in the middle (*g*), or at the end after an appoggiatura (*h*); over a repeated tone (*i*), or a note preceded by a repetition regardless of whether the note is reached by a step (*j*) or a leap (*k*); without an appoggiatura, with one, over one (*l*), after one, etc.

[3] E. F. Baumgart (Foreword to his edition of the *Kenner und Liebhaber* collections, Breslau, 1863) expressed the opinion that in the Moderato example *f*-sharp should be a sixteenth, the additional beam being an oversight. Cf. Figures 68, 128, and H. Schenker, *op. cit.*, p. 45, note 1.

[4] Example *a* from ed. of 1787.

Figure 119

7. This lovely ornament is almost too obliging. It fits almost everywhere and consequently is often abused. Many seem to believe that the sum and substance of the keyboardist's art consists in introducing turns at every slightest instance. Hence its correct use must be carefully investigated, for, despite its complaisance, many apparent opportunities arise which are not actually suitable to it.

8. In most cases the turn serves to add brilliance to notes. Hence, passages which must be played undecorated and sustained because of the affect are ruined by those who insert a turn because of the length of the notes, in ignorance of style and touch. Also, the error of excessive use common to all ornaments applies to this one.

9. A general understanding of its correct use can be gained by considering the turn a normal, suffixed trill in miniature.

10. In most cases the turn is performed rapidly and its upper tone is snapped in the manner already described. Hence it is wrong to play it instead of the normal trill on a long note. While the trill

would occupy the entire duration of the note, the turn, much shorter, would leave a part of the length unfilled.

11.   While discussing this matter, I must point out an exception in slow tempos where, because of the affect, a trill may be replaced by a soft turn, the last tone of which is held until the following note enters. As illustrated in Figure 120 this may occur in cadences and also after an ascending appoggiatura (a).

Figure 120

12.   It follows from its similarity to the suffixed trill that the turn prefers an ascending to a descending following tone. It is easy to move upward (but not downward) through an octave or even further by means of a series of turns. Aside from the keyboard this frequent use of successive turns is indicated in the manner of Figure 121. The turn should not be applied to rapid, descending notes. It [5] may replace the trill in those cases where the latter is difficult to perform owing to the presence of another voice in the same hand. The substitution may be made only on a relatively short note, for others cannot be completely filled in by the turn (a).

Figure 121[6]   Presto

13.   Again, like the related trill, our embellishment may be applied to leaping notes without further concern. Figure 122 illustrates its use in both ascending and descending leaps.

[5] Remainder of paragraph from ed. of 1787.
[6] Example a from ed. of 1787.

Figure 122

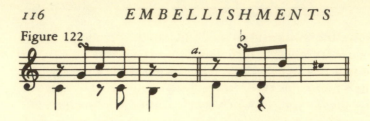

14.   Although the turn is well used over a repeated tone, the following tone, at [7] least in the case of rapid notes, should rise a second. When it descends, the compound appoggiatura [8] is better (Figure 123).

Figure 123

15.   Further, the turn often appears over a long note which follows an appoggiatura as previously shown in Figure 119, Examples *c, e,* and *f.* Note that a turn over an appoggiatura (most of the repeated notes mentioned in the preceding paragraph are appoggiaturas) will not suffer a decoration over the following tone (Figure 124). The exception to this occurs before a *fermata,* where the appoggiatura is lengthened beyond its normal value. The last note of the turn must then be held to create a slight but not an awkward break before the entry of the long mordent (*a*).

Figure 124

16.   Appoggiaturas which do not repeat the preceding tone are not turned (Figure 125), although the following resolution may be (*a*).

Figure 125

17.   Despite the musical worth of this ornament, its symbol is little known apart from the keyboard. It is often indicated by the signs of the trill or even the mordent, these two also being often confused. In Figure 126 there are many examples in which the turn is better and easier than the trill. Examples *a, g, p,* and *q* are the true home of the turn, for no other ornament can be applied to them. Those marked *j, k, l,* and *m,* are as well suited to the trill as the turn in rapid tempos. Note that in these fragments the last note repeats the middle one. In example *n* an appoggiatura is occasionally appended to the turn in slow tempos.

Figure 126[9]

[9] Example *o* from ed. of 1787.

18.   The lack of symbols aside from the keyboard often leads to the setting of the trill's sign in places where this ornament is ill at ease. Sometimes the speed of a piece makes it impossible to execute. Figure 126,[10] Example *o*, illustrates such a case in a passage typical of Tartini, and many allegro movements. The performer should play a turn here, for it is not merely acceptable but in keeping with the speed and the desired effect. In other cases legato phrasing makes for an awkward trill. The last two examples are entitled "Recit.," and differ from each other only in the melodic endings. Both call expressly for a turn. In the first of these·the last note of the turn is not held in the usual manner, in order to imitate the declamatory style of the voice. Since it is impossible to set the sign of a trill here, the passage must be left to the discretion of the performer when other signs are lacking.

19.   As illustrated earlier in Figure 119, Example *e*, the turn may appear over a *fermata* preceded by an ascending appoggiatura. It is never found, however, over a final note approaching in a like manner (Figure 127). Yet it does appear in both cases after a descending appoggiatura (Example *a* and Figure 119, Example *h*).

Figure 127

20.   Although the turn and the trill are similar, there are two respects in which they differ from each other. First, since the final tones of the turn are played less rapidly than the preceding ones, there is always a small space between them and the following tone. Second, the turn occasionally lays aside its brilliance for a purposely broad execution in slow, expressive movements (Figure 128). This kind of performance is also specified in the manner of Example *a*.

Figure 128

10 This sentence and the next from ed. of 1787, footnote.

21. The turn by itself may appear between a note or appoggiatura and the following tone in three situations: First, when the note is fairly long, as in Figure 129, Example *a;* second, over a tie (*b*); third, after a dotted note (*c*). These [11] uses of the turn are very frequent in all kinds of music and cannot be clearly enough indicated without our distinctive symbol, although some call for it by setting the trill sign after a note. In all three cases it serves to fill out notes.

22. The first case occurs in all kinds of motions, but not very well before a stepwise descent. When a performer wishes to avoid a cadential trill he may execute a turn after an appoggiatura which ascends to the final note, as illustrated in the asterisked example of Figure 129. When such is the case a mordent should not be played over the final note. The execution of all turns in example *a* is shown in the last illustration of that group.

23. In the second case, the tying note acquires a dot and the tied note becomes the last tone of the turn. When the tempo is rapid the

Figure 129[12]

11 Remainder of paragraph from ed. of 1787.
12 Examples *d, e, f, g, h* from ed. of 1787.

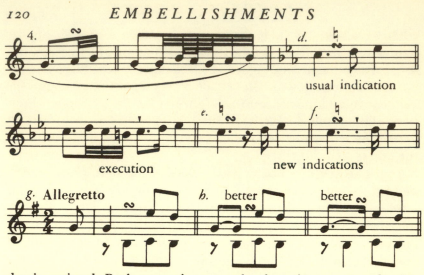

dot is omitted. Both executions are clearly written out under Example *b*. This use of the turn is frequent at cadences.

24. In the third case (Figure 129, Example *c*), two tones acquire dots and the turn is placed between them as illustrated in the notated execution of Example 2. The division of the tones is unvariable. This kind is often used when the tempo is so slow that the dotted note, undecorated, sounds listless; it is also found in caesurae (Example 1) and before cadences when a dotted note is followed by a short one which anticipates a trilled tone (Example 2). Such a turn is not employed after descending dotted notes of only moderate length. Example 3, set with this ornament, is the true home of the turn, for a substituted trill, whether it is placed over or after the first note, is unconditionally wrong. Example 4 shows that the turn may be placed over the second note as well as after the first. The accompanying written-out division of the tones demonstrates conclusively that this employment requires a slow tempo. How [13] is it possible to indicate a desired detaching of the final note of a turn (*d*)? Either by notating a rest (*e*) or by placing a vertical stroke to the right of the symbol and just above a second added dot. (*f*). Although this new indication looks strange, it is necessary, for all means which lead to correct performance should be adopted, even though they seem excessive. Occasionally a turn appears after a relatively long note against which the bass has two or more notes or

---

[13] Remainder of paragraph from ed. of 1787.

a rest, as in Example *g*. In the interests of greater clarity, divide the long note into two tied parts (*h*). The proper entrance of the turn will be thereby made apparent. Otherwise, many uninitiated performers might introduce the ornament too soon, thus necessitating a slow performance of it in order to fill out the note. This would be unsatisfactory and contrary to the rule stated in Paragraph 10.

25.   Accidentals which occur in turns are brought about, as in the case of trills, by preceding or following notes and modulations. Like the trill, a turn must not be used in the interval of an augmented second (Figure 98, Example *d*).

26.   The required snap in the turn, at which the little finger is not adept, requires an occasional slightly forced fingering (Figure 130).

Figure 130

27.   The turn allies itself with the short trill when its first two notes are alternated with extreme rapidity by means of a snap. The effect of the combined ornaments can be most easily realized by thinking of a short trill with a suffix. This trilled turn [14] introduces a unique charm and brilliance to the keyboard. It is a miniature but lively, enclosed and suffixed trill with which, however, it must not be interchanged, for there is as great a difference between the two as there is between the short trill or the turn and the normal trill. It has no distinctive symbol. I specify its use in the manner of Figure 131, which also depicts its execution. With regard to the long slur over the second illustration, I refer the reader to the discussion of the short trill in Paragraph 30 of the section on trills.

Figure 131[15]

28.   The trilled turn occurs either with or without a preceding appoggiatura. However, like the short trill it is used only in a descending second, the first note of which is drawn into the embel-

---

14 *Der prallende Doppelschlag.*
15 The first two notes are not tied in the original illustration.

lishment as illustrated in Figures 131 and 132. Inasmuch as the
trilled turn contains more notes than either of the ornaments which
comprise it, it fills out relatively long notes better than either one
alone. Consequently it is better to use it instead of the short trill in
passages such as the first three of Figure 133. On the other hand, the
short trill alone is better in the asterisked example when the tempo
is allegretto or faster. As a general rule it can be stated that neither
the simple nor the trilled turn is good in passages which are suitable
for an unsuffixed trill. In [16] moderately fast movements the trilled
turn is often performed in the manner of Example *a*. Such an execution is acceptable so long as it does not create bad voice leading with
the bass. Hence, while the example marked (1) is good, that marked
(2) is not. It is used at half (3) and whole cadences (4). Further, this
execution is more readily comprehended when, instead of setting
both symbols, the notation of Example *a* is adopted.

Figure 132   Figure 133[17]

[16] Remainder of paragraph from ed. of 1787.
[17] Last six bars from ed. of 1787.

29.   In slow tempos when three notes descend, the second, over
which a trilled turn may appear, takes an appoggiatura, as does the
final note. This is illustrated in undecorated form (*a*), with the ornaments (*b*), and with the execution written out (*c*), in Figure 134.
The first appoggiatura is quite usual before slow notes, for it helps
to fill them out. Moreover, it is necessary here for the convenience
of the trilled turn, which must not enter before half the duration
of the principal note has passed, precisely the time taken up by the
appoggiatura. The second appoggiatura not only serves to shorten
the final tone, thereby bringing it into agreement with the preceding; it also satisfies the ascending tendency of the turn which this
ornament has in common with the suffixed trill. There are three
reasons against playing the second appoggiatura ahead of its beat,
thus separating it from its following principal tone and incorporat-
ing it in the turn: First, because it is a prefix and not a suffix;
second, because in accordance with our explanation of the turn, its
final tone must never run directly into the following tone (the
appoggiatura in this case) but must always delay a bit in order to
avoid the fault of a trill whose suffix acquires an additional tone; [18]
third, because the appoggiatura serves to divide the following tone
in a manner similar to the other parts of the passage. Here again we
see the amount of harm which can be caused by separating an appoggiatura from the beat of its following tone. To avoid this error,
perform the body of the trilled turn according to the rule, so rapidly
that the final tone, *c*, may be made to sound like a simple sixteenth;
this will create an adequate separation of the ornament from the
following appoggiatura. The illustrated execution of this passage
looks rather alarming. Indeed, were it written out according to the

Figure 134[19]

18 Cf. Ch. II, "The Trill," ¶ 21 and Figure 101.

19 In example *c* the second and third notes are not tied in the original illustrations.
Cf. Ch. II, "The Trill," ¶ 30.

manner in which it must often be played over sixteenths in an adagio, with each note of the turn once again as fast, it would look even worse. Nevertheless, the entire art of execution depends on the ability to perform a rapid trilled turn, one whose execution sounds natural and facile. Example *d* is different from the others, but the performance of the last two notes is the same as in the other examples.

30.   In performing the simple turn or the suffixed trill, at least three fingers must always be employed. Because, beyond this, the snap in these ornaments and particularly in the trilled turn can be well executed by only certain fingers, there often arise great difficulties of performance, in the solution of which extreme expedients must be employed. Figure 135 illustrates a few such cases. In Example *a,* after *e* has been played by the second finger the hand shifts slightly to the left and the third finger takes *d.* It must not, however, as incorrectly taught, strike its tone by crossing over the second finger. In Example *b* our compounded embellishment forces the third finger to glide from a black key to the white one below. The easiest fingerings are those in Example *c.* Nevertheless it is advisable to practice the trilled turn with all fingers because they will thereby increase in strength and dexterity, and above all, because we are not always in a position to employ only the best fingers in performing an ornament.

Figure 135

31.   Embellishments are not easily introduced into the bass unless they are expressly called for. Nevertheless the trilled turn may be interpolated when opportunities such as those of Figure 136 present themselves.

Figure 136

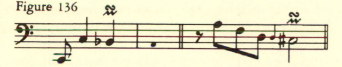

32.   The short trill and the related trilled turn provide unfail-ing tests of a harpsichord's quilling, for an instrument in poor con-dition will be unable to enunciate them. Keyboardists must be pitied who are robbed of these most essential and superior orna-ments because of the poor repair of an instrument. Without them most pieces can be but poorly performed.

33.   When a turn is introduced over detached notes it gains acuteness through the prefixing of a note whose pitch is the same as the decorated one. I notate this ornament, discussed in no other writings, by placing a small thirty-second before the turned note. The thirty-second is unvariable regardless of the tempo or the value of the following note, for it is always played with a very rapid stroke delivered by a stiff finger and immediately connected with the following snapped note. This makes for a new kind of trilled turn, which may well be called the snapped turn [20] to distinguish it from the other. It is better suited to rapid notes than the trill, for I feel that a trill is at its best over a note whose value allows for generous alternation; otherwise another decoration should replace it. Through the added small note the turn acquires a brilliance equal to that of the trilled turn but applied to just the opposite situation.

34.   While the trilled turn may be introduced solely after a descending slurred second, it is precisely this situation alone which will not suffer a snapped turn. In Figure 137 we find its symbol (*a*), its execution (*b*),[21] and a few of its characteristic uses (*c*). It may ap-pear at the beginning of a passage, in the middle, before stepwise motion or a leap, but not over a final tone, staccato or otherwise.

[20] *Der geschnellter Doppelschlag.*

[21] It will be seen from the illustration that Bach is discussing the full turn, which is pressed into service by performers and editors far more frequently than it should be. The indication used here was not widely adopted. It appears, for example, in some of Haydn's early sonatas. In fact, Bach's heroic attempt to indicate by symbol or notation all of the fine variants of the turn went for naught. Most of his contem-poraries and later composers used the same sign (∼ or *tr.*) for all types indiscrimi-nately or they wrote out the ornament in both small and large notation. Such prac-tices make the entire section with its many examples all the more important, for it should serve to sharpen our sensitivity to the kind and amount of refinement that reside in the turn.

It should be noted that aside from the keyboard the snapped turn is indicated by the sign of a trill and, even in keyboard pieces, often by the simple sign of the turn. It [22] may be introduced over the second of a pair of slurred notes in stepwise ascent, as in Example *d*. In such a situation it replaces the ascending trill or the ascending turn.[23] Example *e* shows the snapped turn over the first of a pair of slurred notes in stepwise descent. This use is justified by the preceding detached notes. When these are also slurred, as they may be in a slow tempo, a simple turn or the compound appoggiatura [24] is better, as in the asterisked example.

Figure 137[25]

35.   This embellishment cannot be performed, or at least it is not easy to play with its essential briskness, when it appears over a note which must be taken by the thumb or by the fourth or the little finger. The other fingers are much more adept at executing it.

36.   The snapped turn should not be confused with the simple turn after a note. They differ from each other in that the latter is performed appreciably after the principal tone and is found after slurred and sustained notes. In order to differentiate the two more clearly their execution is illustrated in Figure 138.

Figure 138

[22] Remainder of paragraph from ed. of 1787.
[23] Cf. ¶ 37.
[24] Cf. Ch. II, "The Compound Appoggiatura."
[25] Example *d* to end from ed. of 1787.

37.   Finally, the turn may be preceded by two small thirty-seconds. These small notes are incorporated in the ornament and joined to it as rapidly as possible. The threefold beam is unvariable. This variant, discussed here for the first time, represents a miniature ascending trill for which it may be substituted over short notes. It might be called an ascending turn.[26] Its indication and execution are illustrated in Figure 139. When [27] it is used instead of an ascending trill over the second of two slurred notes, a better effect can be achieved by tying the preceding note to the first note of the turn as illustrated in Example *a*.

Figure 139[28]

THE MORDENT

1.   The mordent is an essential ornament which connects notes, fills them out, and makes them brilliant. It may be either long or short. The symbol of the long mordent is shown in Figure 140. Its execution may be lengthened (*a*) if necessary, but the symbol remains the same. The short mordent and its execution are illustrated in Example *b*.

Figure 140

2.   Although it is customary to play the long mordent only over long notes and the short over short notes, the symbol of the long ornament is often found over quarters or eighths, depending on the tempo, and that of the short mordent over notes of all values and lengths.

3.   Example *c* of Figure 140 illustrates an unusual manner of performing a very short mordent. Of the two tones struck simultaneously, only the upper one is held, the lower one being released immediately.[1] There is nothing wrong in this execution, provided

---

[26] *Der Doppelschlag von unten.*

[27] Remainder of paragraph from ed. of 1787.

[28] Example *a* from ed. of 1787.

[1] Usually called the *acciaccatura*, but not by Bach. He reserves the term for auxiliary tones that are introduced into arpeggios. Cf. Ch. III, ¶ 26, Ch. VII, ¶ 13.

that it is employed less frequently than the other mordents. It is used abruptly only, that is, in unslurred passages.

4. The mordent is especially good in a stepwise or leaping ascent. It seldom appears in descending leaps and never in descending seconds. It may be found at the beginning, middle, or end of a composition.

5. It connects slurred notes in conjunct or disjunct motion, with and without an appoggiatura (Figure 141). In such passages it is employed most frequently over ascending steps and also occasionally after an appoggiatura, as in the asterisked examples. When the mordent is applied to an appoggiatura which is joined to its principal tone by an ascending leap, the principal tone must be long so that it can lend enough of its value to make the mordent full and impressive (*a*). This use of the mordent serves both to connect and to fill out notes. It appears occasionally in recitatives.

Figure 141

6. When it follows an appoggiatura, a mordent is played lightly in accordance with the rule covering the performance of appoggiaturas.

7. The mordent is used to fill out sustained tones. Thus, as illustrated in Figure 142, it is found over tied (*a*), dotted (*b*), and syncopated notes. Syncopations may be fashioned out of a single tone (*c*) or various tones (*d*). In the case of the latter the mordent is best used over the second tone of a single repetition (*e*). It fills out syncopated notes and, in addition, makes them brilliant.

8. With reference to Examples *a* and *b* of Figure 142, it should be noted that when the tempo is so slow that even a long mordent will not fill out the notes adequately, they may be shortened, re-

Figure 142

peated, and performed generally as illustrated in the second set of examples under the same lettering. This liberty must be indulged circumspectly and out of necessity only. The expedient is wrong when it distorts the composer's intentions. To lessen the possibility of such an error, strike a tone with due pressure and hold it. In so doing, one realizes that our instrument sustains tones longer than generally believed. In using mordents the performer must be careful not to destroy the beauty of a sustained tone. Hence, as with other ornaments, he must not apply them to every long note nor overextend them. When mordents serve to fill out a note, a small fraction of the original length must remain free of decoration, for the most perfectly introduced mordent sounds miserable when, like the trill, it speeds directly into the following tone.

9. Mordents, chiefly the short ones, add brilliance to leaping, detached notes. They are found over tones which in relation to the harmony are called definitive [2] (Figure 143, Example *a*), over certain broken chords (*b*), and in the middle parts of full chords (*c*), although the long mordent may also be employed when the notes are long; further, they appear over detached dotted notes where the dot is not held (*d*), and over notes followed by rests (*e*). They also occur over longer notes preceded by short ones which rise by a step (*f*) or a leap (*g*).

[2] *Anschlagend.* That the term has a rhythmic rather than harmonic meaning is clear from Quantz's term for the appoggiatura, *anschlagender Vorschlag.*

10.   Of all the embellishments, the mordent is most frequently interpolated in the bass by the performer, particularly over apex notes reached by a step (*h*) or a leap (*i*), at cadences and elsewhere, especially when the following note lies an octave below (*j*).

Figure 143

11.   In the matter of accidentals this ornament adjusts itself to circumstances in the same manner as the trill. Its brilliance is often increased by raising the lower tone, as in Figure 144.

Figure 144

12.   Occasionally an unusual fingering must be taken in order to keep the best fingers free and ready to perform a mordent preceded by a short note as indicated in Figure 144. Such a fingering may be used only in a moderate tempo. It is justified by the detached performance [3] of the dotted note, owing to which the fourth finger can strike the following tone in order to leave both the thumb and second finger in good position to perform the embellishment. After the third finger has struck its note it suffices to shift the hand slightly to the right. Undotted passages or faster dotted ones should be played with a normal fingering.

13.   The mordent, which, as we have already learned, is often used to fill out long sustained tones, may be interpolated after a trill. However, it must be separated from the latter by dividing the long note into two parts. Without this precaution it would be wrong to play the two embellishments in direct succession, for ornaments must never be crowded against each other. These remarks are heeded in the illustrated execution of Figure 145. The length of such a mordent is determined by the tempo, which must not be rapid, for if it is there will be no need for such an expedient.

Figure 145

14.   It should be observed that the mordent is the opposite of the short trill. The latter may be used only over a descending step, precisely the situation which is unsuited to the mordent. The one element which they have in common is that both may be applied to the interval of a second; ascending in the case of the mordent and descending in the case of the short trill. Both employments are clearly illustrated in Figure 146.

Figure 146

[3] Dots in certain contexts were performed as rests. The practice is described and criticized in Ch. III, ¶ 23.

15.   While discussing mordents, I must make mention of an arbitrary decoration often performed by singers in slow movements at the beginning and before *fermate* and rests. Characteristic passages and their execution are illustrated in Figure 147. Since the tones are identical with those of the mordent and the situation is one that favors its use (except that as usually performed the ornament would be completed too soon) it may be regarded as a slow mordent, which, however, has no use aside from these few cases.

Figure 147

THE COMPOUND APPOGGIATURA [1]

1.   The compound appoggiatura may be applied to a note in two ways: First, the preceding tone is repeated and succeeded by the step above the principal note; second, the tone below and then the tone above are prefixed to it.

2.   Both types are clearly recognizable in the illustrations of Figure 148.

Figure 148

3.   The first type is less rapid than the second, but both are played more softly than the principal tone [2] (Figure 149). Melodies grow in attractiveness through the use of this ornament, which serves to connect notes and, to a degree, fill them out.

[1] *Der Anschlag.* The *Bibliothek der schönen Wissenschaften* says; "Marpurg calls the *Anschlag* the *Doppelvorschlag,* which was its more appropriate earlier name, for it arises out of two *Vorschläge.*" "Compound appoggiatura" is closer to Marpurg's term than to Bach's. However, cf. ¶ 3 and Note 2.

[2] This difference in dynamics between the *Anschlag* and the *Vorschlag* ("always louder than the principal tone") may have been Bach's reason for differentiating the names of the two ornaments by means of prefixes. Only one sub-type of *Anschlag* agrees with the usual manner of performing the appoggiatura (cf. ¶ 10). Another reason, however, is that *Anschlag* indicates unmistakably that the ornament is played on the beat rather than ahead of it. Remember Bach's difficulties with the *Vorschlag!* (Cf. Ch. II, "The Appoggiatura," Notes 12, 13).

Figure 149[3]

suave expression

4. A dot often appears after the first small note of the second type, but the first type is unvariable and appears only in more deliberate tempos when two notes are separated by an ascending leap. A few characteristic passages are illustrated in Figure 150.

Figure 150

5. Because the notes of the second type are performed rapidly it is employed in fast as well as slow tempos. Figure 151 illustrates a context especially suited to the compound appoggiatura, for no other ornament can be successfully applied to the passage. This example with its decoration is good so long as it is played no slower than andante, although its speed may be considerably increased.

6. In addition to the preceding example, this second type with

Figure 151

3 Andante example from ed. of 1787.

its leap of a third may be used in all of the illustrations of Figure
150. As shown in Figure 152, it is also found before notes isolated
by rests (*a*) and on the repetition of a tone followed by a descending
second (*b*). In such a case it is better than the turn, just as the turn
is better before an ascending second, as in the asterisked example.
In [4] fact, our decoration may not be used in this latter context (*h*).
Further, the compound appoggiatura is better than the turn when,
in a slow tempo, it is placed between tones which stand an augmented second apart, for it softens the dissonant character of the interval (*c*). It may also be placed within an ascending second (*b*), or
seventh (*e*), and before a descending appoggiatura (*f*). Thus, in general, this ornament is better fitted to a melody that descends subsequently rather than one that ascends. Exceptions occur only when
the decorated note is repeated and when the tempo is slow (*g*).

Figure 152[5]

7. The dotted compound appoggiatura is notated either as an
ascending appoggiatura or in the manner of Figure 153. Its divisions

[4] This sentence from ed. of 1787.
[5] Example *h* from ed. of 1787.

being variable, they have all been carefully expressed in the Lessons. The following note loses as much of its value as is needed for the performance of the decoration. Example [6] *d* illustrates its correct and incorrect notation.

8.   It never appears in rapid movements but is well used in affettuoso passages. Correct uses of it occur before the repetition of a tone (Figure 153, Example *a*), or in an ascending step (*b*), both of which must be followed by a descent, comprising an appoggiatura (*b*) or some other note (*a*). Example *a* often appears as a caesura in adagio movements. The asterisked example of Figure 79 is better with this ornament than with an appoggiatura, owing to the long *f*. Its execution is illustrated in Example *c* of the present figure.

Figure 153 [7]

9.   It is easy to avoid errors in performing this dotted ornament once its origin is known. When a note stands one step above a preceding variable appoggiatura (Figure 154, Example *a*) and a short appoggiatura is inserted between them (*b*), the first appoggiatura acquires a dot and our embellishment is complete (*c*), on condition that there is a subsequent descent of one or more notes.

Figure 154

10.   In performing this kind of compound appoggiatura observe that although the dotted tone is emphasized, the others are played softly. The second note is connected as rapidly as possible with the principal tone and all three are slurred.

---

[6] This sentence from ed. of 1787.

[7] Example *d* from ed. of 1787. In the original of the example marked "right" the ornament is notated ♩ . This differs from its notation in Ex. *a* and *b* and in Figs. 420–425, thus suggesting a most unfortunate misprint.

11.   Figure 155 contains several examples with their execution. In order to help the performer recognize the usual indication of this ornament I have purposely retained its inadequate notation as a simple appoggiatura. The slower the tempo and the more expressive the melody, the longer the dot must be held, as illustrated in the example marked N.B.

Figure 155

THE SLIDE [1]

1.   The slide appears both with and without a dot. Its execution is suggested by its name. Melodies are made flowing through its use.

2.   The undotted slide consists of either two or three small notes which are struck before a principal tone.

3.   When it consists of two notes they are notated as small thirty-seconds in the manner of Figure 156. In an *alla breve* they may also appear in the form of sixteenths, as in the asterisked example.

---

[1] *Der Schleifer.*

Occasionally the slide is indicated in the manner of Example *a*, and frequently it will be found in large notation (*b*).

4. The two-toned slide is distinguished from the three-toned in that (1) it is always used in a leap which it helps to fill in, as in Figure 156; the three-toned slide, as we shall see presently, performs other duties in addition to this one; (2) the two-toned slide is always played rapidly (*b*), the three-toned is not.

Figure 156

5. Figure 157 illustrates the execution of the three-toned type. Its pace is determined by the character of a movement and the tempo. Inasmuch as there is no generally accepted symbol for this ornament and, also, because its pattern is an exact inversion of the turn,[2] I find it more convenient to use the symbol of Example *b* than to follow the occasional practice of writing out the notes in small notation. The eyes can more easily assimilate our indication of the ornament, and it takes up less space.[3]

Figure 157

6. The three-toned slide is equally at home in very rapid and very slow tempos, in flowing as well as highly expressive movements. Hence it has two quite opposite employments. In rapid pieces it fills out notes and adds sheen. Further, it takes the place of an unsuffixed, ascending trill which cannot be used because of the short note values. Here it is always performed rapidly and, as illustrated in Figure 158, the following note may stand in either leaping or stepwise relation to it.

[2] The *Bibliothek der Schönen Wissenschaften* remarks: "Marpurg divides the turn more correctly into descending and ascending turns, the latter of which Bach seems to consider more as a kind of slide. For the rest, however, Bach discusses this ornament with exceptional care." In fact, Bach's ascending turn is discussed in the section on that ornament. It is differentiated from the three-toned slide by its symbol and its greater number of tones. Cf. Ch. II, "The Turn," ¶ 37, and in the present section, ¶ 9.

[3] This symbol was not widely adopted. Usually the ornament appears fully written out in small and large notation.

Figure 158

7. In its other use it is well fitted for the expression of sadness in languid, adagio movements. Halting and subdued in nature, its performance should be highly expressive, and freed from slavish dependence on note values. Its most usual position is over a repeated tone as shown in Figure 159, Example *a*: In addition it may appear after an ascending step or leap (*b*). It can be seen that the three-toned slide resembles a slow compound appoggiatura with its interval of a third filled in. Long notes may be expressively divided and decorated by it in the manner of Example *c*.

Figure 159

8. Because the emotions are more stirred by dissonance than consonance the slide is most frequently found over the former. In such cases, it appears over slow notes whose values are incompletely filled out on purpose, or completely filled out in a halting manner. It appears under similar circumstances in allegro movements especially where there is a change from major to minor. The chords which go particularly well with this ornament are the diminished seventh, the augmented sixth when it contains a fifth, the sixth with an augmented fourth and minor third, and other similar constructions. Since the behavior of all ornaments is determined largely by their relation to the accompanying bass, it is easy to conclude, that this one tends to move downward.

9. The slide teaches us two things. First, in certain passages the performer must aim more at an unaffected, subdued expressiveness than at filling out notes. Therefore he should not always feel obliged to select only profuse ornaments when decorating slow notes, for if it were correct to do so, the slide would have to be replaced by the ascending turn, which resembles it. Secondly, and conversely, it must not be concluded that the fewer the notes in an ornament the greater its expressiveness, for then it would follow that the compound appoggiatura consisting of only two tones is more expressive than the slide or its equivalent, the filled-in compound appoggiatura.

10. While the three-toned slide is effective in portraying sadness, the dotted two-toned slide is equally effective in awakening more pleasurable feelings.

11. Its notation appears in Figure 160. No other ornament is so variable as this one in its execution,[4] which is determined by the affect. Therefore, as with the dotted compound appoggiatura, I have notated it and at times even specified its execution as clearly as possible in the Lessons.

Figure 160

12. Several examples with their various executions appear in Figure 161. The asterisked division of the slide is better than the following one because of the bass. Most of the examples present contexts that are especially fitted to this ornament alone. Certainly, as an unembellished performance will readily disclose, there is a need for additional tones, due in some cases to the harshness of the dissonances, in others to the emptiness of the octave. Yet no other ornament can be inserted as well as the slide. The following tone usually descends, although, as illustrated in Example *x*, the melody may continue by repeating the final tone of the embellishment.

13. Remaining details of performance are illustrated in Examples 1 and 2 of Figure 161. These show that although the dotted tone in the ornament is emphasized, the two succeeding tones are

---

[4] Bach provides helpful information on the normal and extended execution of this ornament in Ch. VI, "The Dotted Slide," ¶ 4.

Figure 161

played softly. The dot under the principal tone, *e*, in Example 1 informs us that the finger should be released before the termination of that note's written length; consequently, in Example 2 this dot has been changed to a rest after the corresponding *c*.

THE SNAP [1]

1. Figure 162 illustrates my unvariable notation of the short mordent in inversion, the upper tone of which is snapped, the other tones being played with a stiff finger. Its execution suggests that this ornament, not mentioned by other writers, might be called the snap. In [2] its employment as well as its shape it is the opposite of the mordent, but its tones are identical with those of the short trill.

Figure 162

2. The snap is always played rapidly and appears only before quick, detached notes, to which it imparts brilliance while serving to fill them out.

3. It is in effect a miniature unsuffixed trill. Unlike the suffixed trill, which is best followed by an ascent, the snap is better before a

[1] *Der Schneller*. Bach's term was not generally adopted. It is doubtful that universal agreement will ever be reached on the execution and meaning of the English term *inverted mordent*, a name sometimes given to the ornament under discussion (cf. *Elson's Music Dictionary*, "Mordent"). It is often played ahead of the beat when it should be played on the beat, certainly in music of the eighteenth century. Further, it is just as often made to consist erroneously of the lower auxiliary, its identity being exchanged with the mordent. Unaccented inverted mordents can be found among the examples of Figure 161, although they are recognizable as such neither by their notation nor by their name (dotted slide). The Germans are just as badly off in their attempt to find a name, as revealed in the following remark from the *Bibliothek der Schönen Wissenschaften* (1763!): "It seems more correct to us that Marpurg should regard Bach's snap (*Schneller*) as a short trill (*Pralltriller*). But we would not care to say that both are correct in stating that this brilliantly played ornament is a kind of short mordent in inversion. This opinion appears quite dubious upon closer consideration of the nature of the trill and the mordent. Therefore, we consider Marpurg's criticism well grounded when he condemns those keyboardists who call the *Schneller* a mordent." Bach's *Pralltriller* and *Schneller* are far from identical (cf. Ch. II, "The Trill," ¶ 30). Because terminology is so completely confused, it seemed advisable to take a neutral position and translate *Schneller* as directly as possible.

[2] Remainder of paragraph from ed. of 1787.

descent. Undoubtedly this is because its second tone and the principal tone resemble an inverted suffix. Nevertheless it is different from all trills in that it is never enclosed and never appears under a slur.

4. It must be assiduously practiced before it can be made to sound as it should. Because only the strongest, most dexterous fingers execute it effectively, it is often necessary to play the following tones with a finger that will not interfere with the staccato character of the ornament, as illustrated in Figure 163, Example *a*. It is often used at caesurae (*b*).

Figure 163

THE ELABORATION OF FERMATE

1. Although I have no desire to discuss embellishments more elaborate than those already treated, I find it advisable to say something about them in connection with *fermate*.

2. *Fermate* are often employed with good effect, for they awaken unusual attentiveness. Their sign is a slur with a dot under it, which denotes that a tone is to be held as long as required generally by the nature of the composition.

3. At times a note without the sign may be held for expressive reasons. Aside from this, there are three places at which the *fermata* appears: over the next to the last, the last, or the rest after the last bass note. To be used correctly the sign should be written at the beginning and again at the end of an elaborated *fermata*.

4. *Fermate* over rests occur most frequently in allegro movements and are not embellished. The two other kinds are usually found in slow, affettuoso movements and must be embellished if only to avoid artlessness. In any event elaborate decoration is more necessary here than in other parts of movements.[1]

---

[1] P. F. Tosi puts it as follows in the English translation (*Observations on the Florid Song*, 1743) of his *Opinioni:* "Every Air has (at least) three *Cadences*, that are all three final. Generally speaking, the Study of the Singers of the present Times consists in terminating the *Cadence* of the first part with an overflowing of Passages and Divisions at Pleasure, and the *Orchestre* waits; in that of the second the Dose is en-

5.   With this in mind I have illustrated both types of *fermate* with their elaborations in Figure 164. All of the examples require a slow or at most a moderate tempo. Since such elaborations must be related to the affect of a movement, they can be successfully employed only when close attention is paid to a composition's expressive aim. Other similar cases can be surmised through the figured bass signatures.

creased, and the *Orchestre* grows tired; but on the last *Cadence*, the Throat is set a going, like a Weathercock in a Whirlwind, and the *Orchestre* yawns."

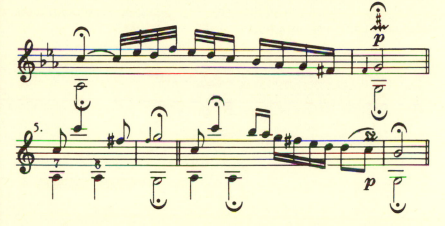

6. Those who lack the ability to introduce elaborations may apply a long ascending trill when necessary to an appoggiatura which stands a step above a final tone (Figure 165, Example *a*).

When the appoggiatura lies a step below, it should be played simply and the final tone trilled (*b*). The same applies to a *fermata* without an appoggiatura (*c*).

Figure 165

CHAPTER THREE

PERFORMANCE

1

KEYBOARDISTS whose chief asset is mere technique are clearly at a disadvantage. A performer may have the most agile fingers, be competent at single and double trills, master the art of fingering, read skillfully at sight regardless of the key, and transpose extemporaneously without the slightest difficulty; play tenths, even twelfths, or runs, cross the hands in every conceivable manner, and excel in other related matters; and yet he may be something less than a clear, pleasing, or stirring keyboardist. More often than not, one meets technicians, nimble keyboardists by profession, who possess all of these qualifications and indeed astound us with their prowess without ever touching our sensibilities. They overwhelm our hearing without satisfying it and stun the mind without moving it. In writing this, I do not wish to discredit the praiseworthy skill of reading at sight. A commendable ability, I urge its practice on everyone. A mere technician, however, can lay no claim to the rewards of those who sway in gentle undulation the ear rather than the eye, the heart rather than the ear, and lead it where they will. Of course it is only rarely possible to reveal the true content and affect of a piece on its first reading. Even the most practiced orchestras often require more than one rehearsal of certain pieces which, to judge from the notes, are very easy. Most technicians do nothing more than play the notes. And how the continuity and flow of the melody suffer, even when the harmony remains unmolested! It is to the advantage of the keyboard that dexterity can be developed beyond the limits of other instruments. But finger velocity must never be misused. It should be reserved for those passages that call for it, without advancing the tempo of the piece as a whole. As proof that I do not disparage speed, nor scorn its usefulness and indispensability, I point to the Lessons in G and F minor [1] and the runs in the C minor Fantasia,[2] all of which must be played as rapidly, but at the same time as distinctly as possible. In certain other countries there is a marked tendency to play adagios too fast and allegros too slow. The contradictions of such faulty playing need not be systematically stated. At the same time it must not be assumed that I condone those whose unwieldy fingers give us no choice but to slumber, whose cantabile is a pretense which hides their inability to enliven the instrument, whose performance, thanks to their lazy fingers, deserves far greater censure than that addressed to shallow fleetness. At least the technicians are subject to improvement; their fire can be damped by expressly checking their speed. The opposite remedy is either not at all or only partially applicable to the hypochondriac disposition which is disclosed, to our greater misery, by flabby fingers. Both, however, perform only mechanically; but a stirring performance depends on an alert mind which is willing to follow reasonable precepts in order to reveal the content of compositions.

2.   What comprises good performance? The ability through singing or playing to make the ear conscious of the true content and affect of a composition. Any passage can be so radically changed by modifying its performance that it will be scarcely recognizable.

3.   The subject matter of performance is the loudness and softness of tones, touch, the snap, legato and staccato execution, the vibrato, arpeggiation, the holding of tones, the retard and accelerando.[3] Lack of these elements or inept use of them makes a poor performance.

4.   Good performance, then, occurs when one hears all notes and their embellishments played in correct time with fitting volume produced by a touch which is related to the true content of a piece. Herein lies the rounded, pure, flowing manner of playing which makes for clarity and expressiveness. With these points in mind, however, it is urgent that the performer test his instrument in advance so that he may avoid either too heavy or too light an at-

---

[1] Sonata II, third movement, and Sonata VI, first movement. Cf. Pt. I, Introduction, Note 17.

[2] Sonata VI, third movement. Cf. Pt. I, Introduction, Note 17, and Ch. III, Note 11.

[3] *Stärcke und Schwäche der Töne, ihr Druck, Schnellen, Ziehen, Stossen, Beben, Brechen, Halten, Schleppen und Fortgehen.*

tack. Many instruments do not produce a perfect, pure tone unless a strong touch is employed; others must be played lightly or the volume will be excessive. I repeat these remarks, first made in the Introduction, in order to encourage a more musical way of portraying rage, anger, and other passions by means of harmonic and melodic devices rather than by an exaggerated, heavy attack. In rapid passages every tone must be played with a fitting pressure or the effect will be turgid and chaotic. The snap, which was introduced during the discussion of the trill, is usually employed in these contexts. A [4] well-rounded manner of performance can be most readily discerned from the playing of rapid pieces which contain alternating light and heavy runs of equal speed. Keyboardists are often found whose ready fingers serve them well in loud runs, but desert them through lack of control in the soft ones, thereby making for indistinctness. They grow nervous, speed onward, and lose control. In the E-flat Lesson [5] the broken chords must be played as distinctly as the runs for both hands. In performing bars 24 to 34 of this piece observe the remarks of Paragraph 16 in the chapter on fingering. Thus, to facilitate the alternate use of hands, employ every slightest pause to bring them to the keys which are to be struck immediately thereafter.

5.   In general the briskness of allegros is expressed by detached notes and the tenderness of adagios by broad, slurred notes. The performer must keep in mind that these characteristic features of allegros and adagios are to be given consideration even when a composition is not so marked, as well as when the performer has not yet gained an adequate understanding of the affect of a work. I use the expression, "in general," advisedly, for I am well aware that all kinds of execution may appear in any tempo.

6.   There are many who play stickily, as if they had glue between their fingers. Their touch is lethargic; they hold notes too long. Others, in an attempt to correct this, leave the keys too soon, as if they burned. Both are wrong. Midway between these extremes is best. Here again I speak in general, for every kind of touch has its use.

7.   The keyboard lacks the power to sustain long notes and to decrease or increase the volume of a tone or, to borrow an apt ex-

[4] Remainder of paragraph from ed. of 1787.
[5] Sonata V, first movement. Cf. Pt. I, Introduction, Note 17.

pression from painting, to shade. These conditions make it no small task to give a singing performance of an adagio without creating too much empty space and a consequent monotony due to a lack of sonority; or without making a silly caricature of it through an excessive use of rapid notes. However, singers and performers on instruments which are not defective in this respect also do not dare to deliver an undecorated long note for fear of eliciting only bored yawns. Moreover, the deficiencies of the keyboard can be concealed under various expedients such as broken chords. Also, the ear accepts more movement from the keyboard than from other instruments. Hence, satisfactory and successful examples of the art of performance can be presented to all but those who bear a strong prejudice against keyboard instruments. A golden mean is difficult but not impossible to discover, particularly in view of the fact that our most usual sustaining devices, such as the trill and the mordent, are also well known to other instruments and the voice. Such embellishments must be full and so performed that the listener will believe that he is hearing only the original note. This requires a freedom of performance that rules out everything slavish and mechanical. Play from the soul, not like a trained bird! A keyboardist of such stamp deserves more praise than other musicians. And these latter should be more censured than keyboardists for bizarre performance.

8.   In order to arrive at an understanding of the true content and affect of a piece, and, in the absence of indications, to decide on the correct manner of performance, be it slurred, detached or what not, and further, to learn the precautions that must be heeded in introducing ornaments, it is advisable that every opportunity be seized to listen to soloists and ensembles; the more so because these details of beauty often depend on extraneous factors. The volume and time value of ornaments must be determined by the affect. In order to avoid vagueness, rests as well as notes must be given their exact value except at *fermate* and cadences. Yet certain purposeful violations of the beat are often exceptionally beautiful. However, a distinction in their use must be observed: In solo performance and in ensembles made up of only a few understanding players, manipulations are permissible which affect the tempo itself; here, the group will be less apt to go astray than to become attentive to and adopt the change; but in large ensembles made up of

motley players the manipulations must be addressed to the bar alone without touching on the broader pace. When [6] a composer ends a movement in a foreign key he usually wants the following movement to begin forthwith. Other reasons as well may require an uninterrupted attack. It is customary to indicate such a procedure by placing only one instead of the usual two-bar lines at the end of the movement.

9. All difficulties in passage work should be mastered through repeated practice. Far more troublesome, in fact, is a good performance of simple notes. These bring fretful moments to many who believe that keyboard instruments are easy to play. Regardless of finger dexterity, never undertake more than can be kept under control in public performance, where it is seldom possible to relax properly or even to maintain a fitting disposition. Ability and disposition should be gauged by the most rapid and difficult parts in order to avoid an overexertion, which will surely result in a breakdown of the performance. Those passages which are troublesome in private and come off well only occasionally should be omitted from public performance unless the performer finds himself in a particularly favorable frame of mind. Also, the instrument should be tested beforehand with trills and other ornaments. There are two reasons for these several precautions: they will assure an agreeable, flowing performance; they will help to remove the anxious mien which, far from enlisting the listener's sympathy, will only annoy him.

10. The pace of a composition, which is usually indicated by several well-known Italian expressions, is based on its general content as well as on the fastest notes and passages contained in it. Due consideration of these factors will prevent an allegro from being rushed and an adagio from being dragged.

11. Every step must be taken to remove accompanying parts from the hand that performs the principal melody so that it may be played with a free, unhampered expression.

12. As a means of learning the essentials of good performance it is advisable to listen to accomplished musicians, as stated in Paragraph 8. Above all, lose no opportunity to hear artistic singing. In so doing, the keyboardist will learn to think in terms of song. Indeed, it is a good practice to sing instrumental melodies in order

[6] Remainder of paragraph from ed. of 1787.

to reach an understanding of their correct performance. This way of learning is of far greater value than the reading of voluminous tomes or listening to learned discourses. In these one meets such terms as Nature, Taste, Song, and Melody, although their authors are often incapable of putting together as many as two natural, tasteful, singing, melodic tones, for they dispense their alms and endowments with a completely unhappy arbitrariness.[7]

13.   A musician cannot move others unless he too is moved. He must of necessity feel all of the affects that he hopes to arouse in his audience, for the revealing of his own humor will stimulate a like humor in the listener. In languishing, sad passages, the performer must languish and grow sad. Thus will the expression of the piece be more clearly perceived by the audience. Here,[8] however, the error of a sluggish, dragging performance must be avoided, caused by an excess of affect and melancholy. Similarly, in lively, joyous passages, the executant must again put himself into the appropriate mood. And so, constantly varying the passions he will barely quiet one before he rouses another. Above all, he must discharge this office in a piece which is highly expressive by nature, whether it be by him or someone else. In the latter case he must make certain that he assumes the emotion which the composer intended in writing it. It is principally in improvisations or fantasias that the keyboardist can best master the feelings of his audience. Those who maintain that all of this can be accomplished without gesture will retract their words when, owing to their own insensibility, they find themselves obliged to sit like a statue before their instrument.[9] Ugly grimaces are, of course, inappropriate and harmful; but fitting expressions help the listener to understand our meaning. Those opposed to this stand are often incapable of doing justice, despite their technique, to their own otherwise worthy compositions. Unable to bring out the content of their works, they remain ignorant of it. But let someone else play these, a person of delicate,

---

[7] Two specimens appeared serially in Marpurg's *Der Critischer Musicus an der Spree*. Both were translations from the French. The first, *Grandvall's Essay on Good Taste in Music*, started on June 3, 1749. Later, starting December 2, 1749, an *Essay on the Decline of Good Taste in Music* by Bollioud de Mermet began. Both contain terms similar to those mentioned here and are marked by "a completely unhappy arbitrariness."

[8] This sentence appeared as a footnote in the ed. of 1787.

[9] Marpurg (*op. cit.*, Sept. 9, 1749) in covering similar material writes, "I know a great composer [Bach?] on whose face one can see depicted everything that his music expresses as he plays it at the keyboard."

sensitive insight who knows the meaning of good performance, and the composer will learn to his astonishment that there is more in his music than he had ever known or believed. Good performance can, in fact, improve and gain praise for even an average composition.

14.   It can be seen from the many affects which music portrays, that the accomplished musician must have special endowments and be capable of employing them wisely. He must carefully appraise his audience, their attitude toward the expressive content of his program, the place itself, and other additional factors. Nature has wisely provided music with every kind of appeal so that all might share in its enjoyment. It thus becomes the duty of the performer to satisfy to the best of his ability every last kind of listener.

15.   As stated earlier, it is especially in fantasias, those expressive not of memorized or plagiarized passages, but rather of true, musical creativeness, that the keyboardist more than any other executant can practice the declamatory style, and move audaciously from one affect to another.[10] A short example is sketched in the final Lesson.[11] As usually notated, common time is indicated but not prescribed for the divisions of the entire piece. For this reason, bar lines are always omitted. Note lengths are determined by the usual superscribed moderato, and by the surrounding values. Triplets can be recognized simply by their beam. Unbarred free fantasias seems especially adept at the expression of affects, for each meter carries a kind of compulsion within itself. At least it can be seen in accompanied recitatives that tempo and meter must be frequently changed in order to rouse and still the rapidly alternating affects. Hence, the metric signature is in many such cases more a convention of notation than a binding factor in performance. It is a distinct merit of the fantasia that, unhampered by such trappings, it can accomplish the aims of the recitative at the keyboard with complete, unmeasured freedom.

16.   Performers, as we have already learned, must try to capture the true content of a composition and express its appropriate affects. Composers, therefore, act wisely who in notating their works in-

[10] For a more extended discussion of the free fantasia cf. Ch. VII.

[11] This sentence is from the ed. of 1787. The Lesson mentioned is the third movement of Sonata VI (cf. Pt. I, Introduction, Note 17). For a score set with a double text that was added later by the poet and Bach admirer, Heinrich Wilhelm von Gerstenberg, see F. Chrysander in *Vierteljahrschrift für Musikwissenschaft*, No. 7, 1891.

clude terms, in addition to tempo indications, which help to clarify the meaning of a piece. However, as worthy as their intentions might be, they would not succeed in preventing a garbled performance if they did not also add to the notes the usual signs and marks relative to execution. With regard to the first point, I hope that I shall be forgiven for using a few unusual terms which, however, fitted the meaning that I wanted to express in the Lessons. I have attended to signs and marks with lavish care, for I know that they are as much needed by keyboardists as by other executants. When one voice is to be brought out above the others it carries pertinent markings. In other cases such signs refer to all parts played by a given hand. The appearance of these signs being better known than their meaning and execution, I shall illustrate and explain the more usual of them in the following paragraphs.

17. Attack and touch are one and the same thing. Everything depends on their force and duration. When notes are to be detached from each other strokes or dots are placed above them, as illustrated in Figure 166. The latter indication has been used in the Lessons in order to avoid a confusion of the strokes with fingering numerals. Notes are detached with relation to: (1) their notated length, that is, a half, quarter, or eighth of a bar; (2) the tempo, fast or slow; and (3) the volume, forte or piano. Such tones are always held for a little less than half of their notated length. In general, detached notes appear mostly in leaping passages and rapid tempos.

Figure 166

18. Notes which are to be played legato must be held for their full length. A slur is placed above them in the manner of Figure 167. The slur applies to all of the notes included under its trace. Patterns of two and four slurred notes are played with a slight, scarcely noticeable increase of pressure on the first and third tones. The same applies to the first tones of groups of three notes. In other cases only the first of the slurred notes is played in this manner. It is a convenient custom to indicate by appropriate marks only the first few of prolonged successions of detached or legato notes, it being

self-evident that all of the tones are to be played similarly until
another kind of mark intervenes. The slurred tones of broken
chords are held in the manner of Figure 168. This applies to the E
major Lesson,[12] where, in addition to the fine effect of such an execution, the advantages of this kind of indication are clearly evident. In
the A-flat Lesson [13] the same execution has been notated in the
French manner, wherein each tone of a chord stands for a separate
voice. I have written it this way so that the student might have an
opportunity to become familiar with both kinds of notation. Generally speaking, slurred notes appear mostly in stepwise passages
and in the slower or more moderate tempos. Passages [14] in which
passing notes or appoggiaturas are struck against a bass are played
legato in all tempos even in the absence of a slur (168 a). As illustrated in the example marked N.B., the same remark applies to
basses which are similarly devised. Note-against-note successions
may be either slurred or detached and therefore require express indications. Successions of thirds like those in Example b would be almost impossible to perform in a fast tempo. At least, a rapid execution might very easily cause stammering or a detaching of the notes
contrary to the composer's intentions. However, played in the manner of the asterisked example with the quarters held for their full
value, the desired effect can be easily produced on the clavichord
as well as the harpsichord. Likewise the succession in Example c
may be played rapidly in the manner of Example d.

Figure 167   Figure 168[15]

[12] Sonata III, third movement. Cf. Pt. I, Introduction, Note 17.
[13] Sonata VI, second movement. Cf. Pt. I, Introduction, Note 17.
[14] Remainder of paragraph from ed. of 1787.
[15] Examples a, b, c, d from ed. of 1787.

19. The notes of Figure 169 are played legato, but each tone is noticeably accented. The term which refers to the performance of notes that are both slurred and dotted is *portato*.[16]

20. A long, affettuoso tone is performed with a vibrato.[17] The finger that depresses and holds the key is gently shaken.[18] The sign of a vibrato appears in Example *a*. The [19] best effect is achieved when the finger withholds its shake until half the value of the note has passed.

Figure 169

---

[16] *Das Tragen der Töne.*

[17] *Die Bebung.* This and the preceding *Tragen der Töne* are clostly related. For one thing, the true and only keyboard home of both is the clavichord. For another, they are executed in the samc manner, the difference being solely in the number of times the key is pressed after the finger stroke. This difference is indicated roughly by the number of dots over each note. Franz Rigler (*Anleitung zum Clavier,* Vienna, 1779) explains the distinction by saying that the *portato* arises "when the key is rather slowly rocked," and the vibrato, "when the tone is quite clearly rocked (*herausgewieget*) according to the number of dots, and without repeating the finger stroke." Daniel Gottlob Türk (Clavierschule, 1789) explains the *portato* as "a joining of tones in such a manner that in progressing from one to another no break occurs. At the clavichord [*Claviere*] this so-called *Tragen* is easy to express, for after striking the key an additional pressure is exerted."

[18] Dr. Charles Burney in *The Present State of Music in Germany,* Vol. II, p. 268, describes Bach's vibrato (*Bebung*) as follows: "In the pathetic and slow movements, whenever he had a long note to express, he absolutely contrived to produce, from his instrument, a cry of sorrow and complaint, such as can only be effected upon the clavichord; and perhaps by himself."

[19] This sentence from ed. of 1787.

21.   The notes of Figure 170 are played in such a manner that the first of each slur is slightly accented. Figure 171 is played similarly except that the last note of each slur is detached. The finger must be raised immediately after it has struck the key. The *portato* and vibrato of Figure 169 apply only to the clavichord; Figures 170 and 171 may be played on both the harpsichord and the clavichord, but [20] more effectively on the latter. The execution of Figures 170 and 171 must not be corrupted into that of Figure 171, Example *a*, an error frequently committed by beginners.

Figure 170   **Figure 171**

22.   Tones which are neither detached, connected, nor fully held are sounded for half their value, unless the abbreviation *Ten.* (hold) is written over them, in which case they must be held fully. Quarters and eighths in moderate and slow tempos are usually performed in this semidetached manner. They must not be played weakly, but with fire and a slight accentuation.

23.   Short notes which follow dotted ones are always shorter in execution than their notated length.[21] Hence it is superfluous to place strokes or dots over them. Figure 172 illustrates their execution. The asterisked example shows us that occasionally the division must agree with the notated values. Dots after long notes or after short ones in slow tempos, and isolated dots, are all held. However, in rapid tempos prolonged successions of dots are performed as rests, the apparent opposite demand of the notation notwithstanding. A more accurate notation would remove such a discrepancy. Lacking this, however, the content of a piece will shed light on the details of its performance. Dots after short notes followed by groups of shorter ones are held fully (Figure 173). When [22] four or more short notes follow a dot they are played with dispatch, there being so many of them. The same applies to Example *a* and, when the tempo is not too slow, to Example *b*. Short notes, when they precede dotted ones, are also played more rapidly than their

[20] Remainder of sentence from ed. of 1787, footnote.
[21] However, cf. Ch. VI, "Performance," ¶ 15.
[22] Remainder of paragraph from ed. of 1787.

notation indicates. All of the short notes of Example *c*, even the sixteenths, when the tempo is not too slow, follow this rule. It would be a better practice to add a beam to all of the notes. It is only generally true that the short notes described here should be played rapidly, for there are exceptions. The melodies in which they appear should be carefully examined. Should ornaments of length, such as the trill or turn, appear over them, their performance must be broader than that of undecorated short notes. Likewise, in sad or expressive passages and in slow tempos the exception is less accelerated than in other cases.

Figure 172

Figure 173[23]

24. The first notes of Figure 174, being slurred, are not played too rapidly in a moderate or slow tempo. If they are, an excess of unfilled space will follow their execution. The first note is accented by means of gentle pressure, but not by a sharp attack or a rapid release.

[23] Examples *a, b, c,* from ed. of 1787.

Figure 174

25. The performer may break a long tied note by restriking the key (Figure 175). Occasionally [24] a short tie must be broken in order to clarify the leading of a voice (*a*). When in legato passages a voice is assigned to a tone directly after it has been taken by·a held note, the hold should not be broken. Rather than violate the legato, the second tone's claim should be denied, for such notes are often written merely for the sake of notation (*b*). Should the two tones be well separated, the second must be struck, but in such a manner that the right hand will regain the key before the left hand has released it (*c*). If the long note is trilled it must not be broken.

Figure 175[25]

26. The usual signs of arpeggiation and their execution appear in Figure 176. The asterisked example represents an arpeggio with an *acciaccatura*. The word "arpeggio" written over a long note calls for a chord broken upward and downward several times.

[24] Remainder of paragraph from ed. of 1787.
[25] Examples *a, b, c* from ed. of 1787.

Figure 176

27. With the advent of an increased use of triplets in common or 4/4 time, as well as in 2/4 and 3/4, many pieces have appeared which might be more conveniently written in 12/8, 9/8, or 6/8. The performance of other lengths against these notes is shown in Figure 177.[26] The unaccented appoggiatura,[27] which is often disagreeable and always difficult, can be avoided in the ways illustrated in these examples.

Figure 177

28. Figure 178 contains several examples in which certain notes and rests should be extended beyond their written length, for affective reasons. In places, I have written out these broadened values; elsewhere they are indicated by a small cross. Example *a* shows how a retard may be applied opportunely to a melody with two different accompaniments. In general the retard fits slow or more moderate tempos better than very fast ones. There are more examples in the opening allegro and the following adagio of the B Minor Sonata, No. 6, of my second engraved work;[28] especially in the adagio,

[26] This discrepant practice of eighteenth-century notation offers many problems to the modern performer. See, for example, J. S. Bach's E minor Partita, *Tempo di Gavotta,* and the E minor Fugue, Bk. II, *The Well-tempered Clavier.*

[27] Cf. Ch. II, "The Appoggiatura," ¶ 25 and Note 12.

[28] The Württemberg Sonatas (Nagels Archiv, Nos. 21, 22). They were preceded by the first published works, the Prussian Sonatas, two years earlier, in 1742 (Nagels Archiv Nos. 6, 15).

where a melody in octaves is transposed three times against rapid notes in the left hand. Each transposition can be effectively performed by gradually and gently accelerating and immediately thereafter retarding. In [29] affettuoso playing, the performer must avoid frequent and excessive retards, which tend to make the tempo drag. The affect itself readily leads to this fault. Hence every effort must be made despite the beauty of detail to keep the tempo at the end of a piece exactly the same as at the beginning, an extremely difficult assignment. There are many excellent musicians, but only a few of whom it can be said truthfully that in the narrowest sense they end a piece as they began it. Passages in a piece in the major mode which are repeated in the minor may be broadened somewhat on their repetition in order to heighten the affect. On entering a *fermata* expressive of languidness, tenderness, or sadness, it is customary to broaden slightly. This brings us to the tempo rubato. Its indication is simply the presence of more or fewer notes than are contained in the normal division of the bar. A whole bar, part of one, or several bars may be, so to speak, distorted in this manner. The most difficult but most important task is to give all notes of the same value exactly the same duration. When the execution is such that one hand seems to play against the bar and the other strictly with it, it may be said that the performer is doing everything that can be required of him. It is only rarely that all parts are struck simultaneously. The beginning of a caesura which terminates a tempo rubato may be drawn into the manipulation, but the end, as in all endings of this tempo, must find all parts together over the bass. Slow notes and caressing or sad melodies are the best, and dissonant chords are better than consonant ones. Proper execution of this tempo demands great critical faculties and a high order of sensibility. He who possesses these will not find it difficult to fashion a performance whose complete freedom will show no trace of coercion, and he will be able to manipulate any kind of passage. However, practice alone will be of no help here, for without a fitting sensitivity, no amount of pains will succeed in contriving a correct rubato. As soon as the upper part begins slavishly to follow the bar, the essence of the rubato is lost, for then all other parts must be played in time. Other instrumentalists and singers, when they are accompanied, can introduce the tempo much more easily than

[29] Remainder of paragraph from ed. of 1787.

the solo keyboardist. The reason for this is the one just stated.[30] If necessary, the solo keyboardist may alter the bass, but not the harmony. Most keyboard pieces contain rubato passages. The division and indication of these is about as satisfactory as can be expected. He who has mastered the tempo rubato need not be fettered by the numerals which divide notes into groups of 5, 7, 11, etc. According to his disposition but always with appropriate freedom he may add or omit notes.

Figure 178

29.   P. means piano or soft; two or more of the letters standing together denote greater softness. M.F. means mezzo forte or half loud. F. means forte; to denote greater loudness two or more of the letters are placed together. In order to control all shades from pianissimo to fortissimo the keys must be gripped firmly and with strength.[31] However, they must not be flogged; but on the other

---

[30] I.e., it is easier for two performers to play in contrived disagreement than it is for the two hands of a single performer.

[31] Throughout this paragraph Bach is speaking of graded as well as terraced dy-

hand there must not be too much restraint. It is not possible to describe the contexts appropriate to the forte or piano because for
every case covered by even the best rule there will be an exception.
The particular effect of these shadings depends on the passage, its
context, and the composer, who may introduce either a forte or a
piano at a given place for equally convincing reasons. In fact, complete passages, including their consonances and dissonances, may
be marked first forte and, later, piano. This is a customary procedure with both repetitions and sequences, particularly when the
accompaniment is modified. But in general it can be said that dissonances are played loudly and consonances softly, since the former
rouse our emotions and the latter quiet them [32] (Figure 179, Example *a*). An exceptional turn of a melody which is designed to create a
violent affect must be played loudly. So-called deceptive progressions are also brought out markedly to complement their function
(*b*). A noteworthy rule which is not without foundation is that all
tones of a melody which lie outside the key may well be emphasized
regardless of whether they form consonances or dissonances and
those which lie within the key may be effectively performed piano,
again regardless of their consonance or dissonance (*c*). Because of
the brevity of Example *c*, I have been obliged to crowd the forte and
piano indications. I know that this constant changing from light to
dark shadings is of no value, for it leads to obscurity rather than
clarity and in the end turns a striking relationship into an ordinary
one. Although each forte and piano in the Lessons has been carefully
marked, it is important to keep in mind that certain ornaments as
discussed in the chapter on embellishments are very much charac-

namics. The terms *crescendo* and *diminuendo* appear in his later compositions, but
only sparingly. Modern signs for graded changes were only evolving in his time. Cf.
R. E. M. Harding, *Origins of Musical Time and Expression*, Oxford Press, 1938,
Ch. IV, and *Harvard Dictionary of Music*, Cambridge, Mass., 1945, "Expression," III.
Bach's older practice is the use of successive abbreviations, such as ff, f, p, pp, or a
more widely spaced ff., pp.

[32] Bach writes here with reference to an elaborate theory of shading advanced by
Quantz (*Versuch einer Anweisung die Flöte traversiere zu spielen*, 1752). It appears
in translation in Arnold, *Art of Accompaniment from a Thorough-Bass*, pp. 407 ff.
The leading point of the theory is that the dynamic level at which chords are to be
played is determined by the kind of dissonances that they express. For example, $4\!\!+^{6}$
is played mezzo-forte; $4\!\!+^{6}_{2}$, forte; $4\!\!+^{2}_{2}$, fortissimo. Bach has many reservations; so many,
that he accepts the theory only in its broadest sense, relieved of all particulars. In
this broadest sense it represents a common practice of the eighteenth century.

terized by dynamic shadings. If the Lessons are played on a harpsichord with two manuals, only one manual should be used to play
detailed changes of forte and piano. It is only when entire passages
are differentiated by contrasting shades that a transfer may be
made. This problem does not exist at the clavichord, for on it all
varieties of loud and soft can be expressed with an almost unrivaled
clarity and purity.[33] A loud, boisterous accompaniment must always
be balanced by a stronger melodic touch.[34]

Figure 179

30. Elaborated cadences [cadenzas] [35] are like improvisations.
In keeping with the substance of a piece they are performed freely
in an unmeasured manner. The notated lengths, therefore, at such
cadences in the Lessons are only approximate and represent merely

---

[33] Johann Fr. Cramer, in his *Magazin der Musik* (Vol. I, p. 1217), wrote, "All who
have heard Bach play the Clavichord must have been struck by the endless nuances of
shadow and light that he casts over his performance."

[34] This material is discussed at length in Ch. VI, "Performance," ¶¶ 5–13.

[35] The common eighteenth-century term was "cadence," which had several meanings, all but one of which have dropped out of use. The Italian word *"cadenza,"*
which came to acquire a specific, and hence clearer, meaning, has been adopted here.
In defense, a quotation from Quantz (*op. cit.,* Ch. XV, ¶ 1) revealing the varied
meanings of "cadence" in his own day, should suffice: "By the word 'cadence' I understand here neither the end nor the interruption of a melody, much less the trill
which is called 'cadence' by some Frenchmen. I shall treat only those elaborate embellishments which are furnished by a concertizing part out of free will and pleasure
at the conclusion of a piece over the penultimate bass note, namely the fifth of the
key of the piece." Bach's discussion of such cadenzas from the point of view of the
accompanist appears in Ch. VI, "Closing Cadences." The soloist's cadenzas are treated
in the last section of Ch. II.

the general pace and differentiation of notes. There is always a slight pause between statements in two- and three-voice cadenzas before a new voice enters. In the Lessons [36] I have indicated these held endings with whole notes instead of the more usual ties. The white notes serve no other purpose and are to be held until relieved by another note in the same voice. Observe that if another note is assigned to the key occupied by one of the whole notes, the key must be relinquished, but reoccupied by the original note after the intervening voice has left. Should both hands be engaged in this procedure, the original hand must retake the key before it has been released finally by the other. In this way continuity of sound will be achieved without an additional attack.[37] With regard to the length of the pauses indicated by white notes, imagine two or three persons in conversation, each one of whom waits for the other to complete his statement before rejoining with his own. Played any other way, the cadenza loses its distinguishing character and sounds more like a clearly measured and barred piece with tied notes. At the same time the pause is not observed when the resolution of a chord preceding the white note must be played by the other voices directly on the white note's entrance.

31.   The F major Lesson [38] is an illustration of the present practice of varying extemporaneously the two reprises of an allegro. The concept is excellent but much abused. My feelings are these: Not everything should be varied, for if it is the reprise will become a new piece. Many things, particularly affettuoso or declamatory passages, cannot be readily varied. Also, galant notation is so replete with new expressions and twists that it is seldom possible even to comprehend it immediately. All variations must relate to the piece's affect, and they must always be at least as good as, if not better than, the original. For example,[39] many variants of melodies introduced by executants in the belief that they honor a piece, actually occurred to the composer, who, however, selected and wrote down the original because he considered it the best of its kind. Simple melodies can often be made into elaborate ones and

---

[36] Sonata IV, second movement, and Sonata VI, second movement. Cf. Pt. I, Introduction, Note 17. A similar dialogue cadenza appears in J. S. Bach's *Werke*, 36.4, p. 31, where, in the D major Toccata, the section marked *con discrezione* begins. Quantz gives many examples (*op. cit.* XV. *Hauptstück*, ¶¶ 19–31).

[37] Cf. ¶ 25 of the present chapter.

[38] Sonata V, third movement. Cf. Pt. I, Introduction, Note 17.

[39] This sentence from ed. of 1787, footnote.

vice versa. All this must be done with no small deliberation. Constant attention must be given to preceding and succeeding parts; there must be a vision of the whole piece so that the variation will retain the original contrasts of the brilliant and the simple, the fiery and the languid, the sad and the joyful, the vocal and the instrumental. In keyboard pieces the bass too may be modified so long as the harmony remains unchanged. Despite the present popularity of elaborate variations, it is of first importance always to make certain that the lineaments of a piece, by which its affect is recognized, remain unobscured.[40]

[40] Of interest in this connection is Bach's Foreword to the first collection of *Sonatas with Varied Reprises* (1760). He writes: "Today varied reprises are indispensable, being expected of every performer. A friend of mine takes every last pain to play pieces as written, purely and in accord with the rules of good performance. Can applause be rightfully denied him? Another, often driven by necessity, hides under bold variations his inability to express the notes as written. Nevertheless, the public holds him above the former. Performers want to vary every detail without stopping to ask whether such variation is permitted by their ability and the construction of the piece.

"Often it is simply the varying, especially when it is allied with long and much too singularly decorated cadenzas, that elicits the loudest acclaim from the audience. And what abuses of these two refinements arise! No longer is there patience enough to play the first part of the piece as written; the long delay of the Bravos would be unendurable. Often these untimely variations are contrary to the construction, the affect, and the inner relationship of the ideas—an unpleasant matter for many composers. Assuming that the performer is capable of varying properly, is he always in the proper mood? Do not many new problems arise with unfamiliar works? Is not the most important consideration in varying, that the performer do honor to the piece? Must not the ideas that he introduces into the repetition be as good as the original ones? Yet, regardless of these difficulties and abuses, good variation always retains its value." Two later sets of pieces with varied reprises from 1766 and 1768 were published in 1914 by Universal Edition (No. 5395) under the title *Klavierstücke*.

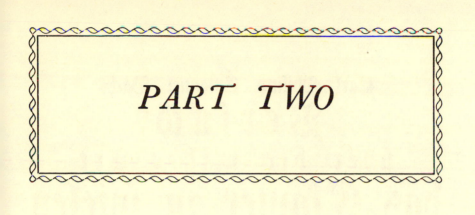

PART TWO

Carl Philipp Emanuel Bachs
Versuch
über die wahre Art
das Clavier zu spielen
Zweyter Theil,
in welchem die Lehre von dem Accompagnement
und der freyen Fantasie
abgehandelt wird.

Nebst einer Kupfertafel.

In Verlegung des Auctoris.

Berlin, 1762.
Gedruckt bey George Ludewig Winter.

Title page of the first edition of *Essay on the True Art of Playing Keyboard Instruments*, Part II

FOREWORD TO PART TWO

I
T HAS finally become my pleasure to present the second part
of this Essay to my friends and admirers. My original intention
was to engrave the musical examples on copper plates, and I
made a start with a fantasia [1] which has been appended to the last
pages. However, I changed my mind later and chose the excellent
invention of music printing [2] so that illustrative matter might appear in the text, thus eliminating the tedious search for examples
in separate tables. The most notable feature of this book is the
attention given to artistic accompaniment, and in this respect
it differs from all previous manuals on thorough bass. The observations are not speculative but rest on experience and wisdom. With
no desire to boast, it may be said that this experience can hardly be
rivaled, for it has grown out of many years of association with good
taste in a musical environment which could not be improved.[3]

[1] Cf. Figure 480.

[2] The examples and Lessons to Part I were engraved and bound under separate
cover. Bach's similar plans for Part II were happily altered by the perfection of a
method of music printing by Johann Gottlob Breitkopf in 1755, consisting in the use
of minute fragments of type which were assembled to form musical characters. The
process was an improvement over sixteenth-century methods of type printing, which
had been abandoned. The new method proved eminently successful and led to mass
production of musical scores. Today, because of the troublesome nature of the process,
its use is limited mostly to short illustrations in books.

The friendly relations between Bach and J. G. Breitkopf are traced by H. von Hase
in the *Bach Jahrbuch* of 1911. Breitkopf, son of Bernard Christoph Breitkopf, founder
of the firm of music publishers (Leipzig, 1719) ran the establishment successfully for
many years. The additional name by which the modern firm is known was added
in 1795, when Gottfried Christof Härtel joined it.

[3] The *Bibliothek der Schönen Wissenschaften* observes: "Those who remember
that the author was first instructed by the greatest master in this element of practical
music; developed under him and already in Leipzig distinguished himself in the
happiest way; how later he became a member of the royal court at Berlin, where the
finest taste flourished under the direction of Graun, who died too early for the
good of music; where the art was practiced with extraordinary delicacy and true
sensitivity, especially because a monarch himself, a great connoisseur of the art, par-

I have written the examples on one system only, in order to keep the size and cost of the work within reasonable bounds. The reader must always find the reason underlying each example and must not restrict his performance of it to the notated register. With regard to the distribution of tones, all necessary observations will be found in the text. For purposes of instruction the niceties of accompaniment and the second part of each section should be treated last. These should be preceded by the first principles of thorough bass. The short sections have no subdivision.

The three-part examples are figured throughout with Telemann bows,[4] a sign which could well be used by all figurists who wish to indicate a three-voiced construction. I use a special sign, $\overset{6}{4}\,3$, for the six-four with a suspended third which has a doubled sixth in four-part construction, in order to differentiate it from the six-four whose fourth part duplicates the bass.[5] I explain these signs in advance so that those who merely leaf through my book will not grow critical or become dismayed by them, but rather will understand immediately that their aim is clarification. There are two examples which seem to contradict the rule which is stated in Paragraph 4 of the first section on the chord of the major seventh. The first is the second example of Figure 301, and the second is Figure 357, Example *f*. In both cases an ascending seventh is accompanied by the figure 9 rather than 2. I have purposely included these just as I have found them, so that the performer might be apprised of them. For, although the indication is not as clear as mine, it is used by some figurists.

If I had restricted the illustrations in the first chapter to the matter at hand, I would have been obliged to omit certain essential observations or at least strip them of their context, and many harmonic changes based on preparation and resolution could not have been treated. An examination of various introductions to thorough

---

ticipated in it; those who remember all this will understand that only a virtuoso like Bach could transform a stiff thorough bass into a fine accompaniment and show the world of music how it must be played sensitively after the nature of the piece."

[4] *Telemannschen Bogen.* A sign, $\overset{\frown}{5}$, which indicated that the diminished triad was to contain in realization only its three original tones without the sixth which was customarily included. (cf. Chapter V, "The Diminished Triad," ¶ 3). In its more general sense it indicates a three-part accompaniment. As suggested by its name, the sign is said to have been introduced by the prolific composer, Georg Philip Telemann, C.P.E. Bach's godfather and his predecessor at the *Johanneum* in Hamburg.

[5] Cf. Ch. V, "The Six-four Chord," I, ¶ 9.

bass will reveal the inadvisability of withholding new progressions until they have been exhaustively discussed. I have avoided this and placed a greater trust in the instructor. Various reasons have led me to repeat certain examples and basic principles. For this, I beg the reader's forbearance. Such excesses can do no harm, for the importance of the matter justifies its repetition, and the reader will gain the advantage of finding all things in their proper order on looking up a passage.

I hope that this work will be as warmly received as the first part, and trust that it will prove as practicable for the student. Although my various duties leave little time for writing, it is my desire to bring out a few supplements, particularly to the last chapter. I have withheld several examples and useful observations on improvisation in order to check the mounting expenses of publication. Perhaps these supplements will appear with those to the first book.

INTRODUCTION TO PART TWO

1

THE ORGAN, harpsichord, pianoforte, and clavichord are the keyboard instruments most commonly used for accompaniment.

2. It is unfortunate that the bowed clavier, Hohlfeld's fine invention,[1] has not yet come into general use. Until it does, its characteristics cannot be described in detail. Certainly, it will prove a useful accompanying instrument.

3. The organ is indispensable in church music with its fugues, large choruses, and sustained style. It provides splendor and maintains order.

4. However, in all recitatives and arias in this style, especially those in which a simple accompaniment permits free variation on the part of the singer, a harpsichord must be used. The emptiness of a performance without this accompanying instrument is, unfortunately, made apparent to us far too often.

5. It is also used for arias and recitatives in chamber and theatrical music.

6. The pianoforte and clavichord provide the best accompaniments in performances that require the most elegant taste. Some singers, however, prefer the support of the clavichord or harpsichord to the pianoforte.

---

[1] Johann Hohlfeld (1711–1771), originally an apprentice passementier, invented a machine for the recording of improvisations and a *Bogenklavier* whose strings were bowed rather than struck or plucked. This was one of a long series of attempts, reaching as far back as sketches by Leonardo da Vinci, to produce a sustained tone and graded dynamic changes at the keyboard. It was demonstrated at the Royal Court in 1753, on which occasion Bach played on it and praised it highly, as did Marpurg. Bach wrote a sonata for the instrument and a song to its inventor on his death (Wotquenne, No. 65, Andantino, Hamburg, 1783, and No. 202c). Cf. Ch. VI, "Performance," ¶ 5.

7. Thus, no piece can be well performed without some form of keyboard accompaniment. Even in heavily scored works, such as operas performed out of doors, where no one would think that the harpsichord could be heard, its absence can certainly be felt. And from a position above the performers all of its tones are clearly perceptible. I base these observations on experiences which may be duplicated by anyone.

8. Some soloists take only a viola or even a violin for accompaniment. This can be condoned only in cases of necessity, where good keyboardists are not available, even though it creates many discrepancies. If the bass is well constructed, the solo becomes a duet; if it is not, how dull it sounds without harmony! A certain Italian master had no reason to introduce this kind of accompaniment.[2] What confusion when the parts cross! Or when the melody is distorted in order to avoid a crossing! As written by the composer, the two parts remain close to each other. How feeble the full chords of the principal part sound, unsupported by a real bass! All harmonic beauty is lost; and a great loss it is in affettuoso pieces.

9. The best accompaniment, one which is free of criticism, is a keyboard instrument and a cello.

10. As regards performers of thorough bass, we are worse off now than we used to be. The cause of this is the refinement of modern music. No one can be content any longer with an accompanist who merely reads and plays figures in the manner of a born pedant, one who memorizes all of the rules and follows them mechanically. Something more is required.

11. The "something more" provides the reason for this continuation of my Essay, and it shall furnish the principal material of its teachings. I aim to instruct those accompanists who, in addition to learning rules, desire to follow the precepts of good taste.

12. In order to become a skilled performer of thorough bass, due time must first be given to the playing of good solos.[3]

13. Good solos are those that have well-constructed melodies and correct harmony, and provide sufficient exercise for both hands.

[2] Bach is obviously not inveighing against unaccompanied duets, at which he himself tried his hand (cf. Nagels-Archiv No. 35) as early as 1752 (Wotquenne No. 141). Rather, it is something like the Opus 4 of Emanuele Barbella (1704–1773), Six Solos for a Violin and Bass or Two Violins, published by R. Brenner. The score contains a prefatory "Scale for teaching to play the Bass part on the Violin."

[3] *Handsachen.* Cf. Pt. I, Foreword, Note 2.

14. In playing these the ear grows accustomed to good melody, an important factor in accompaniment, as we shall see presently.

15. The performer also becomes familiar with all types of meter and tempo along with their characteristic passages. He forms a quite useful acquaintance with most of the problems of thorough bass, and acquires finger facility and practice in sight reading. In brief, solos provide exercise for the eyes, ears, and fingers.

16. Especially recommended are constant listening to good music and careful observing of good accompanists. This will cultivate the ear and teach it to become attentive.

17. Such attentiveness will permit no nuance to pass unnoticed. Observe how musicians always listen to each other and modify their performance so that the ensemble may reach the desired goal. Alertness is required of all performers, including the accompanist, regardless of how exact the figures may be.

18. Our present taste has brought about an entirely new use of harmony. Our melodies, embellishments, and manner of performance often call for unusual chords. At times they must be played in few parts, again, in many. Thus, the range of the accompanist's duties has greatly increased and the recognized rules of thorough bass, which must often be modified, are no longer sufficient.

19. An accompanist must fit to each piece a correct performance of its harmony in the proper volume with a suitable distribution of tones.[4] He must try to follow exactly the composer's intentions, and to this end pay unrelenting attention to the ripieno parts. When there are no middle parts to fill out the harmony, as in solos and trios, the keyboard accompaniment by itself must be constructed in accord with the affect of the piece and the performance of the other players so that the desires of both the composer and the executants will be satisfied.

20. As in reading at sight, the accompanist must always look ahead to the approaching notes.

21. In pursuit of the observations of paragraph 19, I shall give

---

[4] "... *In der gehörigen Stärke und Weite.*" This is one of the essential, guiding principles of Part II, to which Bach refers repeatedly. A discussion of the means to be used in achieving proper volume, i.e., by reducing or adding parts, by changing from one manual to another, etc., will be found in Ch. VI, "Performance," ¶¶ 5–13. In fact, the entire section is an extended treatment of each of the factors mentioned in ¶ 19 here.

as clear and brief an exposition as possible of the usual rules and their modifications, and make many observations on accompaniment in general, as well as on each progression. I shall be attentive to means by which the various progressions may be recognized. Lurking errors and ways of overcoming them will be correctly shown. I shall indicate the best distribution of tones for certain progressions and shall differentiate the essential, less essential, and inessential intervals and their doublings.

22. This latter is necessary because sometimes chords must be thin, sometimes full, and, with reference to the number of parts, there are pieces that require all kinds of accompaniment.

23. Accompaniment may be in one, two, three, four, or more parts.

24. A uniform four- or more-voiced accompaniment is used in heavily scored music, pieces in the learned style which feature counterpoint, figures, etc., and principally in works that consist of music alone, in which taste plays a minor role.[5]

25. In treating four-part accompaniment I shall discuss good construction as well as smooth progression of intervals. Many examples will demonstrate that in order to retain a good distribution of tones it is better to allow two voices to take a unison than to maintain four separate, stiff parts with their needless leaps and awkward progressions.[6] There will also be examples to illustrate the ways in which the left hand must help the right to avoid these defects, which are sometimes ascribed to accompanists' four-part progressions.

26. Three- and fewer-voiced accompaniments are used in delicate works where the taste, performance, or affect of a piece requires a husbanding of harmonic resources. We shall see presently that such pieces often allow for delicate accompaniment only.[7]

---

[5] Marpurg (*Der critische Musicus an der Spree,* p. 216) writes, "Most Symphonies, Fugues, and Trios are played in a manner that might be called the most usual kind of musical expression. I include those Symphonies, etc., in which nothing magnificent, noisy, playful, or very impassioned is sought. Neither the heart nor the understanding is touched to any great degree."

[6] Telemann (*Singe-Spiel- und Generalbass Übungen,* 1734, p. 9) writes: "We have not given place to the unison, another consonance, because through its use one of the four voices which we are using here is lost." This expresses the view of the older school, from which Bach departs, at least in this respect (cf. Ch. V, "The Chord of the Seventh," I, ¶ 12, par ex.).

[7] The learned style of ¶ 24 and that described here, and identified elsewhere as the galant style, are the two chief objects of Bach's discussion of thorough bass. The

27.   In the case of poor and awkward compositions in which there is often no clear middle voice at all, owing to the ineptness of the bass (out of which middle parts should flow) the keyboardist must hide the errors as best he can in a thin accompaniment. He must use chords sparingly and in cases of necessity realize only one figure. He must seek refuge in pauses, divided beats,[8] etc. When his accompaniment is not duplicated by other instruments and the piece allows it, the accompanist may modify the bass extemporaneously as a means of winning correct, flowing middle parts, just as he would change incorrect figures. And how often must this be done!

28.   One-part accompaniment consists of the notated bass alone or its duplication by the right hand.

29.   In the first case, *t. s., tasto,* or *tasto solo* [9] appears over the notes; in the second, *all' unisono* or *unisoni.*[10] Since the indications are often lacking, I shall describe through examples and observations those places where such accompaniments are employed.

30.   The principal part is that which performs the leading melody of a piece in which all other parts play a supporting role, as in solos, concertos, arias, etc.

31.   The upper part is the highest played by the accompanist.

32.   The student, in receiving instruction, must first play each example and then write it out in two staves.[11] The ear and eye will thereby learn to distinguish clearly between the good and the bad.

33.   However, nothing must be taken for granted; both written and played versions must be judged. Every note must be justified. Objections should be raised which the student must answer by giving reasons why, for example, this or that note and no other must be used.

34.   It is best to begin with four-part accompaniment and es-

---

distinction is maintained throughout, as it was by most writers of the time, for these were the two prevailing styles of the period. The distinction is elaborated by Arnold in *The Art of Accompaniment from a Thorough-Bass*, p. 359, note 11, where the terms "strict style" and "free style" are used in the same sense as our "learned" and "galant" styles.

[8] *Nachschläge.* Cf. Ch. II, "The Trill," Note 2.

[9] Cf. Ch. VI, "One-Part Accompaniment for the Left Hand."

[10] Cf. Ch. VI, "The Unison."

[11] For a description of the manner of playing thorough-bass exercises see Ch. VI, "Performance," ¶ 14.

tablish its foundations. Those who learn this style thoroughly will find it easy to go on to others.

35.   Progressions must be practiced in all distributions of tones [12] so that they will become known to the student. In doing this, it is clear that awkward progressions and poor distributions will arise. In meeting these the student will learn to differentiate the good progressions and distributions from the poor. However, whenever it is possible, the remedy for awkward voice leading must be shown immediately.

36.   Although the voice leading may prove awkward, it must not be incorrect. Proper preparation and resolution must be attended to, and forbidden fifths and octaves must be strictly avoided.

37.   In studying the three tonal distributions of four-part chords the student, as suggested in paragraphs 25 and 35, should also learn the use of four expedients: first, the playing of a middle voice by the left hand; second, the bringing together of two voices on the unison; third, the momentary adding of a fifth part to the right hand as a means of averting fifths while avoiding a return to a previous distribution; fourth, the changing of a tonal distribution by the repetition of a chord over a single bass note, as a means of regaining a higher register when the accompaniment goes too low. All four expedients are not only allowed in thorough bass, but are often required, as we shall soon learn.

38.   Unavoidable awkward progressions, hidden fifths and octaves, and certain permissible fifths against the bass must be placed in the middle parts. The upper part must always sing and maintain a pure relationship with the bass.

39.   Instruction should commence with the easy progressions and proceed systematically through the remainder. A brief exercise must illustrate every progression. Brevity does not try patience. This is an important consideration, for the student must not take up a new example until the old has been well committed to the mind and hands. Contrarily, nothing is gained by holding up the progress of a student with unnecessarily long illustrations, for, following his mastery of the progressions, he should diligently practice the accompaniment of various, complete pieces. As preparation for such study, short examples suffice. Through the practice of these

---

[12] *"In allen Lagen";* i.e., with each tone of the chord taking its turn in the upper part. See ¶ 37 of this section.

and the gradual elimination of errors, a satisfactory competence will eventually be won.

40. The teacher should transpose these short examples in all tonal distributions to all keys, major and minor, so that the student will become familiar with them and their notation. Later, this task should be carried out by the student alone.

41. I consider it better, in transposing, to take keys at random rather than move stepwise from one to another, for some students like to play and copy from the untransposed example, depending on their memory to make the necessary changes without giving the matter any real thought. The loss here is considerable. On the other hand, by taking keys at random a student soon acquires facility in reading figures and simultaneously maintaining a good distribution of parts. This last factor assumes many forms and constantly offers opportunities to make use of acceptable expedients as a means of remaining in a good register. In a word, he eventually masters all intervals, regardless of where they lie.

42. While studying transposition, the teacher must explain key signatures to his student and familiarize him with them. Notate the C major and A minor scales and let him, using these as models, write out all major and minor scales. It is hardly necessary for me to point out that it is customary to construct each scale in stepwise descent (*c, b, a, g, f,* etc.) and to correct with accidentals those steps that are too large or too small compared with the model. By this procedure, he will soon memorize the number and position of accidentals in each scale, such as, for example, the number of flats in D-flat, or sharps in C-sharp. If the keys are related by fifths and fourths the gradual increase in the number of accidentals will be made apparent to him.

43. Such knowledge will prove both useful and indispensable. Inescapable situations can very easily arise: The performer is suddenly required to provide an accompaniment and is allowed to give his part nothing more than a cursory examination; he is not given time enough to determine the key from the final note; he can glance only hastily at the key signature. What an unhappy position for anyone who is aware of the rare services and heavy obligations of ripienists, who knows all too well that by rights all ripieno parts should be carefully studied in advance to ensure a good performance! Aside from this matter of execution the part may contain

copyist's errors or, at least, illegible, ambiguous notes, unexpected changes of meter, tempo, figures, keys, etc., which would require preparation from even the most experienced executant.

44.   However, should there be sufficient time to look through the part, examine first the key signature, which can be written in more than the one correct way described above. In the past the signature of D minor rarely contained *b*-flat, or C minor, *a*-flat. Some composers still write this way from habit, love of the obsolete, or perhaps, for other reasons. Others correctly hold to only one signature or none at all, especially in highly chromatic works, freely modulating recitatives, etc., in order to avoid frequent changes, which might prove confusing to the performer. In such cases, many of the accidentals are not even included in the figured bass, it being assumed that the executant is conversant with every key.

CHAPTER FOUR
INTERVALS AND THEIR
SIGNATURES

1

ALL composers who desire good accompaniments to their works must make certain that the bass is correctly and fully figured. The rules which pertain to unfigured basses are often wrong and, in addition, leave many questions unanswered.

2. When the upper part of solos is written in over the bass, or, in larger pieces, when all parts are scored, the keyboardist can, of course, fashion his accompaniment from an unfigured bass, provided he has had experience in composition. If, in addition, an exact figuring is included, the accompaniment may prove to be good. By good accompaniment, I mean only the very best. But aside from this, I know that unfigured basses are often given to a certain keyboardist who is not always able to disentangle himself from the accompaniment.

3. With this in mind I shall discuss means by which an experienced accompanist will find it much easier to make a satisfactory realization of unfigured basses. However, my principal concern will be figured basses.

4. Pupils must learn the figures with dispatch. For this reason, I am no defender of great masses of numerals. I oppose everything that makes for unnecessary trouble and destroys incentive. At the same time, no one can gain a comprehensive knowledge of thorough bass nor learn to accompany properly who does not have an exhaustive vocabulary of figures. Once the executant has triumphed over his fear of signatures, he will be ready to direct his attention to the refinements of accompaniment. These refinements require more figures than were formerly needed for the usual realization of

basses. Can the present-day composer disclose his intentions at all without recourse to figures?

5.   Teachers should let their students accompany pieces with chromatic basses, for these require an ample use of figures. With this purpose in mind, I have assigned many of my father's basses to students, without endangering their lives. Also, they do no harm to the fingers. It is good practice to use the correctly figured works of many composers, so that the student may grow familiar with the various types of signatures and chromatic changes. These should be analyzed, once the student's understanding is adequate, for the insight which is gained hereby will later prove very useful. Such an undertaking increases his knowledge of figures by making it an indispensable part of the study.

6.   Thorough bass would be an easier and more agreeable study, if there were general agreement on the matter of figuring. The main contribution to this cause must be made by accomplished keyboardists who themselves can fashion a good accompaniment. There are many excellent composers and musicians who, while appreciative of a good accompaniment, might find it difficult to indicate their intentions with regard to the keyboard in an idiomatic and requisite manner. The following are among the principal points on which all should agree: Everything essential must be indicated exactly; neither too many nor too few figures should be written; figures must be chosen with an eye to performance; they must be correctly placed; where there are no figures, it must be made known by some sign; all styles of accompaniment, especially the three-, two-, and one-part, must be specified at the point where each is to be used, etc.

7.   The relationship of one tone to another is called an interval.

8.   All signs in thorough bass that pertain to accompaniment are called signatures.

9.   All intervals are measured upward by steps from the bass and are identified by the resultant numeral.

10.   The most usual intervals are those in Figure 180.

11.   An interval retains its name as long as its step is not changed, regardless of changes in accidentals. Thus, all seconds are on the second step, all thirds on the third, etc.

12.   Differences in the size of intervals of the same step, whether

Figure 180

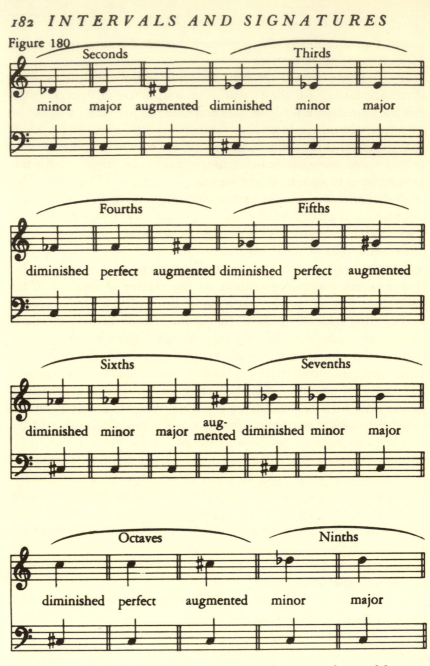

brought about by accidentals or without them, are denoted by certain adjectives.

13. In order to recognize such variation, observe that the rela-

tionship of adjacent keys is called a half tone. Two half tones make a whole tone.

14.   The minor second comprises a half tone, the major, a whole tone, and the augmented, a tone and a half.

15.   The diminished third comprises a whole tone, the minor, a tone and a half, and the major, two whole tones.

16.   The diminished fourth contains two whole tones; the perfect lies a half tone above the major third; the augmented comprises a whole tone more than the major third.

17.   The diminished fifth lies a half tone above the perfect fourth; the perfect comprises a whole tone more than the perfect fourth; the augmented lies a half tone above the perfect.

18.   The diminished sixth contains the same number of tones as the perfect fifth; the minor sixth lies a half tone above the perfect fifth; the major sixth lies a whole tone, and the augmented sixth a tone and a half above the perfect fifth.

19.   The diminished seventh contains a half tone more than the minor sixth; the minor seventh lies one tone below the octave; the major, a half tone below.

20.   The diminished octave is a half tone lower than the perfect; the perfect contains five whole and two half tones; the augmented lies a half tone above the perfect.

21.   In practice the minor ninth and the minor second, the major ninth and major second express the same tones. Actually an octave separates each ninth from its parallel second.

22.   Primes, tenths, elevenths, and twelfths are nothing more than octaves, thirds, fourths, and fifths. They are denoted by the numerals, 1, 10, 11, and 12, and appear often in galant notation and three-part accompaniment. Such figures are used to specify the exact progression of voices, as in Figure 181. It can be seen that the succession 1–2 or 2–1 is more natural and easier to read than 8–2 or 2–8 (Example *a*). The same applies to 10, 11, and 12 (*b*). Successions of these numerals are written as a general rule only before or after a simple 7–8–9 (*c*). Also, by this means it is possible clearly to determine whether two voices should progress in thirds or sixths (*d*), a point not always to be decided on arbitrarily in a fine accompaniment.

23.   The unison in its narrow sense occurs when two or more voices occupy the same key. Hence, it cannot very well be called an

Figure 181

interval. Very often it denotes an octave, a meaning which we shall later discuss in detail. Some use the term "unison" instead of "prime," designating it also with the numeral 1.

24. Intervals express the same tones and retain their names in all octaves.

25. The second and ninth express the same tones but otherwise differ greatly from each other, as we shall soon learn.[1]

26. With regard to quality, intervals follow the construction of the staff. They are thus affected by key signatures without any further indication in the figured bass. For example, if the key signature contains an *f*-sharp, the sixth above *a* is not *f*, but *f*-sharp, and this is indicated simply by 6 over the *a*.

27. However, all chromatic alterations, aside from those included in the key signature, must be expressly indicated.

28. An interval is said to be naturally major, etc., when it agrees with the key signature, and artificially major, etc., when it is altered by an interpolated accidental.

29. A stroke through a figure or a sharp next to it raises an interval a half tone, as in Figure 182.

Figure 182

---

[1] Cf. Ch. V, "The Chord of the Ninth," ¶ 5, and "The Chord of the Major Seventh," I, ¶ 4.

The use of strokes is generally known to Germans and customary with them. The Italians also use them; it is only the French who cause confusion by departing from the practice. In Leclair's figured basses one finds both natural major and artificial minor intervals indicated by a stroke.

30. A flat sign before a figure or after it lowers an interval a half tone, as in Figure 183.

Figure 183

31. A natural sign before a figure or after it restores an interval to its natural size. It is hardly necessary for me to remark that a natural sign lowers intervals in sharp keys and raises them in flat keys, as in Figure 184.

Figure 184

32. Two strokes, two sharps, or a single sharp drawn before a figure or after it raise an interval a whole tone, as in Figure 185.

Figure 185

The use of two sharps is rare and not clear.

33. Two flats or one large flat before a figure or after it lower an interval a whole tone, as in Figure 186.

Figure 186

The large flat, despite its convenience, is not yet widely used.

34. The combinations of natural-flat and natural-sharp which follow a double alteration and restore an interval to its normal size are not as frequently met as would be required by an exact notation. But since they do appear occasionally I mention them here in order to forestall the performer's alarm on meeting them.

35. It should not be considered strange that some write flats or strokes where naturals should appear. The double meaning of the natural sign, which raises and also lowers tones, is responsible for this practice, as in Figure 187.

Figure 187

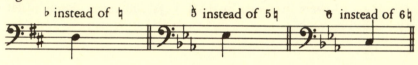

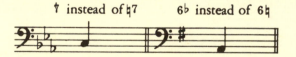

It is customary to indicate the diminished fifth [2] and minor and diminished sevenths by means of a flat.

36. The third may be indicated simply through the accidentals that alter or restore its normal size, as in Figure 188.

Figure 188

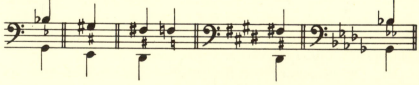

---

[2] Even when it is naturally diminished, a common practice of thorough bass.

37.   Strokes, and flats and naturals which are drawn before the figures, are the easiest to read and, when figures appear in close succession, eliminate all uncertainty over the figures to which they pertain.

38.   Unless an accidental is canceled it continues to be effective.

39.   This rule also applies to figures which appear over repeated tones each one of which expresses a chord. The first figure is effective until another appears, as in Figure 189.

Figure 189

In this example the sixth is struck on each of the first four notes, after which it is replaced by the fifth.

40.   Figures that are placed directly over a note are realized immediately; but when they are placed to the right they are realized after the note has been struck, although they pertain to it and are measured from it, as in Figure 190.

Figure 190

41.   It is not good to place figures under the notes, for this position should be reserved for piano and forte signs. But at times it is not possible to write them elsewhere; for example, when two voices, one for the cello, the other for the keyboard, are written on one staff.

42.   When the subject of a fugue is given to the bass, play the notes as written, omitting chords until figures appear. The same rule applies to short passages where the right hand plays an obbligato accompaniment, which is usually written in small notation, as in Figure 191.

43.   Figures that appear over the dots that lengthen notes are realized at the point where the dot takes effect, although they pertain to the preceding note.

Figure 191

44. Figures that appear over short rests are played on the rest but pertain to the following note, as in Figure 192.

Figure 192

45. Figures over long rests are also played on the rest, but pertain to the preceding note, as in Figure 193.

Figure 193

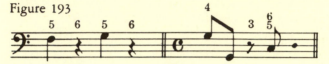

A trained musician can very easily determine which of these two cases applies to a given rest by examining its context.

46. Figures that are placed after a note are realized on divided beats according to its length. If it is duple, the figure or figures are played on the second half of its length, as in Figure 194.

Figure 194

If two successive figures appear over a bass note of duple length, each figure is given half of the note's value, as in Figure 195.

Figure 195

If three successive figures appear over such a note, the first figure, directly over the note, is given half of its length and the others take equal parts of the remaining half, as in Figure 196.

Figure 196

47. If two successive figures appear over a note of triple length or two unequal lengths, which is the same thing, the first figure receives two-thirds or the larger part of the value and the second the remaining third or smaller part, as in Figure 197.

Figure 197

If there are three successive figures, each is given a third of the value, as in Figure 198.

Figure 198

48. These are the usual divisions; any departure from them must be expressly indicated, as in Figure 199.

Figure 199

In both examples the appoggiatura calls for a modification of the rules. The dash which often serves to indicate the prolonging of a figure clearly expresses the desired division. Some omit the dash and separate the last figure from the others. This is not a reliable practice, for it may prove ambiguous. Often the performer cannot be certain whether the composer or the copyist made the grouping, as in Figure 200.

Figure 200

In this particular case another sign is lacking, as we shall see presently.

49.   In the following examples the figures are realized in equal lengths, as in Figure 201.

Figure 201

50.   Because the position of figures is so important, the composer as well as the copyist must be careful to leave enough space in the score to be able to write them in their proper place, especially when there are a great many slurs and other signs relative to performance.

51.   Intervals are either consonant or dissonant.

52.   A consonant interval is one that may be played without preparation (that is, without being present in the preceding chord), that may be doubled, and quitted by ascending or descending leap or step.

53.   This may be done with minor and major thirds, perfect fifths, minor and major sixths and perfect octaves. Consequently, these are the consonant intervals.

54.   In this connection, observe that the octave and fifth are called perfect, first, because they cannot be altered and remain consonant (as soon as they are made smaller or larger they become dissonant); second, because, struck once, they satisfy the ear to such

a degree, that they are never allowed to be played in succession. Out of this arises the well-known first principal rule of harmony: Two octaves or perfect fifths in a pair of voices may never be played in parallel motion, either by leap or by step. Violations are called simply "fifths" or "octaves," as in Figure 202.

Figure 202

Parallel motion occurs when two or more parts move in the same direction upward or downward (Figure 203, Example *a*), and contrary motion, when they move in opposite directions by leap or step (*b*):

Figure 203

55.   It is obvious that the parallel octaves rule does not apply to those places where good reason prompts a composer to lead two voices in unison. It does apply to chord progressions.

56.   Thirds and sixths are called imperfect consonances, because both forms of them, major and minor, sound well; the ear will accept successions of both intervals.

57.   Basically the remaining intervals can not be treated in the manner of consonances as described in paragraph 52. Hence, they are dissonant.[3]

58.   The basic characteristics of dissonances are suggested by their name, which expresses the fact that they sound bad. From this it follows that they may be used only under certain conditions. Their natural harshness must be mollified by preparation and resolution; that is, the dissonant tone must be played, previously, as a consonance and it must succeed to a consonance. By itself, a

---

[3] Thus the perfect fourth, which has shifted its allegiance from consonance to dissonance many times in theoretical writings, becomes a dissonance here. Cf. Ch. V, "The Six-Four Chord," I, ¶ 7.

dissonant tone is sufficiently disagreeable; hence it is wrong to double it; moreover, because it must be resolved, doubling would induce forbidden octaves.

59.   As a means of gaining a clear understanding of the use of dissonances, observe the preparation in the first bar of each of the examples of Figure 204 and, in the second bar, the resolution, which calls for descending or ascending stepwise motion.

Figure 204

60.   Resolution is a constant requirement of all dissonances, but not preparation. Later, however, we shall discuss two cases where even resolution may be omitted.[4]

61.   All dissonances may be struck unprepared over a stationary or repeated bass. The lack of motion in the bass precludes preparation, but at the same time compensates for it.

62.   There are many other ways of introducing unprepared dissonances.

63.   An accidental which lowers a dissonance does not disrupt its preparation (Figure 205). This follows from the discussion of paragraph 11.

Figure 205

64.   A moving bass often causes dissonances to resolve to dissonances (Figure 206, Example *a*) or to remain stationary (*b*). Eventually, however, there must be a resolution to a consonance.

---

[4] Cf. ¶ 77–79.

Figure 206

Such a relationship is called a delayed resolution [5] (*retardatio*).

65.   Occasionally, the right hand does not wait for the arrival of the bass that resolves its dissonance but expresses its resolution prematurely (Figure 207, Example *a*); the bass also does this at times (*b*).

Figure 207

Both are known as an anticipated resolution [6] (*anticipatio*).

66.   When a tone in the bass is interchanged with one in the right hand prior to the resolution of a dissonance, a transfer of chordal tones [7] is said to occur, as in Figure 208.

Figure 208

67.   When the bass strikes the tone to which a dissonance in the right hand should resolve, a transferred resolution [8] is said to oc-

[5] *Eine Aufhaltung der Auflösung.*

[6] *Eine Vorausnahme der Harmonie.* Thus, if the chord arrives before its bass or the bass before its chord, regardless of rhythmic position, an anticipation takes place. This gives the term a broader meaning than it has today, when anticipations and suspensions are distinguished by rhythmic position. Thus only the examples under *b* are analyzed as anticipations today, while those under *a* are analyzed as bass suspensions or appoggiaturas. This point comes up repeatedly when Bach discusses the rhythmic dislocation of chordal tones.

[7] *Eine Verwechselung der Harmonie.*

[8] *Eine Verwechselung der Auflösung.*

cur. The dissonant tone is freed by this action of the bass, which satisfies the need for resolution, as in Figure 209.

Figure 209

Our aim here is merely to introduce the accompanist to these liberties; we leave it to the composer to employ them with discrimination.

68. It is rare that each tone of a succession of rapid notes takes a separate chord. Such unaccompanied notes are said to pass.[9]

69. A single passing tone is not indicated by a sign, but several in succession are denoted by a dash which extends to the point where the right hand resumes. Passing tones appear in all styles, meters, and tempos. Sometimes half of the notes are passing (Figure 210, Example *a*); sometimes fewer (*b*); but often in rapid tempos with short notes most of them are passing (*c*).

Figure 210

[9] *Sie gehen durch;* later, ¶ 69, *die durchgehende Noten.* These terms are general in meaning and apply to all types of connecting or filling tones regardless of whether they proceed by step, leap, or simply repetition (cf. ¶ 72). The passing tone in its narrow meaning is *Der Durchgang,* standing for a stepwise transition from one tone to another (cf. ¶ 73). It can be seen that the terms overlap, since both are concerned with stepwise motion, the first partially, the second exclusively. We have no ready English equivalent for the broader concept unless we extend the connotation of our term *passing tone.* This proved to be the most advisable thing to do here, especially since Bach uses both terms loosely. For the accompanist, it is important to distinguish between principal tones that require chords, passing tones which are not accompanied,

70. In the case of an extended succession of passing tones the chord may be repeated, as in Figure 211.

Figure 211

71. In certain cases which will be treated later, the intervals may be said to pass. This happens in three ways: (1) Over a stationary bass (Figure 212).

Figure 212

(2) Over a moving bass with a stationary right hand (Figure 213).

Figure 213

(3) When both hands move (Figure 214).

Figure 214

72. In rapid drum basses the playing of which may cause a stiffening of the wrist, notes are occasionally passed over, or omitted. An extended discussion of this expedient will be found in the Introduction to Part I, Paragraph 9*a*.

---

and those over which chords are played. This matter is discussed in Ch. VI, "Passing Tones" (cf. ¶ 3) and "Changing Notes." Chordal by-products of horizontal motion are called passing chords. Cf. Arnold, *The Art of Accompaniment from a Thorough-Bass,* Ch. XVIII.

73. The term "passing tone" (*transitus*), refers in its narrow sense to a stepwise bass.

74. When the accompaniment is played with its proper bass on the long part of a bar, the passing tone is called regular (*transitus regularis*). With notes of equal value, the first, third, etc., are long according to the meter and the second, fourth, etc., short (Figure 215).

Figure 215

75. When the accompaniment is played on the long pulse ahead of its proper bass, which falls on the short pulse, the passing tone is irregular (*transitus irregularis*) and is known as a changing note (Figure 216).

Figure 216

76. When the composer prefers not to figure changing notes he may set figures over only the succeeding tones, or place over the changing notes an oblique stroke, a circle, a semicircle, or an *m*, which, on occasion, may be lengthened (Figure 217).

Figure 217

The oblique stroke under Example 2 is the best.

77. Changing notes also occur as anticipations, illustrations of which appear in Figure 207, Example *a*.

78. The dissonances which result from the introduction of both types of passing tone do not always require resolution, even when they are prepared (Figure 218).

Figure 218

79. The same freedom of treatment applies to dissonances which become consonances through an enharmonic change as in Figure 219.

Figure 219

80. On the other hand, we shall learn later that consonances sometimes lose their freedom and require the same preparation and resolution as dissonances.[10]

---

[10] This is a reference to an old dilemma of thorough bass. All intervals were computed solely from the bass, and their consonance or dissonance was determined by this relationship. Thus, in the six-five chord, the second formed by the fifth against the sixth is not mentioned as an interval. Instead Bach writes: "Die Quint wird wie eine Dissonanz gebraucht; sie lässt sich . . . von der sexte binden und gehet allezeit herunter." (The fifth is treated as a dissonance; it is restricted by the sixth and always progresses by stepwise descent). Thus does a consonance lose its freedom. This statement recurs in all cases where chords contain a tone which is consonant with the bass, but dissonant in its relation to another upper part. Cf. in Ch. V: "The Four-Three Chord," I, ¶ 4; "The Six-Five Chord," I, ¶ 4; "The Seven-Six Chord," ¶ 5; "The Chord of the Major Seventh," II, ¶ 2; "The Five-Four Chord," ¶ 4. The fourth in this last chord is a dissonance, but a mild one, and is not always obliged to descend in other contexts.

CHAPTER FIVE

THOROUGH BASS

THE TRIAD,[1] I

1

THE most perfect consonant chord, that with which most works begin and all end, is the triad.

2. It consists of a ground tone, fifth, and third.

3. When the octave is added it becomes the common chord, the fifth of which must be perfect. It is only the third that is variable, appearing as either major or minor.

4. The chord is major when its third is major, and minor when its third its minor.

5. The unnatural triad contains either a diminished or an augmented fifth.

6. In the first case it is called the diminished triad, in the second, the augmented.

7. These chords, which contain dissonances, will be discussed on the completion of our study of consonant chords.

8. The tones of the common chord may be distributed in three ways: with either the fifth, octave, or third in the upper voice (Figure 220).

Figure 220

---

[1] Cf. Arnold, *Art of Accompaniment from a Thorough-Bass*, pp. 498–503.

9. The common chord is played when there appears over a bass which is not passing, either nothing at all, an isolated accidental, or 8, 5, 3, each by itself, or combined with one or both of the other numerals.

10. Since the fifth is always perfect, it is played as such without any indication (Figure 221).

Figure 221

11. According to circumstances, the octave of the bass [2] may be omitted and either the third or the fifth doubled.

12. However, when the third becomes major by chromatic alteration it is not doubled.

13. In three-part accompaniment the octave of the bass is omitted, although a resolution or the melody of the principal part may require that the fifth be omitted instead.

14. In two-part accompaniment, other things being equal, only the third is played.

15. In order to recognize the common chord from its notation, observe that its tones fall on adjacent lines or adjacent spaces.

16. When I strike two notes which are separated by three keys, I play the major third; but separated by two keys, the minor third.

17. Contrary motion makes the best and safest accompaniments, especially when triads are employed. With it, open and hidden fifths and octaves can be avoided.

18. Hidden fifths and octaves become apparent when two voices which move in similar motion are filled in, thereby creating open fifths and octaves (Figure 222).

[2] Throughout, Bach distinguishes between a doubling by the right hand of the bass note and a doubling within the right hand. The first has been translated as "duplication" or "the octave of the bass" (Bach writes simply *die Octave*) and the other as "doubling" (Bach, *die Verdoppelung*).

Figure 222

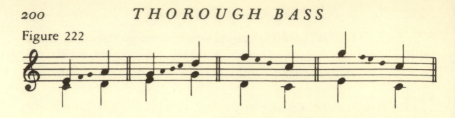

19.   These are more permissible between inner voices or an inner voice and the bass than between the upper voice and the bass, for these parts must always be constructed with a view to absolute purity and good melody. Since such progressions create impure relationships, they are bad.

20.   Nevertheless, the following hidden fifths may appear in the outer as well as inner parts (Figure 223).

Figure 223

21.   Two open fifths of different quality may be played in succession.

22.   In any pair of voices a perfect fifth may descend to a diminished fifth (Figure 224).

Figure 224

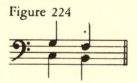

But a diminished fifth may succeed to a perfect fifth only out of necessity, and preferably not in the outer parts (Figure 225).

Figure 225

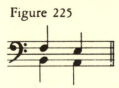

23.   In ascending motion the progression of a perfect fifth to a diminished fifth (Figure 226, Example *a*) is better than a diminished

fifth to a perfect (*b*) because of the descending tendency of the diminished fifth.

Figure 226

Both progressions belong to inner parts.

24. The right hand should not play above the two-lined *f*, unless the bass is written very high, or the bass clef is replaced by a higher one;[3] or unless a special effect is intended, as, for example, when a passage is varied on its repetition by a change of register, etc.

25. The right hand should not play below the upper half of the unlined octave, unless conditions the reverse of those mentioned in the preceding paragraph are present.

26. For purposes of instruction, students may exceed this range in order to practice successions in various distributions and thereby become familiar with all registers.

27. At first, however, it is customary to restrict the right hand to the confines of the descant clef,[4] and the bass to the bass clef.

28. The foundations of accompaniment can be best established when students are required to learn thoroughly all twenty-four common chords.[5] This should occur gradually. The chords in their three distributions should be played up and down the entire keyboard. At first it is sufficient to let this be done slowly, but later the speed must be regularly increased so that finally the hands will develop the ability to strike any common chord without hesitancy.

29. To begin with, only a few chords should be assigned and reassigned until the requisite knowledge and facility have been acquired.

30. All lessons must be related to each other so that old material will be constantly reviewed and not forgotten.

---

[3] Known as *Bassetto* or, in German, *Bassett, Bassetgen*. Cf. Arnold, *op. cit.*, pp. 373 ff.

[4] That is, the C-clef on the first line.

[5] I.e., major and minor triads on each degree of the chromatic scale.

31. Here, as in other exercises, the student must be asked numberless questions about intervals so that he will develop the ability to recognize them automatically without reflection. This suggestion is based on experience. There are many who by virtue of long practice and a good ear realize chords and figures, and even accompany entire pieces without any knowledge, intervals as well as rules being little known to them. Useful and essential as a good ear is, it will prove undependable and harmful when the executant depends on it alone without exercising his mind.

32. Chords succeed to each other in the most direct manner. This should be observed in all accompaniments.[6]

33. Hence, when the bass rises a third, retain the intervals common to both tones and take anew only the fifth over the second tone (Figure 227).

Figure 227

And when the bass falls a third, only the octave of the second tone must be sought (Figure 228).

Figure 228

34. But when the bass rises or falls a second, all upper voices must move contrary to it (Figure 229).

[6] Cf. Ch. VI, "Accompaniment," ¶ 14.

Figure 229

35.   When the bass ascends a half step and both chords have major thirds, the fifth and third of the first chord move to either an octave or unison. Hence, the second chord has a doubled third and no octave (Figure 230).

Figure 230

Played in reverse, the first chord must have a doubled third and no octave (Figure 231).

Figure 231

If this precaution is not taken, one of the voices will express an augmented second, which is to be avoided (Figure 232).

Figure 232

36.   In a final cadence the fifth must never appear in the upper voice. The octave is the best interval when it can be reached; next best is the third; but the closing note of the principal part must not lie below this third.

37.   When the hands come too close to each other, or the right hand moves too low, the chord may be shifted to a higher register by repeating it over a single bass note, provided there is sufficient time; if there is not, a new voice may be added on top, and the lowest one over the bass relinquished. These expedients may be used, first, only in an emergency, for I believe that under normal conditions the accompanist should restrict himself to four parts and not increase their number; second, only with consonances, for dissonances impose limitations on the accompaniment.

THE TRIAD, II

1.   The student should be urged to use contrary motion even when it is not required. In his exercises all kinds of treacherous progressions should be introduced so that he may learn clearly how to avoid them. For this purpose it is good practice to write out realizations.

2.   But when it becomes apparent that he is fully aware of lurking errors, he may be shown those successions in which parallel motion is sometimes preferable to contrary, as in Figure 233.

Figure 233

3.   It can be seen in Figure 233 that it is good to lead the upper voice in parallel thirds with the bass. The major third has a tend-

ency to ascend unless it is hindered from doing so by a prepared dissonance or a poor doubling (Figure 234).

Figure 234

4. Because of this tendency, the major third of the upper voice in the first chord of Figure 235 must not descend in contrary motion to the fifth of the second chord.

Figure 235

A lesser evil, hidden octaves (Figure 236), should be chosen at a cadence in preference to the unnatural progression of Figure 235.

Figure 236

5. Most disposed to an ascent is the chromatic major third (Figure 237, Example *a*). Therefore when the octave of such a chord

moves to the seventh, a voice must be added to the next chord so that it will be complete (*b*). If, however, the fifth of the major chord leaps to the seventh, the expedient is not needed (*c*).

Figure 237

6. In four-part accompaniment the major third in an inner part does not require such close attention. It may progress by a descending leap (Figure 238).

Figure 238

·7. In three-part accompaniment, however, the major third in the middle part ascends, regardless of the resultant incomplete triad (Figure 239).

Figure 239

8.   Normally, the common chord does not require a signature. There are times, however, when it is necessary to write the numeral or numerals which denote its intervals. The reasons are: dissonances struck and resolved into our chord over a stationary tone (Figure 240, Example *a*); a dissonance which follows our chord, the bass being held (*b*); a chordal change over a single tone (*c*); a tone in the bass which might otherwise be considered passing (*d*). In all of these cases the entire chord is played.

Figure 240

9.   But there are times when a series of threes is written over a rapid passing bass as a means of informing the accompanist that the right hand is to play only parallel thirds with the bass [7] (Figure 241).

Figure 241

10.   Exercises on common chords must not go beyond simple modulations. Otherwise the ear will grow confused in its attempt to take in all twenty-four keys at a time. It is far better to hold extravagances in reserve and concentrate on natural chord successions. Besides, when short studies are transposed to the various keys, all chords put in an appearance anyway. Further, in transposing, the

[7] Cf. Ch. VI, "Some Refinements of Accompaniment," ¶¶ 6–8, where the use of thirds without indication is discussed.

student learns why some tones are written with sharps or flats and yet retain the same relative sound (Figure 242).

Figure 242

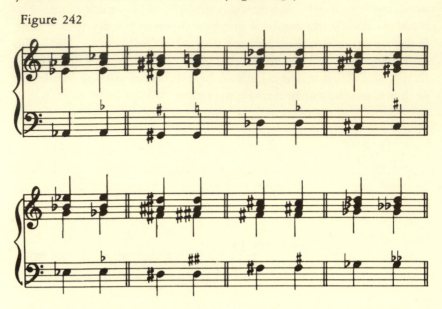

11. The following short examples will perhaps suffice to illustrate the meaning of Paragraph 10. The numerals denote the best intervals for the upper voice (Figure 243).

Figure 243[8]

8 Cf. Arnold, *op. cit.*, p. 503, Note 15.

12.   Divided accompaniment is used either out of necessity or to achieve elegance. Everything that the accompanist must know about this technique will be illustrated at a later time. Divided accompaniment occurs when the left hand realizes some of the figures without increasing the normal number of parts. Chords are spread out and often made more attractive by this means. Occasionally the resolution of a dissonance requires it.

13.   Our earlier discussion of primes, tenths, and twelfths applies to divided accompaniment also.[9]

THE CHORD OF THE SIXTH,[1] I

1.   The chord of the sixth that contains a major or minor sixth consists entirely of consonances, namely, the sixth, third, and octave.

2.   The usual signature of the chord is 6 alone, but at times the other intervals are specified for various reasons.

3.   In figuring the bass, required accidentals must not be overlooked.

4.   The third below the bass note becomes the sixth above it, and the triad that is built from this third or sixth provides the tones of the chord of the sixth.

5.   The chord of the sixth containing the octave of the bass is rare, being used on single bass notes marked 6, or out of necessity, when required by dissonances, etc. More frequently, the third or sixth is doubled and the octave of the bass omitted.

6.   In these doublings, which may be in the unison as well as the octave, none of the figures is unrealized. The tones of the common chord (Figure 244, Example *a*) which comprises the position of the sixth are present in all of its doublings.

Figure 244

But by means of this position many errors can be circumvented and good voice leading maintained, as we shall see later.

9 Cf. Ch. IV, ¶¶ 22–23.
1 Cf. Arnold, *op. cit.,* pp. 516–533.

7.   The following rules of doubling should be observed:

(1)   When a diatonic sixth and third are major, either interval may be doubled (Figure 245).

Figure 245

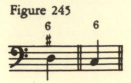

(2)   When a diatonic or chromatically raised sixth is major, but the third is minor, the sixth is not doubled (Figure 246).

Figure 246

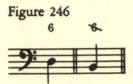

(3)   When a chromatically raised sixth and third are major, either may be doubled. Also when only the third of this chord is raised chromatically, it may be doubled (Figure 247).

Figure 247

(4)   When the bass is raised chromatically it is not duplicated (Figure 248, Example *a*) unless the sixth is similarly raised (*b*):

Figure 248

8.   Three-part accompaniment comprises only the third and sixth.

9.   In two-part accompaniment one of the intervals must be omitted; hence the position cannot be used readily. A typical case

occurs when the principal part moves piano in notes that lie a sixth above the bass while the accompanist plays thirds [2] (Figure 249).

Figure 249

10. When the bass of the position of the sixth moves through successive steps or thirds, the doubling must be alternated with a duplicated bass in order to avoid octaves (Figure 250).

Figure 250

Although it is more urgent to attend to the doubling when the bass moves by step, when it moves by leaps an alternated doubling helps to create a better upper part.

11. When the tempo is rapid, such successions are best expressed in three voices, in which case only one distribution of tones is possible, for in the other the fourths become fifths. In short, the sixth should always lie in the upper voice. Even in four-part accompaniment this is the safest and, for melodic purposes, the best distribution.

12. When the octave of the bass is taken, it is best not to place it in the upper voice.

[2] However, see Ch. VI, "One-part accompaniment for the left hand," ¶¶ 3, 4.

13.   The unmelodic progressions marked with an asterisk can be avoided by doubling [3] (Figure 251).

Figure 251

14.   When 6 succeeds to 5, the part that expresses the sixth progresses to the fifth while the other parts are held. This progression often appears in succession. All three dispositions of the position of the sixth may be employed here, provided that the rules of doubling are heeded. On redistributing the tones of the following examples, it will be found that a unison doubling must be used occasionally. In a few cases where the third is doubled, one of the doubled tones progresses to the fifth while the sixth is held. By this means leaps, otherwise unavoidable on single appearances of the

Figure 252

[3] I.e., instead of a duplication of the bass. Cf. Ch. V, "The Triad," Note 1.

progression, can be eliminated and a uniform disposition maintained (Figure 252).

15. When 5 6 appears over a bass note, the common chord is struck and its fifth moves to the sixth while the other voices are held. When this progression appears in succession, a three-part accompaniment is the easiest. Also it is the best fitted for the accompaniment of rapid notes in pieces which do not call for a full setting.

16. When the accompaniment is in four parts, errors are easily avoided by doubling, since the progression consists entirely of consonances. Best are the examples in which the two kinds of doubling are alternated. An exception to such a uniform procedure occurs on the appearance of the diminished fifth (Figure 253, Example *a*). Further, the leap of an augmented fourth should be avoided (*b*). A leaping accompaniment with or without a doubling in the right hand is acceptable, but not always attractive (*c*). Example *d* illustrates a divided accompaniment.

Figure 253

The diminished fifth seems to abandon its descending tendency in Figure 253, Examples *a, c,* and *d.* But a closer examination of the voice leading discloses its resolution (Figure 254).

Figure 254

17. Occasionally, $\overset{8}{6}$ will be found in the galant style, where it calls for a three-part realization. Since the same signature is also employed in four-part accompaniment, the performer must be care-

ful to distinguish the one setting from the other. A sign of differentiation would be helpful here, for the indication by itself is often ambiguous. The figures are found over basses which, if not set in three parts, might take for the fourth part a third (Figure 255, Example *a*) or a fourth (*b*); and at times any additional interval would sound extremely harsh.

Figure 255

18. In four-part settings, the signature $\frac{8}{6}$ often indicates the resolution of a preceding dissonance (Figure 256, Example *a*) and also specifies the exact course of a part (*b*). But inasmuch as this latter use applies also to three-part realizations, and no sign of differentiation is employed, the best advice that can be given to an accompanist is to listen and judge.

Figure 256

19. The presence of compound signatures before and after $\frac{8}{6}$ is usually a sign of three-part accompaniment. If a Telemann bow were placed above the signature ($\overset{\frown}{\underset{6}{8}}$), chord and context would be immediately recognizable as three-part.

20. When the sixth appears with a diminished octave, no additional interval is played. The octave descends and can most frequently be regarded as a retardation of the next tone. The examples of Figure 257 are noteworthy. In the last one, $\frac{7}{5}$ precedes an embellishing $\overset{\natural\ 8}{6}$.

Figure 257

21.　The augmented sixth is a dissonance which appears with preparation (Figure 258, Example *a*) or without it (*b*) and always ascends. The required accidental is included in the signature. If no other figure appears, the third is added in three-part accompaniment and doubled in four.

Figure 258

22.　The diminished sixth, a dissonance, is rare. It demands a distinct type of admirer. Those who use it, prepare it and resolve it by stepwise descent. It sounds passably well when accompanied solely by the minor third. The required accidental must not be omitted from its signature (Figure 259).

Figure 259

THE CHORD OF THE SIXTH, II

1. The accompanist must remember that it is most necessary to look ahead in the case of those chords that permit more than one kind of realization. He will not always enjoy a free choice but must know how to adjust his chord to those that follow.

2. When the minor sixth and chromatic major third appear at cadences instead of $\begin{smallmatrix}6&5\\4&\sharp\end{smallmatrix}$, it is best to take the octave of the bass with the sixth (Figure 260, Example *a*). Moreover, the octave is required when it prepares (*b*) or resolves (*c*) a dissonance. In the last example the octave serves to eliminate a leap. Here again the signature should include a Telemann bow (6) as a warning.

Figure 260

3. When a bass note marked 6 ascends a step to one marked $\begin{smallmatrix}6\\5\end{smallmatrix}$ it is best, when possible, to add the octave of the bass to the sixth, for it makes the smoothest voice leading (Figure 261, Example *a*). If the third is doubled, one of the voices must leap (*b*). Composers may have valid reasons for introducing leaps into inner parts, but accompanists avoid them for equally valid ones. A doubled sixth in our progression can easily cause fifths (*c*). Two parts must leap in order to avoid them (*d*). I repeat, add the octave of the bass *when possible,* for there are times when only the sixth or third can be doubled. A chromatically raised bass (which is not to be duplicated) may necessitate a doubling of the third (*e*). Correct resolution of dissonances may require a doubled sixth, as in the case of the seventh and augmented fifth of Example *f*.

Figure 261

4. When a bass expresses several sixths, moving by stepwise ascent or descent interspersed with unaccompanied tones, close attention must still be given to doubling in four-part realizations (Figure 262).

Figure 262

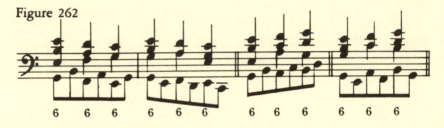

5. In certain distributions even contrary motion cannot be counted upon to avoid fifths, as illustrated in Figure 263. Such errors can be corrected through doubling (*a*). But in *b*, contrary motion is good in all distributions of tones except the case illustrated in *c*.

Figure 263

6. Doubling in the unison is often preferable to that in the octave, for it helps maintain close position and makes a better upper voice, as illustrated in Figure 264.

Figure 264

7. If the accompanist does not look ahead as he should, errors will be avoided only by good fortune. In the first of the following examples, the octave of the bass must be retaken over the unaccompanied note in order to prepare the following seventh (Figure 265, Example *a*). Such basses are convenient to the accompanist, for they give him an opportunity to decide beforehand how each chord shall be realized. At the same time the expedient of Example *a* never adds to the attractiveness of a setting. In Example *b* the third of the chord of the major sixth must be doubled unless recourse is taken to a divided accompaniment following a duplication of the bass. The reason is that the fourth in the second chord must remain stationary. For a similar reason the sixth of the six-four chord in the asterisked example must be doubled or, as an alternative (*c*), the tone *a* must enter as an eighth note in order to prepare the following seventh.

Figure 265

8. In the first of the examples of Figure 266 we see the use of a varied doubling as a means of avoiding octaves. In the second example the same means must be more extensively employed for the same reason. A consistent distribution of tones is thereby maintained and unnecessary leaps are avoided.

Figure 266

9. The major sixth accompanied by the minor third tends to ascend. For this reason the second of the following realizations is preferable to the first. This precaution is most essential when the sixth lies in the upper part.

Figure 267

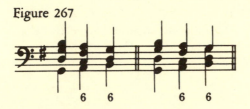

10. The unison doubling may be employed more freely than octave doublings. It may be used on a chromatic tone as a means, for example, of avoiding a leap (Figure 268). Inasmuch as composers write inner parts in this manner, even though both tones of the unison doubling can be heard, the keyboardist is certainly justified in availing himself of the resource, for on our instrument we strike and hear only one tone in such a doubling.

Figure 268

11.   When Figure 250 is realized in three parts, the right hand must not be widely separated from the bass or the fourths will become too pronounced. But beyond this the accompanist need not feel uneasy about them. They may ascend and descend by step or leap, for the interval is created by upper parts and does not pertain to the bass. The only caution that must be heeded is to see that they do not become fifths by inversion.

12.   When the third or sixth of a chord is chromatically altered by a short note in the principal part over an unfigured bass, the accompanist may ignore the change and retain the chord he has already realized, even when the tempo is slow (Figure 269).

Figure 269

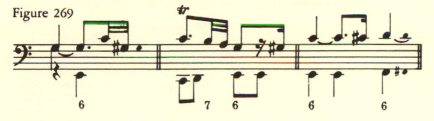

13.   At times a succeeding chord or progression necessitates a five-part realization of the chord of the sixth (Figure 270).

Figure 270

14.   It has been stated repeatedly that the augmented second must not be used in an accompaniment. Yet, since this progression, which is as good as the diminished third,[4] is often used as a melodic refinement, there are times when the accompanist cannot be taken to task for employing it. In fact, in such cases, an attempt to eliminate it would distort the setting (Figure 271, Example a). But aside from such a situation it is correctly avoided.

[4] ". . . Which is as good as the diminished third" inserted in ed. of 1797. Since the accompanying Figure 270 included, in the original, examples of the diminished third, it would seem reasonable to conclude that the clause had been overlooked.

Figure 271

THE DIMINISHED TRIAD [1]

1.   The diminished triad contains a minor third and an octave in addition to the diminished fifth. In three-part accompaniment the octave is omitted.

2.   It is denoted by either no figure or the usual signature of the diminished fifth (5♭). In sharp keys a natural sign (5♮) sometimes replaces the flat. Occasionally the remaining figures are included in the signature.

3.   For the sake of convenience the sign of the diminished fifth is often placed over a bass which is to be realized as a six-five chord. Hence, voice leading alone must be the judge of whether the diminished triad or the six-five chord is intended. For the first meaning Kapellmeister Telemann [2] wisely places a bow over the 5 (5̑). When necessary the accidental is included (5̑♭). By this means confusion is ended, and novices who lack a penetrating knowledge of voice leading are spared embarrassment.

[1] Cf. Arnold, *op. cit.*, pp. 506–510.
[2] Cf. Pt. II, Foreword, Note 4.

4.   The diminished fifth is a dissonance which is introduced with preparation (Figure 272, Example *a*) or without it (*b*). It resolves by stepwise descent.

Figure 272

5.   The diminished fifth appears more often with other figures than it does with the octave and third, as we shall see later. Its triad sounds well in three parts but rather empty in four. When the third is doubled in place of a duplicated bass, all of the upper parts form consonances with each other, thus making the chord more acceptable. It sounds poorest when the octave of the bass is in the upper part. The principal responsibility of the cautious accompanist is the disposition of the chord rather than its doubling, for a choice of the latter is occasionally restricted by the required resolution of a dissonance (Figure 273).

Figure 273

6.   When the bass of this chord is chromatically raised, the octave is omitted and the third doubled (Figure 274, Example *a*). The same doubling is often used in order to maintain good voice leading and to avoid awkward leaps (*b*).

Figure 274

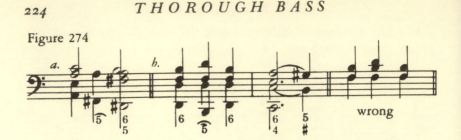

7. In the minor mode, the chord on the second step contains a diminished fifth regardless of whether the octave or the major sixth is also present. In Figure 275, when the bass is unfigured but the principal voice is written in, the figures which have been placed under the bass are best because of the succession. A leap may be made to an unprepared diminished fifth (*a*). As part of a triad this dissonance is treated more freely than in other relationships.

Figure 275

THE AUGMENTED TRIAD [1]

1. In four-part accompaniment, the augmented triad consists of a major third, an octave, and the augmented fifth. In three-part accompaniment the octave is omitted.

2. Its bass carries the indication of the augmented fifth (5, 5♮); or the altered fifth and the appropriate remaining intervals.

3. The augmented fifth is a dissonance which is not easily introduced unprepared. It resolves by stepwise ascent. Composers some-

[1] Cf. Arnold, *op. cit.*, pp. 512–513.

times use it as a melodic refinement in place of the perfect fifth (Figure 276, Example *a*). More often it appears before a retarded sixth (*b*). On occasion a chromatic change calls for its employment without its being indicated (*c*).

Figure 276

4. It does no harm to the triad to omit the octave and double the third, for this establishes consonant relationships among the upper parts (Figure 277).

Figure 277

5. Inasmuch as the augmented fifth is most frequently used as a refinement, it is better fitted to three- than to four-part accompaniment. The latter is normally used when the signature includes additional figures.

6. A slow chromatic progression that features the augmented fifth is accompanied in three parts. Such half steps in the principal part are not easily adaptable to rapid tempos; but when they occur the accompanist omits them (Figure 278).

Figure 278

THE SIX-FOUR CHORD,[1] I

1. In four part accompaniment the six-four chord contains an octave in addition to the intervals which give it its name. In three parts the octave is omitted.

2. The signature, $\frac{6}{4}$, is all that is required to denote the chord.

3. The minor and major sixth and all three kinds of fourth may be expressed by it. Hence it contains only one dissonance, the fourth. The qualities of the intervals are recognizable from the key signature and the accidentals added to the signature of the chord.

4. The diminished fourth requires preparation (Figure 279, Example *a*), but the perfect and augmented fourths may be introduced either with or without it (*b*). Because [2] the six-four chord with the augmented fourth offers the fewest useful examples, I have had to call on the chord of the second, with which this interval is most frequently used, in order to illustrate its characteristic behavior. The diminished and perfect fourths resolve by stepwise descent, but the augmented fourth by stepwise ascent over a descending bass.

Figure 279

5. Those who know the triad that is built on the fourth above the bass will recognize the tones of the six-four chord.

6. We shall learn soon that the sixth, a consonance, may be doubled when there is good reason to do so. Even though the octave of the bass is omitted when this takes place, no tone of the chord is thereby lost.

7. Of the three kinds of fourth, the perfect is the least dissonant in this chord. Nevertheless it must be resolved, unless it is used as a passing interval. In this latter case it may be doubled if necessary and if permitted by the preceding signatures. The examples of Figure 280 illustrate the passing fourth.

[1] Cf. Arnold, *op. cit.*, pp. 536–540.
[2] This sentence appears in the original ed. as a footnote.

Figure 280

8. The perfect fourth may be accompanied by either the major or minor sixth. It may resolve directly to a five-three chord (Figure 281, Example *a*), although it is not always required to do so. The bass may remain stationary or progress, for the succeeding figures are often different from the expected ones, and this sometimes retards but never disrupts the resolution (*b*).

Figure 281

9. When the third of a chord of the sixth is retarded by a fourth, the progression, a delicate one, is best expressed in three parts. If a four-part accompaniment is required, the octave is omitted and the sixth doubled. Examples *a* and *c* of Figure 282 illustrate the occurrence of this chord before a six-five chord with a diminished

fifth. All three kinds of fourth and the two consonant sixths may be employed, provided that the fourths are prepared and move by stepwise descent. The progression is much used in our present, agreeable style, but it never contains the octave. How essential therefore is some indication that might make it recognizable to the uninitiated! We shall choose the sign $\overset{\wedge}{\underset{4}{6}}$.

10. When the fourth is diminished, the sixth is minor (Figure 282, Example *a*); when it is augmented, the sixth is major (*b*); but when it is perfect, the sixth may be either quality (*c*) as we have already learned. With regard to the asterisked example, it does not occur freely unless the bass first ascends and then descends. In the last two examples the best distribution is that which follows $\overset{4}{3}$ and $\overset{6}{5}$ in open position.[3]

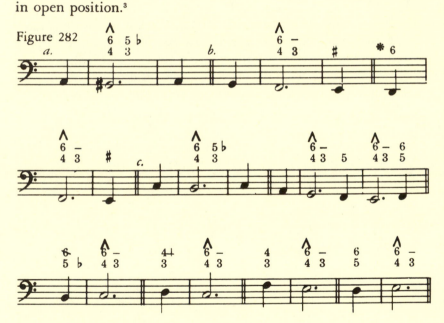

Figure 282

11. When this kind of six-four chord follows a diminished fifth over a stationary bass, a three-part accompaniment is best. If a fourth part is required, the sixth is doubled and the octave of the bass omitted (Figure 283).

[3] Perhaps because the initial chord sounds more sonorous when the upper parts lie a seventh rather than a second apart. At least, neither disposition presents any challenging problems of voice leading.

Figure 283

The $\overset{6}{4}$ in the examples of Figure 283 is a passing chord. The under-lying relationships are those of Figure 284.

Figure 284

12.   When the sixth is major in this six-four chord and the re-tarded third is minor, the four-part accompaniment is $\overset{6}{\underset{3}{4}}$ (Figure 285).

Figure 285

13.   When the augmented fourth is used in a passing relation-ship, the bass is not always required to progress by stepwise descent (Figure 286, Example *a*). The second example takes only a three-part setting. In *b* the augmented fourth over *f* anticipates its normal entrance, which is on the following eighth, *c*, where it functions as a passing tone moving to a major sixth. In the last example the sixth above *f* may be doubled when the third above *b* lies on top. This is the best disposition here.

Figure 286

14. When the bass of a common chord or the six-three chord descends one step to a six-four chord, the doubling of the first chord must be such as will avoid octaves (Figure 287).

Figure 287

15. When the bass of a six-three chord ascends a step to a six-four chord, the bass may be duplicated or the other intervals doubled unless the third lies on top. When it does lie on top, this third should be doubled in either the octave or unison (Figure 288, Example *a*). If this is not done, even opposite motion cannot prevent fifths (*b*). When the sixth is major and the third minor in this progression, the octave of the bass may be taken, provided that the sixth, if possible, but not the third, is placed in the upper part (*c*).

Figure 288   **Wrong**

THE SIX-FOUR CHORD, II

1. In the examples of Figure 289, it is perhaps better to transfer the resolution of the diminished fifth to the bass of the six-four chord and double the sixth than lead the voices in a strictly correct manner with the diminished fifth resolving to the octave of the second note in the bass. The latter progression always makes the six-four chord sound ugly. For this reason the figuring of Example *b* is better than that of *a*.

Figure 289

2. In Figure 290 the doubled sixth of the six-four chord in a four-part setting must be released immediately on the entrance of the diminished triad:

Figure 290

3. The augmented fourth in the six-four chord sounds rather empty in four-part settings but is improved by the addition of a second or a third. This chord, the signature of which must include the sixth along with the fourth, may have a duplicated bass or a doubled sixth. The latter construction is used not only because it sounds well with its upper parts consonant with each other, but also

Figure 291

because it is sometimes required (aside from those cases where $\overset{\wedge}{4}^{6}$ is specified) in order to maintain flowing parts and avoid errors (Figure 291.)

4.   The six-four chord with a perfect fourth sometimes arises out of a retardation of $\flat \overset{7}{5}$, in which case it is realized in three parts. The perfect and augmented fourths must not be confused with each other, especially when the former is indicated by accidentals which normally pertain to the augmented fourth, as in the following examples (Figure 292).

Figure 292

5.   A six-four chord which is created by the action of an ascending changing note after $\overset{\wedge}{6}^{8}$, is realized only in three parts (Figure 293).

Figure 293

6.   In Figure 294 it is wrong to denote the chord of the sixth on the second note as either $\overset{\wedge}{4}\overset{6-}{3}$ or $\overset{6}{4}_{2}$. The fourth on the last sixteenth serves only as a refinement which passes decoratively to the appoggiatura before the final note. The underlying progression is illus-

trated under *a*. In passing, observe that the octave above *f*-sharp rather than the fifth should be taken as a fourth part because of the preceding *c*.

Figure 294

THE FOUR-THREE CHORD,[1] I

1. This chord consists of a third, fourth, and sixth.

2. Its signature is $\frac{4}{3}$. The eye is more accustomed to this indication than it is to the occasional $\frac{3}{4}$. The sixth is included in the signature when it is chromatically altered (Figure 295, Example *a*), resolves a dissonance (*b*), or moves to a passing tone over a held bass (*c*).

Figure 295

3. The intervals that appear in the chord are the minor, major, and augmented sixth, the perfect and augmented fourth, and the minor and major third.

4. The exceptional features of the chord are that the third is treated as a dissonance and the fourth enjoys more freedom than usual. The former is usually [2] restricted by the latter, and always resolves by stepwise descent. The fourth remains stationary or ascends. These progressions will be clearly illustrated and discussed in detail when we examine all types of four-three chords, an undertaking which is necessitated by the great variation in the behavior of both fourths, the stationary and the ascending.

5. When the chord consists of a major sixth, perfect fourth, and

[1] Cf. Arnold, *op. cit.*, pp. 628–646.
[2] I.e., except when the fourth is omitted (cf. ¶ 7, par ex.).

minor third, either the fourth or the third must be prepared. Most frequently it is the third, which then moves by stepwise descent. The fourth remains stationary. This progression also appears over a tied bass, and it is sometimes denoted by a simple 6 rather than $\frac{4}{3}$. The bass progresses by stepwise ascent or descent. In ascent it proceeds to a chord of the sixth, in descent to a common chord. Those who know the tones of the six-four chord can easily find the four-three chord by omitting the octave of the bass and replacing it with the third (Figure 296).

Figure 296

6. The rather unusual examples of Figure 297 require the signature $\frac{4}{3}$ expressly. In the second example the chord of the sixth is clearly better than $\frac{4}{3}$:

Figure 297

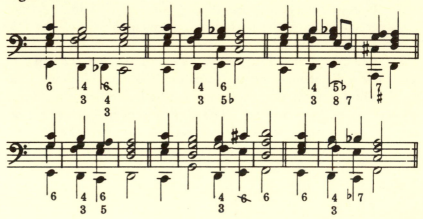

7.   In three-part accompaniment one tone of the chord is lost.
Yet certain refinements are met on occasion which are not suitable
to four parts. For example, the expression may require a soft performance which an accompanist might not be able to achieve on a
resonant instrument unless he used a thin setting, etc. In such a
case one interval must be omitted. In Figure 296 the fourth may be
left out, but in Figure 297 a four-part realization is presupposed.

8.   When the chord consists of a major sixth, augmented fourth,
and major third, either the fourth or the third must be prepared.
The latter descends afterwards while the fourth remains stationary
or ascends. The bass may be tied or not, and it progresses by step-
wise ascent or descent. Here the signature $\overset{4}{3}$ or $\overset{4+}{3}$ is required more
than in Figure 296, for a simple 6 or $\overset{6}{4}$ as the signature can easily
cause confusion. The disposition which sounds best is that in which
the fourth and third are separated from each other. Example *a* of
Figure 298 may express fifths if the third of the preceding chord of
the sixth is doubled. Such being the case, they can be avoided by
placing the fourth on top (*b*). In three-part accompaniment the
sixth of the four-three chord may be omitted except in Example *a*.
The [3] figures that stand below the notes have no bearing on those
which stand above.

Figure 298

9. [4]   When the chord contains a minor sixth, perfect fourth, and
minor third, either the fourth or the third must be prepared. The

---

[3] This sentence appeared in the original ed. as a footnote.

[4] In all eighteenth-century editions this paragraph was misnumbered 8. In correct-
ing it, all following paragraph numbers have had to be increased by one.

fourth remains stationary and the third descends. The progression
may be introduced over a tied or untied bass which descends afterwards. Example *a* of Figure 299 will be found occasionally, although it is not especially good. The major sixth makes a better

progression (*b*). The signature of the chord is $\overset{4}{3}$, but when the sixth
is lowered it is included with its accidental. In the second and third
examples there is only one good disposition. The sixth must lie on
top, because of the succeeding six-five chord. Other realizations contain fifths. In three parts the fourth is omitted from *a* and *b*:

Figure 299

10.   When the chord contains a major sixth, augmented fourth,
and minor third, the fourth or the third is usually prepared. In
Example *a* of Figure 300 both enter freely over a passing note whose
initiating tone has been elided (*b*). The third resolves by stepwise
descent, the fourth by ascent. The bass may, but need not be, tied;
subsequently it descends by a step. The signature is $\overset{4+}{3}$, $\flat\overset{4}{3}$, or $\flat\overset{4+}{3}$
Those who know the tones of the chord of the second with a raised
fourth can locate this four-three chord quite easily by taking a
third above the bass instead of the second. Except in the asterisked
example, the sixth is omitted from three-part realizations.

11.   When the chord contains a major sixth, perfect fourth, and
major third, either the fourth or the third is prepared. The third
resolves by stepwise descent; the fourth remains stationary. The

bass may remain on a single tone as in the organ point, or it may progress. This chord sounds best when the third and fourth are separated from each other. Its signature is ⁴₃. When the bass is held, the chord is realized in four parts; otherwise the fourth is omitted. A chord of the sixth is better than the four-three chord in the last two examples of Figure 301.

12. When the chord contains an augmented sixth, augmented fourth, and major third, preparation of the sixth is optional, but it is required of either the fourth or third. The third progresses subsequently by stepwise descent. The fourth remains stationary or ascends. The bass may, but need not be, tied. In either case its subsequent motion is stepwise descent in parallel motion with the third. Many denote this chord ambiguously with only a sixth and

its accidental. The best signature expresses all of the intervals. **In**
three-part accompaniment the fourth is omitted (Figure 302).

13. Occasionally an octave must be taken in addition to the
other intervals, not merely for the sake of a full setting, but more
in order to resolve a preceding dissonance (Figure 303, Example *a*),
or to prepare a succeeding one (*b*). This being the case, it is best to
place all four intervals in the signature and thus preclude conjec-
ture. In Example *a*, $^{6}_{4}$ enters prematurely as the result of an elision.
Actually, the ninth, seventh, and fourth should be resolved first, as
in Example *c*. Our chord thus turns out to be merely a passing

chord, which accounts for the leaping rather than stepwise movement of the bass.

THE FOUR-THREE CHORD, II

1. To the chord of the major sixth and minor third, the perfect fourth is sometimes added without express indication (Figure 304, Example *a*) in order to avoid the errors of *aa*, to gain a uniform disposition (*b*) without the leaps of *c*, or to create a good upper part (*d*).

Figure 304

2. In Example *a* of Figure 305 the six-four-three chord sounds very well against the long appoggiatura. The succeeding figures are in most cases already present in the first chord. The upper voice

continues melodically in thirds with the bass. Example *b*, set simply, suffers neither a doubled third above *d*, nor an ascent of the third to *g*, for this third, *f*, is also the seventh above the second eighth, *g*, and must therefore be properly resolved (*c*). The dissonances of Example *d* are conveniently prepared by the four-three chord:

Figure 305

3.   In the examples of Figure 306 the chord of the sixth is taken over each *d*. The four-three chord sounds ugly against the repeated *a* (*a*). A chromatic alteration sometimes prevents the taking of $\frac{6}{4}$ $_3$ (*b*). Again, passing notes may require the simple chord of the sixth, as illustrated here by the *f* (*c*). Other factors which oblige the accompanist to play an indicated chord of the sixth rather than $\frac{6}{4}$ $_3$ are: the succeeding figures, which may be more easily realized by holding or repeating the chord of the sixth (*d*); the succeeding notes, which may prevent a proper resolution of the third of $\frac{6}{4}$ $_3$ (*e*); errors of voice leading which are caused by $\frac{4}{3}$ (*f*). Those progressions in

thorough bass that allow for variants and yet cannot always be realized optionally make it all the more necessary to look ahead and listen carefully.

Figure 306

4. Some consider it sufficient to signify $^6_4$ after $^7_5$ in the following example, since this specifies the progressing parts (Figure 307, Example *a*). However, an inexperienced accompanist might add the octave of the bass to the six-four chord according to the rule of construction of this chord rather than hold the third. The figuring of *b* is clearer and more correct, despite the fact that the eye must scan an additional figure.

Figure 307

5. Figure 308 is exceptional, and its accompaniment can give rise to several errors. The third of the first $^4_3$ does not resolve but remains stationary to become a fourth, for the chord is to be re-

garded as passing. The augmented fourth, however, ascends charac-teristically. The second $\frac{4}{3}$ behaves normally. In order to realize the first signature completely and make it possible for the augmented fourth to ascend, the second of the chord should be doubled.

Figure 308
Adagio

6.   In Figure 309 a unison doubling of the sixth (*a*) makes a better progression than a doubled third (*b*):

Figure 309

7.   One of the best uses of the augmented fourth with the aug-mented sixth is the following. In other cases this latter interval usually sounds better with the fifth or a doubled third. The *b*, through its presence in most of the chords, provides an intended obstinacy which heightens the effectiveness of $\overset{\sharp6}{\underset{3}{4}}$ (Figure 310).

Figure 310

8.   In Figure 311 the melody of the principal part, and to a greater degree the preparation of the third, necessitates a violation of the rule prohibiting the progression of a diminished third.[5] The preceding chromatic alteration of the sixth is automatically can-

[5] Changed in ed. of 1797 from the earlier "augmented second."

celed in the $\overset{4}{3}$, for the augmented fourth presupposes an accompanying major sixth.

Figure 311

9. Although the earlier statements concerning the three-part realization of our chord are generally applicable, the accompanist must be attentive to the principal part, for at times the tones performed by it may be omitted from a light accompaniment (Figure 312).

Figure 312
piano

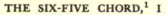

THE SIX-FIVE CHORD,[1] I

1. This chord consists of a sixth, fifth, and third.

2. Its signature is $\overset{6}{5}$, or 5♭ alone when the fifth is diminished. The third, when it is chromatically altered, is included with its accidental. Also, accidentals which pertain to the sixth and fifth must not be omitted from the signature.

3. In this chord there are three sixths, augmented, major, and

[1] Cf. Arnold, *op. cit.*, pp. 602–626.

minor; two fifths, the diminished and perfect; and two thirds, the major and minor.

4.   The fifth is treated as a dissonance. It is usually [2] restricted by the sixth, and always progresses by stepwise descent.

5.   The perfect fifth does not readily occur without preparation (Figure 313, Example *a*); but the diminished fifth may lie in the preceding chord or enter freely (*b*). However, when this latter interval is taken unprepared, the sixth is usually present in the preceding chord. As the fifth, especially the diminished fifth, resolves, the bass normally ascends one step. Example *c* shows us that on occasion the bass may remain stationary or leap upward and downward, in which event the resolution of the fifth is often retarded. In the last example under *c* there is an interchange of chordal tones and an elision, as illustrated in *d*.

---

[2] I.e., except when the sixth is omitted, when the fifth is diminished (in which case it is already a dissonance, hence, restricted anyway), or when the chord is a "passing chord" (cf. ¶ 10 here).

6. Those who know the progression 6 5 or 5 6 can easily locate the tones of our chord by omitting the octave of the bass, playing the adjacent figures simultaneously along with the third, and attending to preparation.

7. At times the octave of the bass must be taken as a fifth part because of the resolution (*a*) or preparation (*b*) of a dissonance (Figure 314).

Figure 314

8. When the signature $\frac{6}{5}\,\overline{4}$ appears over a stationary bass, the third is omitted and the octave of the bass taken as a fourth part, for

the underlying construction is simply a six-four chord with its fourth retarded by a fifth. In such a case the fifth is perfect and prepared (Figure 315, Example *a*). But should the fifth succeed not to $\overline{4}$ but to some other signature (*b*) or should the bass move simultaneously with the fifth (*c*), the usual $\overset{6}{5}$ accompaniment is to be taken. For the benefit of the inexperienced accompanist, the first of these six-five chords (they often appear over organ points) should be distinguished from the normal construction by means of a Telemann bow.[3] The last example under *a* is noteworthy because of the divided accompaniment and the doubled sixth:

Figure 315

---

[3] Cf. Part II, Foreword, Note 4.

9.   When the chord contains an augmented sixth it always takes a perfect fifth and a major third as its remaining intervals. The fifth is usually prepared (Figure 316, Example *a*); but it and the sixth too may be taken freely when the bass is stationary (*b*). Normally, the sixth should enter one eighth later, as illustrated in *c*. Subsequently the sixth progresses by stepwise ascent, and the fifth, momentarily stationary, by stepwise descent:

Figure 316

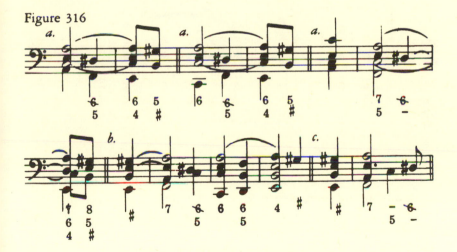

10.   Since three-part accompaniment necessitates the omission of one interval, it should not be employed without good reason. But

when it is required, the omitted interval must be decided upon carefully. The third, the perfect fifth, or the sixth, especially when the last-mentioned is accompanied by the diminished fifth, may be omitted according to circumstances. When the chord is used as a passing construction, the fifth does not resolve. In such a case the third serves no good end and may be omitted in favor of the sixth and fifth. In the examples of Figure 317, the chords that preceed $\frac{6}{5}$ and provide its stationary fifth are set uniformly in three parts. Inasmuch [4] as we have made use of the Telemann bow in other situations in order to distinguish a three- from a four-part realization, it may be included here in the signature of a six-five chord whose third is to be omitted.

Figure 317

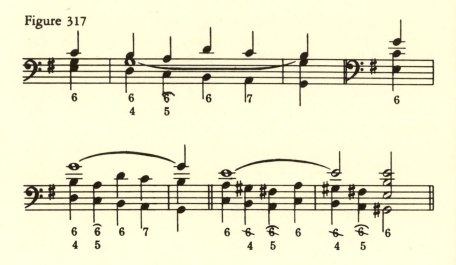

THE SIX-FIVE CHORD, II

1. The examples of Figure 318 show us how the sixth, as well as its accompanying diminished fifth, may enter unprepared (*a*). The underlying progression without elisions is illustrated in *b*. The fifth of the first bass note must not be placed on top, for the diminished fifth progression belongs in the inner parts.

[4] This sentence appeared in the original ed. as a footnote. For Telemann bow, cf. Part II, Foreword, Note 4.

Figure 318

2. Those who set Example *a* of Figure 319 with its unprepared perfect fifths (an occasional but undesirable progression) must defend it as an elision of the succession 6 5 (*b*) or as a manipulation of 8 7 (*c*). Over the bass *g* of bar one, and *f*, bar two, the sixth must be separated from its preparation as a means of avoiding fifths (*d*). The fifths by contrary motion over *a* and *c* in the first bar cannot be, nor indeed need they be, circumvented. Example *e* is even worse than *a*:

Figure 319

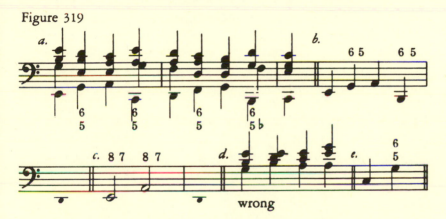

wrong

3. The diminished fifth may enter freely; and even when it can be prepared, it may be separated from its preparatory interval for certain justifiable reasons. They are: the resolution of a dissonance (Figure 320, Example *a*); the retention of a convenient spacing and the continuation of a good melody (*b*); the avoidance of a poor relationship between the outer parts (*c*). In the absence of these

factors, however, strict observance must be made of the rules which call for the preparation and resolution of a dissonance in the voice in which the dissonance appears.

Figure 320

4.   At times it is better to omit the sixth and double the third in a chord containing a diminished fifth, even though the sixth would not clash with chromatic changes. The reasons are: The sixth, taken freely, may add a discordant element to the resolution of a preceding dissonance (Figure 321, Example *a*); the doubled third may help to maintain a good melody (*b*) or to avoid errors. (*c*).

Figure 321

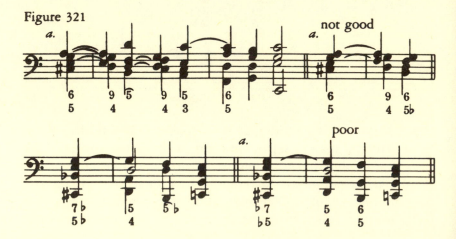

5. As a rule, all chromatic changes that pertain to the third must appear in the signature, as in the case of all figures. Nevertheless there are times when the accidental is omitted, under the assumption that the quality of the third will be known from its context. In Figure 322, if a diminished third is to be played it must be expressly specified by a flat over the bass:

Figure 322

6. Figure 323 should please the devotees of strange chords. It gives passing expression in a slow tempo to $\frac{6}{5}$, $\frac{6}{4}$, and $\frac{6}{4}$, the latter two in open position.

Figure 323

7.   In a slow tempo which requires a soft performance the sixth may be omitted from the six-five chord in the first example of Figure 324 and the third from the same chord in the second example. In the third example the third may be omitted from both the six-five and seven-five chords in order to provide the principal part with sufficient freedom and quiet to express its slow notes in accord with the desired affect.

Figure 324

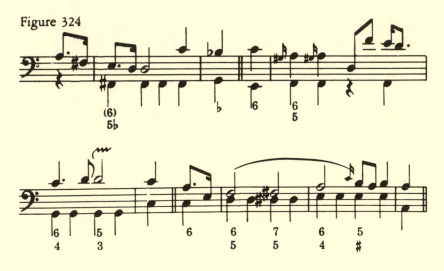

THE CHORD OF THE SECOND,[1] I

1.   This chord consists of a second, fourth, and sixth.

2.   Its signatures are: 2, 4+, 4♮ (in those cases where the natural sign raises a tone), $\frac{4}{2}$, and $\frac{6}{4}$.

3.   The chord may contain the major or minor sixth, the augmented or perfect fourth, the major, minor, or augmented second.

---

[1] Cf. Arnold, *op. cit.*, pp. 648–672.

4. The dissonance is in the bass and may enter as either a tied note (Figure 325, Example *a*) or a passing tone (*b*), but it always resolves by stepwise descent. Hence, the octave of the bass is never taken by the right hand, even in an inner part, although it may be by the left for re-enforcement. The second itself is treated as a consonance; it may enter freely, remain stationary, or leap; and it may be doubled.

Figure 325

5. When the chord contains a major second, major sixth, and perfect fourth, the last-named interval may subsequently ascend, descend, remain stationary, or leap downward (Figure 326, Example *a*). It enjoys the same freedom when it is associated with the major second and minor sixth (*b*); or the minor second and minor sixth (*c*):

Figure 326

6. When the augmented fourth is associated with the major second and major sixth, it may remain stationary, or ascend (Figure 327, Example *a*); this also holds when it appears with the augmented second and major sixth (*b*). Although it descends momentarily in a passing relationship in the last example, it ascends immediately thereafter:

Figure 327

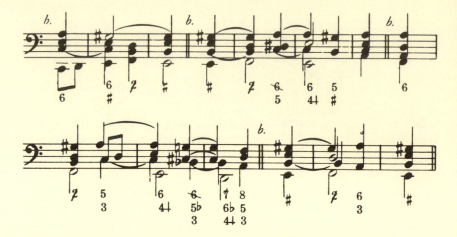

7. In order to win four individual tones in four-part accompaniment, the augmented fourth must sometimes leap downward. In fact, I see no other means of attaining such an end, should this progression be prohibited. At the same time, the parts progress much more smoothly and this interval behaves much more characteristically when it progresses by stepwise ascent while unison and octave doublings are alternated. Further, by this means all dispositions of the chord may be employed, whereas in the other case the leap from the augmented fourth must be assigned to an inner part if the progression is to be acceptable (Figure 328).

Figure 328

8. The chord of the second is easy to find. Its tones form the triad that lies a second above the bass.

9. Since this chord is founded on a triad, the accompanist must be careful to avoid fifths when it is preceded by a triad or by a chord which comprises one (Figure 329).

Figure 329

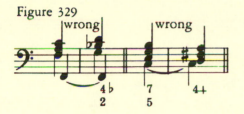

10. For purposes of re-enforcement, a fifth part may be taken at times which doubles the major or minor second. Moreover, this provides a means of disguising the poor downward leap from the augmented fourth. Such a doubling may not be applied to the augmented second nor to the major second when it is associated with the minor sixth. (Figure 330).

Figure 330

11. In a three-part accompaniment the chord loses an interval. Hence it should not be used freely unless there is sufficient reason, in which case the sixth is omitted.

12. So that the eye will not be overwhelmed by a mass of numerals, certain intervals are to be taken for granted in the absence of specific indications: The major sixth accompanies a specified augmented fourth (Figure 331, Example *a*); the minor sixth accompanies a specified minor second (*b*); the augmented fourth accompanies the augmented second (*c*); and the major second and major sixth accompany a fourth which is augmented by means of a double sharp (*d*):

Figure 331

13. In Figure 332, however, the raised sixth must be expressly indicated. If it is not, an accompanist inexperienced in the ways of chromaticism, far from being provided with a convenient reduction in the number of figures, will be caused no end of difficulty and embarrassment. In the last example the sixth may be replaced by a doubled second in anticipation of the approaching triad.

Figure 332

14. Occasionally when the bass of $\overset{7}{5}$ ascends one step to become the bass of a minor triad, the figures, $\overset{\sharp}{\underset{2}{4}}$ or $\overset{6}{\underset{2}{4}}$ will be found inter-

polated over the second tone. The chord is created by accompanied appoggiaturas; hence its bass does not descend, for $\frac{6}{4}$ is only a decoration of the underlying triad. The second and fourth move to a third and the sixth moves to a fifth. In a light accompaniment the fourth (*a*) or at times the sixth [2] (*b*) may be omitted (Figure 333).

Figure 333

15.   Occasionally $\frac{4}{2}$ will be found over a stationary or a repeated bass. It is to be realized in three parts without any additional tones. The intervals are no more in need of resolution than the bass, for, as passing notes, they may ascend or descend. The preceding and following signatures are also realized in three parts most of the time. Such an accompaniment usually duplicates other performing parts. Once in a while, however, one of these parts sustains the octave or fifth of the underlying chord. If it is the fifth, a major seventh may be added to $\frac{4}{2}$ (Figure 334, Example *a*). As a warning, a Telemann bow [3] may be placed over $\frac{4}{2}$.

[2] The sixth is present in both examples under *b*. Evidently, "sixth" is a misprint for "second," since this interval is omitted from the illustrations. Bach's $\frac{6}{4}$ signature verifies this assumption.

[3] Cf. Pt. II, Foreword, Note 4.

Figure 334

THE CHORD OF THE SECOND, II

1. The second of the successive $\overset{4}{2}$ chords in the following example arrives one eighth too soon as the result of an elision which is illustrated in Example *a* of Figure 335. A perfect fourth may precede the augmented fourth in the same kind of progression (*b*).

Figure 335

2. It is wrong to write the signature of an augmented fourth alone in the following examples. The chord of the second, which is specified by this indication, cannot be realized in the first example of Figure 336 because of the preceding *g*-sharp, nor in the second because of the necessity of resolving the preceding dissonances. The six-four must be taken in both cases. In the notating of parts it is sometimes forgotten in haste that the signature 4+ is an abbreviated sign of an entire six-four-two chord rather than the six-four.

Figure 336

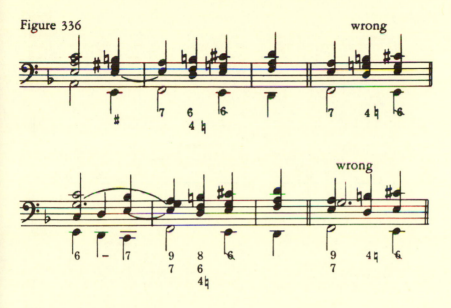

3. When the fifth and third of $5\flat^6$ are retarded by a slow two-part appoggiatura and this rather discordant embellishment must be played by the accompanist, $^4_2$ and $3^{5\flat}$ are indicated over the bass, the sixth of the four-two chord being omitted from the accompaniment as well as the signature (Figure 337, Example *a*). When the second of the chord of the second is retarded by a slow appoggiatura on the augmented octave, the accompanist takes the fourth alone in a light accompaniment and does not add the second and sixth until the second enters in the principal part. However, since the augmented octave is more fearful to the eye than to the ear (which is not unpleasantly deceived by its resolution in a slow tempo accompanied by the fourth), it may be included in the signature and played by the accompanist (*b*). Also, the execution under *c* does not sound bad with the third, as an appoggiatura, moving to the fourth. Those whose ears are oversensitive can withhold the right hand's accompaniment from the appoggiatura in both cases. In any event, when the accompaniment is to be very light, the performance of these refinements should be left to the principal part. The augmented octave is a dissonance that resolves upward, and it is used only as an appoggiatura.

Figure 337

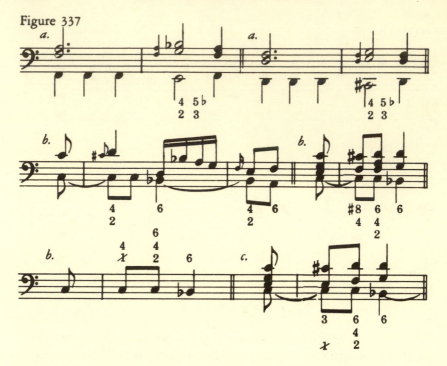

4. In order to avoid octaves, the third or fifth of the last chord must be doubled in Figure 338.

Figure 338

THE FIVE-TWO CHORD.[1]

1. This chord consists of a second and a fifth. For a fourth part either of the intervals may be doubled.

2. Its signature is $\frac{5}{2}$. The second is major and the fifth perfect.

3. As in all chords of the second, the bass is dissonant; it must be prepared, and it resolves by stepwise descent (Figure 339).

---

[1] Cf. Arnold, *op. cit.*, pp. 708–709.

Figure 339

4. Figure 339 shows clearly that $\overset{5}{2}$ results from the premature entrance of the tones of the following chord of the sixth. When the second of the chord is doubled the chord of the sixth becomes $\overset{3}{6}$, and when the fifth is doubled, $\overset{6}{\underset{6}{3}}$.

5. The five-two chord always sounds empty regardless of whether it is realized in three or four parts. It is made sonorous by its resolution. Rare in the galant style, it is more frequent in learned works and in company with syncopations. Consequently it is realized in four parts.

6. Inasmuch as one of the tones, but not the bass, must be doubled, care must be taken to avoid octaves when a preceding chord also contains a doubling. Doublings must be alternated in such a case [2] (Figure 340).

Figure 340

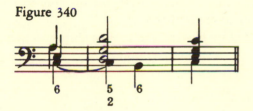

7. The five-two chord with an augmented fifth sometimes results from the action of an irregular passing tone or changing note (Figure 341).

Figure 341

[2] I.e., octave and unison doublings in the right hand.

THE FIVE-FOUR-TWO CHORD [1]

1.   The chord consists of the intervals which give it its name.

2.   Its signature is $\frac{5}{4}$. The second is major, and the fifth and
$\frac{}{2}$
fourth are perfect.

3.   Here too, the bass is tied and resolves by stepwise descent, for it is the bass that is dissonant. The fifth or the fourth must also lie in the preceding chord. By means of this chord the upper parts of the six-five chord with a diminished fifth are anticipated (Figure 342).

Figure 342

4.   Because it appears only in works that require a full accompaniment, it is always realized in four parts; all the more so, because none of the intervals may be omitted.

5.   The chord can be located by playing the six-five chord on the tone that lies one step below the written bass note.

THE THREE-TWO CHORD [2]

1.   This chord consists of a minor second, major third, and perfect fifth.

2.   Its signature is $\overset{3}{2}$ with 2 lowered by an accidental; and when the third is chromatically raised it is represented in the signature solely by an accidental.

3.   Once again, the bass is dissonant; it is tied, and resolves by stepwise descent (Figure 343).

[1] Cf. Arnold, *op. cit.*, pp. 711–712. This chord is not to be confused with the Five-Four Chord, to which a separate section is devoted.
[2] Cf. Arnold, *op. cit.*, pp. 713–714.

Figure 343

4. The three-two chord is always realized in four parts, since it is expressly indicated in order that no interval will be omitted. The tones of this chord can be located by playing a triad and replacing the octave of the bass with a second.

5. Through the action of an irregular passing tone this chord anticipates the upper parts of a four-three chord with a major second (*a*) or a minor third (*b*) (Figure 344).

Figure 344

THE CHORD OF THE SEVENTH,[1] I

1. The chord of the seventh exists in three forms, consisting of: a seventh, fifth, and third; a seventh, third, and octave; a seventh and a doubled third.

2. The signatures are 7 and $\overset{7}{5}$. Accidentals must not be forgotten, especially when the third becomes major or minor through chromatic alteration.

3. Comprising this chord are: Diminished, minor, and major sevenths; augmented, perfect, and diminished fifths; major and minor thirds; the octave.

4. The seventh is a dissonance which appears with preparation (Figure 345, Example *a*) and without it (*b*). It progresses by stepwise descent. The ascending major seventh will be given separate treatment later. In our present study this seventh, like the others, resolves downward. The passing seventh [2] alone may remain sta-

---

[1] Cf. Arnold, *op. cit.*, pp. 542–599.
[2] Or, more accurately, the seventh formed by a passing bass.

tionary on occasion (*c*). But when it enters after the bass it too descends (*d*).

Figure 345

5. The seventh is the same as the second below the bass, and the chord of the seventh with a fifth contains the triad on the third above the bass.

6. The fifth and octave are omitted in three-part accompaniment, but the third must always be represented except in the galant style.

7. Use of one or another of the three forms of the chord is not always optional. Certain great difficulties arise in connection with their employment, as we shall see later. It would be a simple task but of great benefit to practiced as well as inexperienced accompanists if the fifth and octave were included in the signature whenever they were to be played. Their presence would offer nothing new to the eyes, for they are often found in the signature anyway. The most essential consideration with regard to the construction of the chord is that the seventh must appear and resolve in the voice in which it is prepared.

8. The major third must not be doubled when it appears with the minor seventh, regardless of whether it comes by its quality naturally or chromatically.

9. The seventh may resolve on either its own bass or a different one. Both resolutions appear singly and also in succession.

10. A single appearance of 7 6 is better realized with a doubled third, or the octave, than with a fifth. But when the latter is perfect and not contrary to a chromatic context, it too may be taken, provided that care is exercised to avoid fifths. In fact, when it fits

chromatically, even the augmented fifth may be taken in a 7 6 progression, and without being indicated, particularly when it stems from a preceding unresolved augmented fourth. The diminished fifth appears occasionally in this progression and may also be taken without indication on condition that it resolve properly. Examples of all of these variants will illustrate my meaning.

11.   In Example *a* of Figure 346 the octave of the bass may be taken as well as the doubled third. In the case of the former, the third in the right hand moves against the left. The disposition with the fifth of the first chord on top is the poorest; the octave on top is the best. Should the third be doubled in the octave, both hands progress in parallel motion. In Example *b* only the doubled third is possible because of the rule against the augmented second. Neither Example *a* nor *b* can be realized with the fifth because the ascent of the first tone in the bass would create fifths. In *c*, the fifth being perfect, it may be played if necessary, although the other accompaniments are preferable. In *d* the fifth cannot be included because it disagrees chromatically with the augmented sixth over the following tone. The octave must be taken, since, according to Paragraph 8, a doubled third is not permissible in this chord. In *e* the

Figure 346

fifth is diminished, but cannot be resolved. This is a point which must be carefully observed, for it makes the realization of the fifth dangerous. Hence, either of the two remaining forms of the chord must be employed. Successions of sixths must be placed in the upper part in order to avoid errors or awkward voice leading. In *f*, only the octave of the bass is good, for the other constructions introduce awkward and bad progressions.

12.   In Figure 347, Example *a*, all three forms of the chord may be used. The diminished fifth is allowed in this progression because it can move to a fourth on the entrance of the raised sixth. In *b* the fifth must be augmented, if it is to be taken at all, and it moves to a unison doubling on the sixth. Since this fifth is indicated as infrequently as the diminished fifth, who can tell whether a composer wants it to be used? Ordinarily, a dissonant interval which clashes with an already dissonant chord is not realized without its being indicated. Of course it is another matter when the fifths are expressly called for. But unbidden fifths steal in through the use of accompaniments that require the maintenance of four separate parts. Hence, a unison doubling removes any necessity of realizing

Figure 347

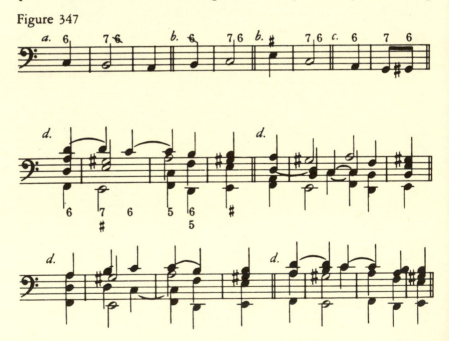

them.[3] Consequently the other two forms of the chord are safer here (*b*). Example *c* is noteworthy: The doubled third is not to be used here according to Paragraph 8, and the octave of the bass does not go well with the following *g*-sharp. Therefore only the fifth is possible. In *d* the easiest accompaniment is the octave of the bass, but the fifth may also be used. A doubled third is ruled out. A unison doubling may be used to good ends in this example.

13.   In Figure 348, Example *a*, the perfect (first example) and augmented (second example) fifths are required because of the preceding augmented fourth. The resolution of the fourth causes both fifths to ascend. When the fourth of a chord of the second is perfect, it is customary to indicate the diminished fifth in a succeeding chord of the seventh (*b*). If the sixth which accompanies the fourth

Figure 348

is minor it is usually followed by a diminished seventh with a diminished fifth (*c*). In *d* the octave must be taken because of the preceding signature. Example *e* calls for a three-part accompaniment. The chromatic course of the principal voice does not allow readily for a full realization. The resolutions must take place neither sooner nor later than required. In order to prepare the seventh in Example *f*, a fifth voice must be taken over the first tone.

The chord of the seventh may be $\begin{smallmatrix}3\\7\\5\flat\\3\end{smallmatrix}$ or $\begin{smallmatrix}8\\7\\5\flat\\3\end{smallmatrix}$, and the seventh and augmented fifth resolve into a unison.

14.　　Successive bass tones in ascent or descent, each expressing a 7 6 progression, are frequent occurrences. In descent, a three-part accompaniment is easiest, and it is preferable in passages which do not need full chords. A four-part setting is preserved from errors by a voice leading which employs alternately all forms of the chords of the sixth and seventh with and without doubling.[4] Everything that has been previously discussed and need not be repeated here must be given constant consideration. In so many words, preparation, resolution, and doubling must agree with the rules.

15.　　Figure 349 may be accompanied in several ways. The best are those in which the doubling is constantly varied (*a*). Where it is too uniform, that is, where the bass is duplicated, and the third or sixth are constantly doubled, errors can be committed easily and the octaves or fifths may become too prominent. Thus, Example *b* is poor because there are too many fifths. Moreover, not all are perfect; the diminished fifth is not resolved. The octaves in the upper voice of *c* make the accompaniment ugly; and the thirds are dangerous, for they can easily lead to a violation of the rule of Paragraph 8. The realization in *d* is poor because of both the thirds and the fifths. Example *e* is worthless on several counts: The diminished fifth is unresolved; worse, the fifths lie in the upper part; eventually the realization must lead to an incorrect doubling. In short, it is wholly bad. Example *f* is acceptable so long as the minor third does not appear with a major sixth. Example *g* is poor on account of the unresolved diminished fifth and the octaves in the upper part:

---

[4] That is, a doubling within the right hand in alternation with the octave of the bass.

Figure 349[5]

16. Ascending basses which express successive 7 6 progressions cannot be easily accompanied in other than four parts. The right hand moves against the left. The octave and third accompany both the seventh and the sixth. Example *a* is the best, and more natural than *b* (Figure 350).

Figure 350

[5] The examples from *b* to the end appeared originally in the text in the form of signatures. I have realized them in order to make them more immediately comprehensible.

17.   Isolated sevenths which resolve as the bass progresses are realized in most cases with a full accompaniment which includes the fifth. Special cases of this type of progression will be treated in the second section. When the fifth is diminished, it too must resolve (Figure 351).

Figure 351

18.   Successive bass tones which express sevenths that resolve on the following chord progress by ascending fourths or descending fifths. When a three-part accompaniment is required, only the third is taken with the seventh. In a four-part realization $\overset{7}{\underset{3}{5}}$ and $\overset{8}{\underset{3}{7}}$ are alternated. This makes the safest and best accompaniment. Doubled thirds can easily lead to a violation of the doubling rule. Nevertheless, I have constructed an example (*b*) in which this doubling is acceptable (Figure 352).

Figure 352

19. The fifth is not easily included with the passing seventh in Figure 353. Moreover, a doubled third or an octave sounds better (*a*). When the fourth is prepared and the third can resolve by stepwise descent, both intervals may be realized with the seventh. Example *b* does not really belong here but rather with the discussion of rapid passing notes over which the right hand holds the initial chord.[6] Hence, in practice it is not figured.

Figure 353

20. A passing seventh which enters after its bass is best when it comes from the octave (Figure 354, Example *a*). However, since the originating chord is consonant, it is not incorrect to leap to the seventh in order to change the disposition of tones (*b*). But this freedom is withheld when 8 7 is followed by other signatures over the same bass (*c*). Although this is not its proper place, our discussion suggests a case where the octave, followed by a seventh, is accompanied by other dissonances and must itself be prepared and resolved. Of course the octave here moves to the seventh (*d*):

Figure 354

[6] Cf. Ch. IV, ¶¶ 68–72, Ch. VI, "Passing Tones" and "Changing Notes."

THE CHORD OF THE SEVENTH, II

1. At cadences, and also elsewhere, if the bass ascends a step or a fourth or descends a fifth, a chord of the seventh may be taken over the first note without indication, provided that the following chord is a triad. The fifth is also taken with the seventh here (Figure 355, Example *a*), and if the right hand threatens to go too low the octave should be held while the fifth moves to the seventh (*b*). By this means a good upper part can be retained and the final chord will be complete. When the bass ascends a step, the third of the second chord must be doubled occasionally (*c*).

Figure 355

2. The examples of Figure 356 require the octave of the bass with the seventh. In *a*, fifths are created by the fifth when it is included with a seventh that lies in the upper part. Hence the octave replaces it in this disposition of the chord. In the other dispositions the fifth may be used. The fifths of Example *b* caused by the

motion of the principal part, *a* to *g*, against a middle voice, *d* to *c*,
are avoided by holding the octave over from the six-four chord
and leading the sixth to the seventh, thus omitting the fifth. Perhaps this observation seems far-fetched; yet, in a slow tempo, deli-
cately performed, such fifths can be heard. Moreover, when the
principal part is written in over the bass, the accompanist is obliged
to avoid them. In *c* the diminished fifth must be prepared by the
octave of the chord of the seventh. There is only one disposition for
this progression. In *d*, both the sixth and the diminished fifth are
prepared when the octave is taken over *g*. The major third above
this tone moves nicely upward in thirds with the bass. In *e* forbidden fifths are eliminated by taking the octave of the bass over *e*.
In *f*, where the retardation of a resolution (as explained in *ff*) creates
successive sevenths, the first seventh must be accompanied by the
octave; if it is not there will be fifths. In *g*, the preparation of the
second seventh requires the octave with the first one. In *h*, there
would be no place for the third over *c* if the fifth were taken in the
preceding chord of the seventh. In *i* the chromatic major third
over *a* can move upward naturally, and the sixth of the succeeding
chord of the second will be prepared, if the octave is taken over *a*.
In *j*, if the fifth is played it will create octaves. In *k*, the tones of a
chord are interchanged, as illustrated in *kk*. The second seventh
seems to be a resolution of the first, but in fact it is nothing more
than a decorative detail of the upper voice, rendered negligible by
the interchange of parts. The octave is taken with the first seventh
in order not to obstruct this figuration and also to prepare the
second of the chord on *c*. In *l* the diminished seventh must resolve
to the octave of the following tone. In *m* the octave is taken with
the seventh in order to avoid fifths, and to prepare the tones of the
ninth chord over *e*. In *n* the octave again eliminates a faulty progression and places in the hand the tones of the four-three chord
over *b*. In *o*, if $\frac{7}{5}$ is expressly called for, the octave must be taken as a
fifth voice over *f* in order to prepare the following diminished
seventh. In *p*, the octave is required with the seventh in order to
prepare the following fifth. In *q* the octave is better than the fifth,
for it eliminates octaves against the divided beats in the bass by
creating contrary motion. In *r* the octave eliminates an unmelodic
progression which would be introduced by the fifth.

wrong   good

3.   The examples of Figure 357 require a fifth with the seventh. In Example *a* it must be taken because of the following six-five

Figure 357

chord. In *b* the diminished fifth accompanies both the minor and diminished sevenths without indication. The disposition with the fifth of the first chord on top is worthless. In *c* octaves are created if the octave is taken over the first *e*, since the octave must be taken over the following *c* in order to prepare the ensuing seventh. It is this last factor that causes the error unless the *g*-sharp leaps to *c* (*cc*) while the resolution of the first seventh is transferred to the bass. It is better to take the fifth and lead it up to *c*. The disposition with the seventh over *e* in the upper voice is not to be used. In *d*, the fifth is required in order to prepare the fourth and thus bring to completion the tones that appear over the following tone. In *e*, the seventh over *c* must be prepared by the fifth of the preceding chord. Over the last chord the third is played as a fifth part. It may enter as the octave of the preceding *e*. In *f*, preparation of the ninth over the final tone is provided by the fifth of the preceding chord of the seventh. In the first illustration under *f* an octave may be taken over *e* as a fifth part in order subsequently to win a complete triad over *a*. Finally, the second and fourth examples of Figure 355 show us that the fifth is better than the octave when the bass of the chord of the seventh ascends one step to a triad.

4.   The examples of Figure 358 are noteworthy for their signatures as well as their realizations. In *a*, a fifth part enters in the second bar. As soon as it has performed its office it may be dropped, attention being directed solely to a normal preparation and resolution. In *b*, care must be taken to avoid octaves and fifths against the passing notes in the bass. The additional illustrations show how easily they can be eliminated by an alternation of octave and unison doublings. In *c*, the seventh over the changing note *f* ascends, for this first seven-five chord is only an anticipation of the six-four chord that belongs to the following *e*. In *d* the fifth of the seventh chord cannot be taken in an undivided accompaniment without causing an error. Since the major third may not be doubled, the octave of the bass must be taken. Otherwise only a three-part realization or a divided accompaniment can be employed. Normally, the ninth should resolve over *c*, thus preparing the following seventh. The nature of the retardation is made apparent in Example *dd*. The realization of Example *d* in an undivided accompaniment is best when the ninth lies in the upper part, and much easier when a seventh accompanies the ninth. In *e* all forms of the chord of the

seventh may be used, provided that the fifth over *e* does not progress to the fifth over *f* as illustrated in the first realization of this example. The correct accompaniment of Example *f* is shown in the first of each pair of illustrations. In short, the octave is taken with the first seventh, and the fifth with the second in order to prepare the last one. Should this preparation be overlooked until the chord has changed, the right hand may play two chords over the second seventh if its length, as here, allows, and take the proper accompaniment on the second chord. In using this acceptable expedient care must be taken not to disrupt any preparation. In *g* the first seventh takes a doubled third and the second a third and a fourth. These latter intervals are played so that the four-three chord will be complete on the resolution of the seventh to the major sixth. The fifth cannot be taken with the first seventh because of the following sixth, *c*-sharp. Nor can the octave be taken, since it would cause fifths in the other parts (*gg*). The progression is illustrated in *x* without the retarded resolution. In *h* the third of the seventh must be doubled, for the chromatically raised bass may not be duplicated; nor can the fifth be taken. Example *i* contains two extraordinary examples which I have come upon. In truth, they should be figured in the manner of *ii*. As they stand in *i,* errors cannot be avoided without resorting to a fifth part or the illustrated divided accompaniment. In *j* care must be taken to avoid unmelodic and incorrect progressions. The illustrated dispositions are good; in the remaining one, fifths are struck over the second and third bass notes. In *k,* too, only two dispositions may be used; the third with the octave on top over *c* leads to errors. In *l,* an alternated doubling is required. In *m,* the chromatic minor third is taken without indication in a four-part realization. An unaltered diminished third above an altered bass must be indicated. This interval is not unsuited to chromatic contexts.

Figure 358

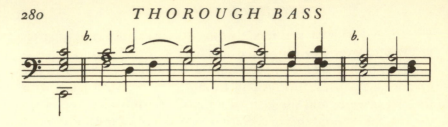

wrong

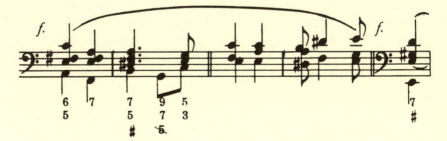

wrong   wrong

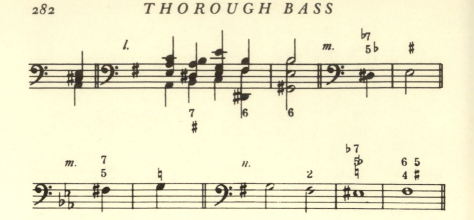

5. In delicate accompaniments the third is omitted from minor and diminished sevenths, especially when it must be chromatically raised (Figure 359, Example *a*). In such a case, some composers prefer to double the diminished fifth in the belief that it is better than the chromatic minor third. The remaining signatures in these examples are also realized in three parts.

Figure 359

6. When a cadential bass note, expressing ^{♭7}_{5♭}, is raised and ascends a half step, the third of the last chord is doubled and the octave omitted in the interests of a more melodic part writing (Figure 360).

Figure 360

THE SEVEN-SIX CHORD [1]

1.   This chord exists in two forms, consisting of a seventh, sixth, and third,[2] or a seventh, sixth, and fourth.

2.   Its signature in the first case is $\begin{smallmatrix}7\\6\end{smallmatrix}$ 5. The third is indicated only when it is chromatically altered. Chromatic alterations of the remaining intervals must not be omitted from the signature.

3.   When the fourth is present instead of the third it must be indicated. Usually it is followed by a three under the succeeding five ($\begin{smallmatrix}7\\6\\4\end{smallmatrix}$ $\begin{smallmatrix}\\5\\3\end{smallmatrix}$).

4.   Comprising the chord are the minor seventh, the major or minor sixth, and the major third, which may be replaced by the perfect fourth.

5.   The seventh may enter freely, and it remains stationary; the sixth is restricted in the manner of a dissonance by the seventh and is therefore present in the preceding chord. It resolves downward to the fifth. When the fourth is present it too must lie in the preceding chord; it resolves to a third with the sixth. The bass may be held or enter freely (Figure 361).

6.   It can be seen in Figure 361 that the underlying relationship is a chord of the seventh whose fifth and third are retarded by a sixth and fourth. The best disposition is that with the sixth on top and the seventh in the lower middle part. However, the accompanist is not always free to take this distribution, for its realization is dependent on the requisite preparation.

[1] Cf. Arnold, *op. cit.*, pp. 701–703.
[2] This chord will be recognized as that which has come to be known as the dominant thirteenth. Thorough-bass writers knew that the sixth was merely a replacement of the fifth. Later the sixth simply graced the fifth, both intervals being present simultaneously. Harmonic theorists explained the chord by accumulating enough thirds to reach to the thirteenth. And having erected this exegetic skyscraper, they promptly forbade their students to use it unless the fifth, ninth, and eleventh stories were first demolished. The chord is still known by the name of this perilously unsound structure.

7. Three-part accompaniment of the chord is rare. It is not easily realized in the galant style, but when it does appear, four parts should be employed unless a light performance necessitates omission of the third.

8. Instead of adding a second section, we shall conclude our discussion here with four noteworthy examples (Figure 362). In the first, an accessory second replaces the fourth in the seven-six chord and moves to a third. This progression, like others that occur over organ points, is best understood when separated from the bass. The essential relationship is illustrated in *a*. In *b* the diminished sevenths appear in company with a minor sixth and minor third. The underlying relationship is illustrated in *c*, where we find that the manipulation consists of a fifth retarded by a sixth. The progression sounds ugly in all dispositions. Even when the sixth is placed on top it is not much improved. Hence I prefer the progression in Example *d*. It is interesting that the diminished octave,[3] once roundly denounced, should be so clearly better here (*d*) than these

---

[3] The diminished octave happens to have been one of Bach's favored intervals. It recurs throughout his works, as pointed out by Marpurg. Cf. Ch. V, "The Chord of the Second," II, ¶ 3, where Bach also expresses approval of the augmented octave. His defense of these intervals may have been prompted by Heinichen's paraphrase of a hoary couplet:

"Octava deficiens & superflua
Sunt duo Diaboli in Musica."
Der General-Bass, p. 101.

other quite familiar intervals (*b*), which have never been criticized. I am little in favor of strange intervals; yet, study of various writings on accompaniment has convinced me that ugliness often

Figure 362

results primarily from unusual combinations of usual sounds. In the third example (*e*) the diminished seventh appears in company with the diminished sixth and minor third. The underlying progression is illustrated in *f*, and shows us that the fifth is retarded by a sixth. When this interval is on top, the progression (*e*) is not too bad. But other distributions require ears which are as extraordinary as the example. A three-part accompaniment (*g*) is more acceptable. In the third bar of the final example (*h*) the resolution of the fourth is retarded until the fifth has descended a chromatic half step. This progression is good when the bass is held before and after, when the tempo is rather broad, and the major third, *g*-sharp, does not appear immediately prior to the entrance of the retarded fourth, as it does in the last illustration of Figure 361. The last example (Figure 362, Example *h*) makes use of the organ point, which will be treated separately later. But in order to restore the confidence of those who are overwhelmed by the mass of numerals, we state that ordinarily the right hand does not play such passages. The signatures are therefore omitted, and *tasto solo* is written over the bass. In our present study they serve to indicate the voice leading and chord changes.

THE SEVEN-FOUR CHORD [1]

1.   This chord really belongs in the discussion of appoggiaturas, still ahead of us. However, since it can be found in pieces in which appoggiaturas are not represented in other signatures, we shall give it special consideration here.

2.   It appears over bass tones that are normally accompanied by the chord of the seventh or the six-four chord.[2]

3.   When this chord replaces the chord of the seventh it takes either of two forms, consisting of a seventh, fifth, and fourth, or a seventh, octave, and fourth. In both cases its signature is $\frac{7}{4}$. Here, as elsewhere, it would be but a small task to include the third figure. This would make it easier for the beginner and eliminate its confusion with the chord of the major seventh, which, as we shall see, is similarly indicated at times.

---

[1] Cf. Arnold, *op. cit.*, pp. 703–708.

[2] The seven-four chord as a manipulated chord of the seventh is discussed in ¶¶ 3–13, the final ¶¶ 14–15 being directed to the seven-four chord as a manipulated six-four chord.

4. Comprising this chord are major, minor, and diminished sevenths; augmented, perfect, and diminished fifths; diminished, perfect, and augmented fourths.

5. As we have already learned, the underlying relationship is the chord of the seventh. The only difference is that the third is retarded by the fourth. Both the seventh and the fourth, or at least one of these intervals, should be prepared. Both resolve by stepwise descent; even the augmented fourth, for it appears only as an inessential appoggiatura rather than a definitive chord tone. The seventh and fourth seldom resolve simultaneously; usually one follows the other. The bass behaves as in the chord of the seventh.

6. Inclusion of the fifth or the octave hangs on the same considerations that govern their appearance in the underlying chord of the seventh.

7. The seven-four chord is only rarely used when the seventh resolves to a sixth over a stationary bass; and even more rarely, here, do the seventh and fourth resolve simultaneously. For one thing, it sounds bad, and for another it can be dangerous, dependent on the distribution of tones, to have appoggiaturas in two voices a fourth apart. I use the expression *appoggiaturas* advisedly, for dissonances, particularly those that resolve over a stationary bass, are in essence nothing more than decorations.

8. In Figure 363 the seventh and fourth resolve simultaneously. Example *bb* is preferable to *b;* $\frac{7}{4}\atop{3}$ may always be taken when the seventh moves to a major sixth, and the fourth, if it progressed, would move to a minor third (*bb*). In *c* and *cc* the augmented fifth must be expressly indicated. Example *d* is best in three-part accompaniment, and *e* is not particularly good inasmuch as the best disposition, with the augmented fourth and major third widely separated, cannot be played because of fifths.

Figure 363

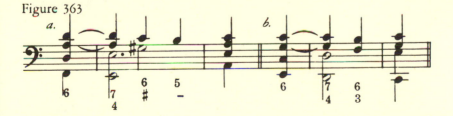

9. In Figure 364, where the fourth resolves before the seventh (*a*) and the seventh before the fourth (*b*), three-part accompaniments should be used. A fourth part is rather forced in *a* and impossible without errors in *b*.

Figure 364

10. In Figure 365 the fourth resolves directly to a third while the seventh awaits the following bass note. When the accompanist is free to take either the fifth or the octave with an unprepared seventh, it is better to take the fifth because it creates a complete chord on the resolution of the fourth (*a*), whereas the octave makes

an incomplete one (*aa*). If the fifth is taken, the fourth is best placed on top. Occasionally, owing to a required preparation of a succeeding interval, the octave must be taken (*b*). Here the fifth may be included as an additional part if it fits. In Example *c* the third (1) or the fifth (2) should be doubled. If this is not done, it is better to separate the fourth from its preparation (3) than keep both in the same part (4). The reason centers around the progression of the bass from *a* to *g*-sharp while the middle part moves from *a* to *f*. When the latter motion is filled in, it creates a cross relation. Although this consideration is no longer as important as it used to be, the progression can be avoided very easily. Certainly no one will deny that the execution of the unelaborated form of this progres-

Figure 365

sion with contrary motion (5) is better than its execution with similar motion (6). Except in the galant style, only 1 and 2 should be
used.

11. When the seventh is prepared, choice of a fourth part is
much more limited. In Figure 366 there are but few examples
where the fifth or the octave is optional. The progression in the
asterisked example sounds best in the notated distribution of parts.

Figure 366

12. When successive sevenths appear over a bass that leaps by
fourths and fifths, alternate sevenths are often accompanied by
4 3. The progression may be realized in four parts if necessary (*a*).
But, should 4 3 appear with all of the sevenths, the accompanist may
with clear conscience limit the setting to three parts. This succession occurs in the galant style only. Its realization is shown in *b*
and its bass, figured, in *bb*. In fact, the seven-four chord is usually
given a three-part setting, for the chord does not readily appear in
the learned style (Figure 367).

Figure 367

13.   In the example of a passing seventh in Figure 368, an inner part moves in thirds with the bass, and the seventh and fourth remain stationary. The signature, $\frac{7}{4}$, used by some, is not clear enough; $\frac{7}{4}$ is better. A doubled third, or a third and an octave, is 3 better than the illustration.

Figure 368

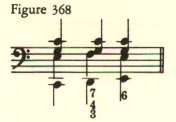

14.   When our chord appears in place of the six-four chord, it is because the sixth is retarded by the seventh. This latter interval with the fourth and octave form the content of the chord. The

seventh is usually minor, but the fourth is always perfect. Both intervals resolve downward, the seventh before the fourth. The signature of this progression is $\frac{7}{4}\frac{6}{}$.

15.   Figure 369 provides more detailed information about this progression. In *a* the bass remains stationary, and neither the seventh nor the fourth is prepared. In *b* the seventh is prepared but not the fourth. Over the first note, $\frac{7}{5}\atop{3}$ or $\frac{8}{7}\atop{3}$ may be taken. In *c*, both intervals are prepared. $\frac{6}{3}\atop{6}$ should be taken over the first note. A doubled third with the sixth (*cc*) creates hidden octaves, and $\frac{6}{8}\atop{3}$ direct octaves. In *d* the seventh is prepared. The triad over the first note may be realized as $\frac{8}{5}\atop{3}$, $\frac{5}{3}\atop{5}$, or $\frac{3}{5}\atop{8}$. The triad with the octave is excellent but not with the fifth on top, for this distribution causes errors. In *e* both dissonances, seventh and fourth, are prepared. Over the first tone $\frac{7}{5}\atop{3}$ or $\frac{3}{7}\atop{3}$ may be taken. Because the octave is required over the second tone, it cannot be taken over the first. In *f* the seventh will be prepared if the first chord is realized as $\frac{8}{6}\atop{3}$. When the third of the chord of the sixth lies on top, fifths are unavoidable. In *g*, both dissonances are prepared. However, in order to prepare the seventh, an octave must be taken as a fifth part over the first bass note. The fourth and seventh are also prepared in *h*. The fifth is taken with 7 6 over the second bass note. In a divided accompaniment the doubled third may be played, as illustrated in the final example. The octave cannot be taken with this 7 6 progression without causing errors.

Figure 369

THE CHORD OF THE MAJOR SEVENTH,[1] I

1. Normally, this chord consists of a major seventh, perfect fourth, and major second.

2. Its most usual signature in four-part accompaniment is $\begin{smallmatrix}7\\4\\2\end{smallmatrix}$

[1] Cf. Arnold, *op. cit.*, pp. 674–682.

with accidentals as required. Confusion is caused by those who expect a four-part realization but omit 2 from the signature or specify
only 7.

3.   This chord appears as a passing relationship over a stationary
bass, and also as the retardation of a triad following a moving bass.
In the first instance, all three intervals are taken freely and ascend
(Figure 370, Example *a*). In the second, the seventh and second
must lie in the preceding chord; the fourth may (*b*), but need not
(*c*), be prepared. The second and seventh ascend; the fourth descends. When the fourth in Example *a* lies on top, it too descends.

Figure 370

4.   The signature $\frac{9}{7}$ is often used instead of our $\frac{7}{4}$. In the course
of our study we shall see that certain forms of the chord may be indicated by either one. The distinction to be observed here is that
the major seventh when accompanied by a ninth always resolves by
stepwise descent, but in our chord the seventh and the second always resolve by stepwise ascent. The second, appearing as it does
over a stationary bass, and being used consequently as a passing
tone or a retardation, enjoys the same right here as it does in similar
cases; namely, the right to ascend.

5.   To locate $\frac{7}{4}$, play the triad on the seventh above the bass.

6.   In three-part accompaniment the second or the fourth is
omitted. When it is necessary to specify one of these settings the
signature is $2\,\frac{7}{3}\,\frac{8}{3}$ or $4\,\frac{7}{3}\,\frac{8}{3}$. Care must be taken to observe the indicated
resolution of the seventh in the latter signature in order to avoid a
realization of the seven-four chord instead of the intended three-
part seven-four-two chord.

7.   Our chord is occasionally realized in five parts. The addi-

tional interval is either a sixth, major or minor, or a perfect fifth. The bass may remain stationary or move.

8.   Either sixth may, but need not, be prepared. Both progress downward to the fifth, thereby making a complete triad on the resolution of the chord. The second is sometimes omitted if four parts are preferred. This is most frequent when a bass note with the signature 6 or $\frac{4}{3}$ descends stepwise to the tone over which our chord appears. Should the sixth over the first bass note be augmented, the interval of the second cannot be taken with the next chord, for it lacks preparation.

9.   The examples in Figure 371 will make my meaning clearer. An exact indication of the intervals is especially needed here. In *a* the second may, but need not, be played, depending on its being specified. In the third and fourth illustrations under *a* the sixth moves to a fifth while the seventh and fourth remain stationary. The first and third examples, illustrating the major sixth, sound good only in the notated distribution of parts. In *b* and *c* five-part

Figure 371

settings of our chord are continued from the opening chord. In *b* all of the tones of our chord lie in the preceding chord; in *c* only the sixth must be sought out. In 1 and 2 the second joins the throng as a detail of decorative motions in the middle parts; hence it should be omitted initially. In 3 the second is optional. The raised seventh resolves before the entrance of the six-four chord. In 4, 5, and 6 the second is omitted for the reason stated in the preceding paragraph.

10.   When the fifth is taken as an additional part, it remains stationary. It may, but need not, be present in the preceding chord. By means of this interval the following triad is made complete and, even when the second is omitted, four correct parts are retained, as illustrated in the last three examples of Figure 372. Here again close attention must be given to the resolution of the seventh in order to forestall confusion with the seven-four chord, whose signature is the same as ours. The fourth and fifth examples are sometimes indicated with 9 instead of 2.

Figure 372

THE CHORD OF THE MAJOR SEVENTH, II

1.   The ascending major seventh may not be prepared as the octave of the preceding bass note. Hence Figure 373 is incorrect:

Figure 373

wrong

2.   When the seventh is retarded by an octave the other parts are not affected but enter with the bass note. The octave becomes a dissonance, being restricted by the second above the bass. Hence it resolves by stepwise descent to the seventh. In the signature of this relationship 8 and 7 stand adjacent to each other, and the remaining figures that enter with 8 are placed below it. In Figure 374, Example *a*, the second as well as the seventh is retarded, but by a

Figure 374

third. Hence, this latter interval, like the octave, assumes the characteristics of a dissonance. In *b* only the second is retarded, again by a third. This third may be doubled in the preceding triad (*c*). The notated distribution of parts is the best in all of the examples.

3. When the fourth, lying in the principal part, is retarded by a fifth, the accompanist plays, on the entrance of the bass note, $\begin{smallmatrix}7\\5\\4\\2\end{smallmatrix}$, $\begin{smallmatrix}7\\4\\2\end{smallmatrix}$, or simply $\overset{7}{2}$, according to the need for a full or thin accompaniment (Figure 375).

Figure 375

4. Figure 376 is best accompanied in three parts. If a fourth part should or must be added, the fifth rather than the fourth is taken. The setting would be made ugly by adding the fourth to the several appoggiaturas already present. The fifth, on the other hand, throws the notated appoggiaturas of the principal part into bolder relief and makes the succeeding triad complete. A fifth part cannot be used to attain completeness, for the progression does not assimilate four parts very well, let alone five.

Figure 376

5. The apparent downward motion of the major seventh in Example *a* of Figure 377 is the result of an ellipsis. The complete relationship is illustrated in *b*. In Example *c* the resolution of $\frac{9}{7}$ is differentiated from that of $\frac{7}{2}$. Although no detail of resolution would be lacking if in the last bar $\frac{9\ 8}{7\ 8}$ were taken instead of our $\frac{4\ 3}{}$ chord, no one can deny that the illustrated progression is closer to the sense of the passage.

Figure 377

THE CHORD OF THE NINTH,[1] I

1. This chord consists of a ninth, fifth, and third.[2]

2. Its signature is 9 8 when the ninth resolves on a stationary bass, but simply 9 when the bass progresses. Accidentals are no more to be overlooked here than in other signatures.

[1] Cf. Arnold, *op. cit.*, pp. 693–694.

[2] Hence this chord is not to be confused with the present-day "ninth chord," which Bach discusses later as the nine-seven chord.

3.   Comprising the chord of the ninth are major and minor ninths, augmented, perfect, and diminished fifths, major and minor thirds.

4.   The ninth is a dissonance which must always be prepared. It resolves by stepwise descent (Figure 378).

Figure 378

5.   The ninth has the same position on the staff as the second but is clearly distinguishable from it in its accompaniment, preparation, and resolution. In the case of the second, the dissonance lies in the bass, which must be prepared and resolved; but in the ninth the dissonance lies in the upper tone, which must be prepared and resolved. Differences in the accompaniment of these two dissonances have already been noted and will be enlarged upon in this and the next section.

6.   To realize the chord of the ninth, take the triad above the bass but strike the ninth instead of the octave. Those who know the $\frac{3}{2}$ chord know the chord of the ninth.

7.   The major ninth may be accompanied by either the perfect or the augmented fifth. With the perfect fifth the third may be major (Figure 379, Example a) or minor (b); with the augmented fifth it is always major. This latter fifth lies in the preceding chord and resolves with the ninth or by itself (c). The minor ninth may be accompanied by either the perfect or the diminished fifth. With the perfect fifth there may be either a major (d) or a minor third (e). In the latter case the fifth sometimes ascends to the sixth on the resolution of the ninth (e). Although the diminished fifth may be taken freely (f), it is better when it lies in the preceding chord (g).

8.   In Figure 380 with its alternating ninth and six-five chords the only disposition free of errors is that in which the ninth is placed in the lower middle part. The fifths that occur in the other two dispositions, no matter how ardently they may be defended, are and

Figure 379

remain ugly.[3] When the best disposition cannot be taken it is better to omit the sixth from the six-five chord and double the third in-

Figure 380

[3] The object of this remark is Marpurg (Cf. Arnold, *op. cit.*, pp. 401 ff.), and possibly Carl Heinrich Graun, whose support of greater tolerance in these matters is cited by Marpurg.

stead (*a*). Otherwise the realization in *b*, employing a divided accompaniment, should be noted and used whenever possible.

9. The fifth is omitted from three-part realizations. Because one interval is thus lost, the accompanist must exercise the same care in using this kind of accompaniment as we have found necessary in other similar cases.

THE CHORD OF THE NINTH, II

1. The ninth is and remains a ninth even when it is placed directly adjacent to the bass. This relationship is often unavoidable. For example, composers frequently meet it who write obbligato parts for bass instruments. A double bass is best fitted here to give the lowest voice its proper gravity. Of course, aside from such a case

Figure 381

as this, it is always better to place the ninth nine degrees above the bass.

2. Examples *a* and *b* of Figure 381 call for a divided accompaniment when they are realized in four parts. In the first the ninth, as a passing interval, is not resolved (*a*) and in the second its resolution is retarded (*b*). When the accompaniment is not divided the third chord is realized in three parts (*c*). In *d* a doubled third or sixth in the chord of the sixth is the best setting, for it eliminates large leaps and prepares the diminished fifth in the chord of the ninth. In *e* three parts are safest. Should a fourth part be used, the sixth must appear on top over the first note (*f*). The remaining two dispositions create fifths.

3. The ninth may not be prepared as an octave over the preceding bass. Hence Figure 382, Example *a*, is wrong. Resolution [4] of the ninth to the octave is the cause of this rule. Hence, when the resolution is not to an octave, the rule may be ignored. Formerly, musicians [5] wrote thoughtlessly in the manner of Example *b*. These octaves on the after beat sound no better than the octave preparation and resolution of the ninth. Proof that this rule was introduced because of the resolution rather than the preparation is provided by the fact that other dissonances may be prepared on the octave (*c*). Despite this, octave preparation of the ninth is never attractive. It must be avoided: (1) in the outer parts; (2) in thin settings; (3) except for contrapuntal reasons. The bass must always be changed on the resolution, if this use of the ninth is to be allowed. I believe that the direct fifths of Example *d* (which some defend by claiming that they are covered, in the notated distribution) sound worse than the after-beat octaves of Example *a*. However, both are poor. [6]

Figure 382 [7]

---

[4] Remainder of paragraph from ed. of 1797.

[5] His father must be included in this stricture. Cf. J. S. Bach, *Choralgesänge* (Br. u. H.) No. 209, *Jesus Meine Zuversicht*, bar 1, bass and tenor.

[6] Cf. Arnold, *op. cit.*, pp. 397–406.

[7] Examples from *b* to end from ed. of 1797.

THE NINE-SIX CHORD [1]

1.   This chord consists of a ninth, sixth, and third.

2.   Its signature is $\overset{9}{6}$ with appropriate accidentals. The resolution of the ninth leads to a chord of the sixth with the bass duplicated. Hence, those familiar with this latter chord can easily find the nine-six.

3.   The three intervals that comprise the chord may be major or minor, as illustrated in Figure 383. The disposition with the ninth on top is generally best. The three examples that bear the letter *a* sound rather poor even in this disposition. An improved progression follows each example.

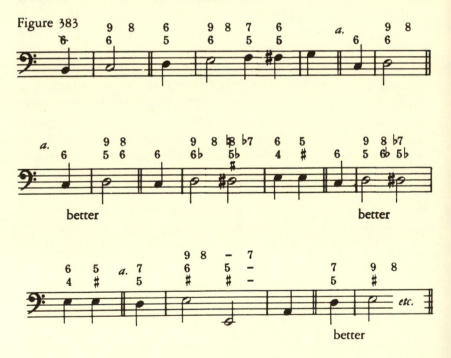

Figure 383

[1] Cf. Arnold, *op. cit.*, pp. 698–699.

THE NINE-FOUR CHORD [1]

1.   This chord consists of a ninth, fifth, and fourth.

2.   Its signature is $\overset{9}{4}$, with accidentals when necessary. When both dissonances resolve over the original bass note, $\overset{8}{3}$ is placed to the right of the signature.

3.   Since both the ninth and the fourth must be prepared, it is only the remaining interval that must be located. In order easily to identify the tones, take the six-five chord on the second below the bass note, for it contains the same tones as our chord and often precedes it. It will also be recognized by those who know the five-four-two chord. Both dissonances resolve simultaneously in most cases (*a*); but on occasion successively (*b*) (Figure 384).

Figure 384

6	9	8	7	9	–	3		6	9	8	8	5♭
5	4	3	5	4	3			5	4	–	♭7	
											3	

4.   The ninth may be major or minor; the fifth, augmented, perfect, or diminished; but the fourth, as we shall see in the following examples, is always perfect. It is better to prepare the diminished fifth than strike it freely. The augmented fifth, too, must lie in the preceding chord (Figure 385).

Figure 385

5.   The sixth must be included in the signature ($\overset{9}{\underset{4}{6}}$) if it is to be taken in place of the fifth. It may be major or minor. The tones of this chord may be identified by playing the chord of the second on

---

[1] Cf. Arnold, *op. cit.*, pp. 697–698.

the given bass note. Often the sixth moves to the fifth while the ninth and fourth resolve. Such being the case, only two distributions of the tones are practicable, for the remaining one creates fifths. The last three examples of Figure 386 illustrate this progression:

best distribution

6. In the galant style the fourth is sometimes played without preparation (Figure 387, Example *a*). This unprepared fourth may even be augmented (*b*). Such fourths are brought about by the introduction of appoggiaturas that are provided with a three-part accompaniment. The first example is better than the second.

7. The examples of Figure 388 are also realized in three parts. In the second illustration under *a* the ninth as well as the fourth seems to lack preparation. In *b*, however, it can be seen that the opposite is true, as soon as the appoggiaturas are removed. The accompaniment to both of these illustrations is the same as the realization in *a*.

Figure 388

THE NINE-SEVEN CHORD [1]

1. This chord consists of a ninth, seventh, and third.

2. Its signature is $\frac{9}{7}$, with accidentals as required. When both dissonances resolve over the original bass note, $\frac{8}{6}$ follows the original signature.

3. The ninth as well as the seventh must be prepared. Both dissonances resolve by stepwise descent, simultaneously in most cases (*a*), but at times successively (*b*) (Figure 389).

Figure 389

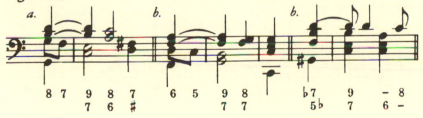

4. As illustrated in Figure 390, the three intervals that comprise the chord may be major or minor.

5. Occasionally the octave of the preceding chord must be taken as a fifth part in order to prepare the seventh. Such being the case, the fifth of our chord should also be played, for it too will lie in the

[1] The equivalent of the present-day "ninth chord." It should be noted that Bach's chord resolves uniformly on a stationary bass. Cf. Arnold, *op. cit.*, pp. 699–701.

Figure 390

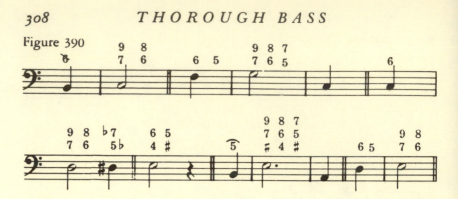

preparatory chord. It may be diminished, perfect, or augmented (Figure 391).

Figure 391

6. If the fourth is to be taken instead of the third of this chord, it must be expressly indicated in the signature. Since this tone, too, will be present in the preceding chord, the entire construction, including the fifth as an additional part, will lie under the fingers. The fourth may be perfect, diminished, or augmented; and as stated above, it is prepared. A fifth part is also taken in order to prepare

Figure 392

the seventh, as illustrated in the last four examples. In the first two examples of Figure 392 the tones of the first chord should be distributed in such a manner as to avoid the seventh in the upper part.

7. Example *a* of Figure 393, similar to several others which have already been illustrated, is realized in three parts. The fourth part is regained on the chord of the second. A three-part setting is also used in *b* and *c,* where the suspended seventh and ninth move upward before resolving. In *d* the chord of the seventh enters prematurely, as explained in *e.* In *f* our chord, unresolved, results from the motion of a passing bass. This kind of passage with varied figuration can be found in heavily scored, noisy pieces, such as symphonies, etc. (*g*).

Figure 393

THE FIVE-FOUR CHORD [1]

1. The five-four chord consists of a fourth, fifth, and octave.

2. Its signature is 4 3 or $\overset{5}{4}$ 3 when the fourth resolves to the third over a common bass note. But when the resolution occurs over a moving bass, 4 or $\overset{5}{4}$ is sufficient. In the first case, 3 is often replaced by an accidental which specifies the size of the third. The accidental must be separated from the preceding 4 in order to indicate clearly that it refers, not to this numeral, but to 3.

3. The perfect and diminished fifth, the perfect fourth, and the octave are the intervals which may appear in the five-four chord.

4. The fourth is always prepared and resolves by stepwise descent. The fifth, which restricts this dissonance, is not always present in the preceding chord, being struck freely at times, even when it is diminished (Figure 394).

Figure 394

5. In order to locate the chord, play the triad on any bass note, but substitute a fourth for the third. This procedure makes it easy to learn the distribution of tones and the resolution of the fourth.

6. To avoid fifths in Example *a* of Figure 395, the octave of the five-four chord must be omitted and the fifth doubled instead. No interval is thereby lost. This step is not necessary after the remaining dispositions of the preceding chord of the seventh. In *b* the third of the chord that precedes $\overset{5}{4}$ must be doubled. If this cannot be done, the accompaniment must be divided (*bb*).

7. In the galant style the perfect or augmented fourth some-

[1] Cf. Arnold, *op. cit.*, pp. 694–698.

Figure 395

times enters unprepared (along with the fifth) in the form of an appoggiatura which cannot be omitted from the accompaniment unless it is replaced by a rest.[2] In Example *a*, Figure 396, the perfect fourth may enter by stepwise or leaping motion. But in *b* the augmented fourth is approached only by step, and $\frac{5}{4}$ must be expressly called for. The notated distribution of tones is the most acceptable. In other cases the augmented fourth may be omitted from the accompaniment and replaced by a quarter rest (*c*). In *d* all forms of the chord of the sixth may be used, and the perfect fourth which follows may be approached by step or leap. But the realizations of *dd* must be avoided.

Figure 396

8.   If for adequate reasons a three-part realization is required, the octave can be most readily omitted.

[2] For an extended discussion of the accompaniment to appoggiaturas, cf. Ch. VI, "Appoggiaturas."

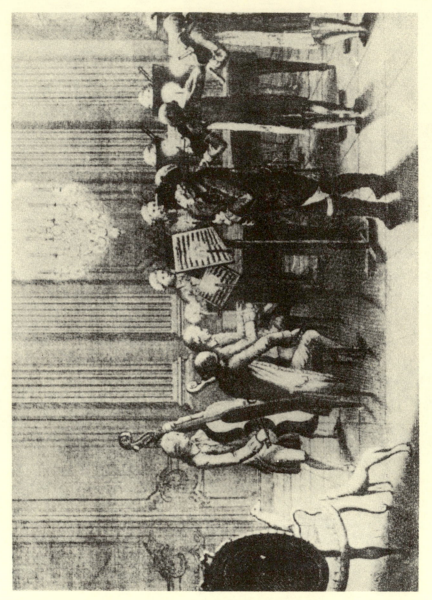

Frederick the Great with his musicians, an engraving by P. Haas

CHAPTER SIX

ACCOMPANIMENT

THE UNISON [1]

1

THE octave is included in the meaning of the term *unison.*
Thus when parts progress either in real unisons or in octaves, they are said to move in unison (*all'unisono*), even
when the figuration of one of the parts is different from that of the
other (Figure 397).

Figure 397

2.   There is no need to commend this technique, which attains
its beauty through the omission of harmony, for the many examples
of it to be found in the works of good composers provide a dependable testimony.

3.   Yet it is surprising that some composers do not always specify
a unison accompaniment in scoring the bass. Figures will be found
where they are not to be realized. The results can only be unhappy.
Imagine a situation: A composer works industriously over a piece,
lavishing on it every last resource of melody and harmony. At a
certain point he feels that his audience must be roused with something different. He searches enthusiastically for a passage whose
splendor and majesty shall be pronounced and striking. He decides
to discard the beauty of harmony for a while; the passage shall be
played in unison; it alone is to occupy the thoughts and actions of

[1] Cf. Arnold, *The Art of Accompaniment from a Thorough-Bass,* Ch. III, Sect. 12.

the performers. This is followed by a resumption of harmony, etc. He completes the work and it is performed. His pleasant expectations of the intended execution of the passage are shattered by the accompanist who, at the keyboard, prepares and resolves the indicated intervals as carefully and regularly as possible. At another time this would be much to his credit, but now it is only a source of annoyance. Fortunately, for him, the composer realizes that he overlooked something in writing out the bass part and is overjoyed when the accompanist, displeased at his inappropriate accompaniment, abandons chords and reinforces the passage in accordance with the first rule of accompaniment as stated in Paragraph 19 of the Introduction: An accompanist must fit to each piece a correct performance of its harmony in the proper volume.

4.   In order to clarify this rule, we shall discuss two cases in which the accompanist is obliged to play in unison. Accompaniment in the unison occurs when the bass is played in octaves with both hands.[2]

5.   The first case relates to passages which are written for one part. When all performers play in unison it is only natural that the accompanist too should follow the unisons and give up his chords. Such passages usually carry the indication, *unisoni* or *all'unisono*.

6.   There is a special case which departs somewhat from the preceding. It occurs when the ripieno parts are in unison with the bass while the principal part has a long held note or a different melody. The ripieno parts must be observed carefully to learn whether their broken chords give expression to the essential intervals, especially the dissonances and resolutions of the underlying harmony.[3] If they do, the accompanist also should play in unison (Figure 398, Example *a*). But if the accompaniment to the principal part is simple and not only calls for harmony, but attains its affect through the use of it, a chordal setting must be chosen (*b*). Especially needed here is an exact indication of the required accompaniment, for free choice demands an insight which is capable of deciding whether a chordal accompaniment helps or hinders the principal part. Furthermore, according to circumstances the case discussed here might take either type of accompaniment.

[2] I.e., one note for each hand.

[3] With regard to the treatment of dissonances in a unison accompaniment, see Ch. VI, "Some Precautions of Accompaniment," ¶ 3, where Bach takes a freer view of the need for resolutions.

Figure 398
Adagio

7. For special reasons, composers sometimes place a melody in the bass and accompany it in unisons in the narrow sense—that is, without any octave doubling either above or below. When the bass is thus to be played only in the notated register, the accompanist, his right hand silent, plays such misleading unisons in one part alone with the left hand. To be played in a similar manner are those melodies which, while not always brilliant, are of striking expressiveness and appear on occasion in the lowest part alone.[4] They should not be hidden beneath a harmonic accompaniment nor raised in register by octave doublings. The composer who contrives such a studied effect must designate it with great accuracy or his plans may fall short of full realization in performance.

8. The second case that calls for unison accompaniment concerns all brilliant passages for the lowest part in the setting of which the composer has a special purpose in mind. They may be fashioned out of leaps, runs, broken chords, successive trills, and countless other figures. From our point of view, such passages must stand out clearly, and this is achieved less by a chordal than a unison accompaniment. It is not yet a general practice to designate this case, *unisoni* or *all'unisono;* hence, the manner of support is left to the discretion of an understanding accompanist. Experience has proved to me the effectiveness of a unison accompaniment in such passages.

9. Brilliant basses are usually provided with a chordal accompaniment only in two-part pieces such as a solo or solo aria.

10. Termination of a unison accompaniment is indicated by figures placed over the bass at the point where a chordal setting is resumed. Should the first note express a triad that is indicated ordinarily without any figures, at least one of its intervals must be designated.

---

[4] One of the most strikingly expressive examples, written later by Bach, is the opening of *Die Auferstehung und Himmelfahrt Jesu* (Wotquenne No. 240).

ONE-PART ACCOMPANIMENT FOR THE LEFT HAND [1]

1.   In this kind of accompaniment, which is indicated by *t.s.,* *tasto,* or *tasto solo,* the left hand alone plays the bass without octave duplication. In certain passages it is as much needed as the unison accompaniment which we have just discussed; and performance will suffer as much from an incorrect indication of it as will the unison accompaniment.

2.   Italians do not use either of these accompaniments. Perhaps they believe that only chords can be played on our instruments and consider it unfitted for the accompaniment of the most beautiful, affettuoso passages. They do not care to have the tinkling sounds of their keyboardists in such places; the more so because it is known that they can play scarcely any chord without rolling it. Hence in Italian works, delicate passages usually carry the direction *senza cembalo* over the bass as a kind of warning. Whole arias sometimes have this indication, which is laughable to the singers of that country when they are shown the words in their own scores.

3.   We use the *tasto solo* to great advantage in suitable passages; for example, when the bass and principal part move in thirds and sixths with no additional voices. The piece may be for two or more parts. Should the bass be marked piano, and the thirds or sixths lie close together, thus precluding octave duplication, no other accompaniment is as natural as ours. The double basses are silent

Figure 399

1 Cf. Arnold, *op. cit.,* Ch. III, § 12.

while the other bass instruments play softly in the notated register along with the keyboard. The examples of Figure 399 are typical.

4.   On the other hand, when such passages are doubled and the thirds or sixths are widely separated, the accompaniment in unison or *all'unisono* may be used, the bass being doubled. If this part does not go too low, the doubling should be in the lower rather than the upper octave. Such settings can be found in symphonies and concertos. The first and second violins play together while the violas and basses move in unison (Figure 400).

Figure 400
  Allegro

5.   At half and whole cadences where the principal part has an appoggiatura whose release is piano, as discussed in the first part of this Essay,[2] an accompanist at the harpsichord plays only the bass; at the clavichord or pianoforte, however, both the appoggiatura and the release may be played, but execution must be adjusted to the volume and length of the ornament in the principal part, so that it will retain the freedom to perform its notes in accordance with the affect. On the pianoforte an alternative is to perform only the bass under the appoggiatura as loudly as necessary and then the release quite softly with the right hand.

6.   *Tasto solo* is also used on a bass over which a melody is set in a low register with no accompaniment above it. But when there is an accompaniment by several instruments, also low, figures may be placed over the bass, which an understanding accompanist who is aware of the construction of the piece will perform only in the low register. However, because the judgment of thorough-bass players, many of whom are dilettantes, is not always trustworthy, it is better and safer in this case also to indicate *t.s.* over the bass and dispense with the harmony of the keyboard than to endure an accompaniment which cries out above the other instruments and

[2] Cf. Chapter II, "The Appoggiatura," ¶ 7.

ruins the passage. This kind of setting occurs in concertos for low-pitched instruments, arias for low voices, etc.

7. The following additional instances of this kind of accompaniment should be noted (Figure 401). In *a,* where the principal voice starts in actual unison with the bass, the first note should be played *t.s.* In *b,* the right hand is silent at those places where *t.s.* appears, even when there are figures. Performance in a slow tempo would suffer here were the accompanist to anticipate the change of harmony of the principal part.

Figure 401

8. The bass in *tasto solo* must never be doubled in the octave by the left hand, unless the passage is so loud and the instrument so

weak that only in this manner can a proper balance be reached. But it is always better and more appropriate to the nature of *tasto solo* when such an expedient is not employed, for it is in respect to doubling that *tasto solo* is distinguished from *unisono*.

9. The resumption of a chordal accompaniment after *t.s.* is indicated by the reappearance of figures, just as in the case of *unisono*.

THE ORGAN POINT [1]

1. The organ point or *point d'orgue* occurs when various harmonic changes, often involving tied notes, are made over a held or repeated bass note.

2. It appears generally in learned things, especially fugues, near the end over the dominant or over the final note. Occasionally it will be found in the course of a piece over the dominant or tonic of a key reached by modulation. In the first case, composers often introduce all manner of contrapuntal devices in stretto.

3. The organ point may be in three or more parts. The harmony is usually complete even without the bass, which however, adds a final, appropriate gravity. In order to comprehend or explain the chords and the unusual combinations of intervals the bass should be disregarded. When this is done, the strange signatures turn out to be indications of nothing more than the ordinary progressions of thorough bass.

4. It is not easy to figure organ points, so they are usually set *tasto solo*. Those who do figure them must accept the fact that they will be played *tasto solo* anyway. The reason for this can be ascribed not only to a justifiable simplification of the accompanist's tasks but often to the impossibility of reading the figures. Assuming that the right hand could accompany all organ points, gratitude would never compensate for the expended anxiety and trouble.

5. To play the organ point *tasto solo* removes the necessity of scanning unusual signatures and successions of towering figures. Parts are often constructed in such a manner that one crosses the other. This might oblige the accompanist to cross parts, which is not allowed in thorough bass, since many errors might be thereby excused without satisfying the ear. In such a case, therefore, the entire organ point must be played in divided accompaniment to en-

[1] Cf. Arnold, *op. cit.*, Ch. XX.

sure correct preparation and resolution, and prevent the right hand from descending too far. This is an excessive demand. Sometimes the chord changes are so rapid that they can scarcely be brought out even when the accompanist tries to realize them.

6.   The examples of Figure 402 will suffice to illustrate these remarks. Figures have been included in order to provide an understanding of the chords. A setting without the organ point follows each example.

Figure 402

Allegro

APPOGGIATURAS [1]

1. It would be superfluous to repeat the discussion of the appoggiatura which is contained in the first part of this Essay. I assume that the reader has read this material carefully, for it is inseparable from the present remarks.

2. It is rare that an accompaniment can be constructed without reference to appoggiaturas, for they are in most cases an integral part of it. They appear most frequently in pieces where taste rules, for they are one of its outstanding refinements. Such pieces require a delicate accompaniment which aims to bring the appoggiatura into relief rather than to obscure or destroy it.

3. Appoggiaturas retard the chords which are called for by the bass. It is common knowledge that, according to the rules of good performance, the ornament is emphasized and its release played lightly. Consequently, it is doubly wrong to omit indication of them from the signature, for without some clue the accompaniment in most cases can only be poor. The chord retarded by an appoggiatura takes on a quite different appearance through an exact indication. But, although knowledge of the usual signatures will not suffice and the accompanist must learn to recognize strange combinations of numerals, he will soon grow accustomed to them. In scores where the principal part is not notated in the continuo part these signatures are indispensable, for the presence of an appoggiatura can not be guessed. And even when the principal part with its ornaments is present, how can the numerals be modified in performance if the figures contain no reference to the appoggiaturas? How can middle parts, if they are required, be realized?

4. In Chapter V much material was covered relative to appoggiaturas. This will not be repeated here. Our present discussion begins with the long, variable appoggiatura. The shortest of these is never more rapid than an eighth note in an allegretto.

5. When a bass note is figured without reference to an accompanying appoggiatura, and this appoggiatura with its release complements the given numerals or is identical with one of them, the accompaniment need not be modified even if it is in four parts. The examples of Figure 403 are constructed in this manner.

[1] Cf. Arnold, *op. cit.*, pp. 422 ff.

Figure 403

6.   But if the appoggiatura is not related to the harmony of the release and therefore differs from the intervals of the bass note over which it appears, the accompanist should play the ornament and as many intervals from the indicated signature as required by its loudness and its suggested harmony. When it is played softly and with great affect, its length dependent on the caprice of the principal part, the accompanist should omit the ornament and play one or at most two supporting parts. This occurs most frequently with chromatically raised appoggiaturas. Two-part appoggiaturas are played in the accompaniment, making a total of three parts. Some appoggiaturas suffer no accompaniment at all. As a corollary to these remarks it should be observed that the greater the affect of a piece, the more delicate must its accompaniment be. Such delicacy is concerned with the selection, entrance, reduction, and omission of chords. My meaning will be illustrated by examples of all characteristic situations.

7.[2]   In Figure 404 the illustrated delicate accompaniment is better than the complete chord of the ninth.

Figure 404[3]

8.   Figure 405 illustrates the three kinds of second,[4] used as ascending appoggiaturas. Even though they are not always played by the accompanist they must be indicated in the signature. Unless they are reckoned as ninths, their signature is usually 2 3. Appropriate accidentals and the remaining figures must be included. One numeral above the 2 indicates a three-part accompaniment. In the examples that follow throughout this section, the first illustration is figured without reference to the appoggiatura; but in the second, which is the accompaniment to the first, the signatures are computed correctly. In *a*, $\frac{5}{3}$ may be taken in the second bar, but in the fourth bar, accompaniment of the augmented second is momentarily replaced by an eighth rest after which only the fifth is taken.

2 From the ed. of 1797.
3 From the ed. of 1797.
4 That is, major, minor, and augmented seconds measured from the bass.

In *b*, only the seventh is realized, but in the two-part appoggiatura of *bb* the second as well as the seventh is played. In *c*, the seventh or both the seventh and the second may be taken, since both tones appear in the preceding chord. The same applies to *d*, where either 6 or $\frac{6}{2}$ may be realized. In *e*, the second is treated as a ninth, that is, it moves to an octave. In a slow tempo the appoggiatura in *f* may, of course, be realized; but elsewhere it is replaced by a quarter rest and the seventh alone is played. The appoggiaturas and their releases are accompanied in *g*. A slur must be placed over $\frac{4}{2}$ to indicate omission of the sixth. In *h*, an eighth rest would be too short, were the accompanist to omit the ornament; hence it should be played, especially since it is present in the preceding chord. In *i*, the second cannot be treated as a ninth because of the following *f*-sharp in the bass; however, the interval may be omitted and $\frac{5}{3}$ alone played. To avoid fifths, the sixth must be omitted from the first *f*-sharp. For reasons of affect, the principal part in a slow tempo frequently retards on the *a*, carrying it over to the next bar. The accompanist should not do likewise but continue to play in strict tempo. In *j*, the second may be treated as a ninth in a slow tempo; but elsewhere it should be omitted and the triad played directly on each bass note. Where many chromatic appoggiaturas appear, as in *k* and *kk*, the harmony must be thin and interspersed with rests in order to bring the ornaments into relief and avoid ugly chords. In *l* the appoggiatura is played, since it appears in the preceding chord, and the fifth is added to it. Although the seconds in *m* may be realized, the illustrated accompaniment is better for a soft performance. Moreover, the rests will help to clarify the appoggiaturas and remove any blurring of their outline. In *n*, where the chromatically raised ornament concurs with a change of bass, the sixth alone should be taken. Any of three accompaniments may be used for *o*, comprising: (1) the fifth alone; (2) the fifth and augmented second; (3) these two intervals and the octave. Choice is governed by the required loudness or softness of the accompaniment. In *p*, the first second is treated as a ninth, but the following one is accompanied by the sixth alone, the third being struck later. Over the bass note *c* only the fifth and ninth are realized, and over the following *f*-sharp, the diminished fifth and third. The fourth over *c* and its resolution are omitted, so that the principal part may perform the resolution with complete freedom. This detail is one of the refinements that are reserved for the principal part. It should be observed here that accompaniments must be so contrived that they clarify or at least do not obscure the various refinements of melodies whether these consist of chromatic intervals, retarded and anticipated resolutions, or, above all, syncopations, especially in slow pieces of an affective nature. Clarity is attained through rests, and obscurity can be avoided by thinning the chords. Were all refinements realized on the keyboard, listeners would not be able to tell whether it was being played as an accompanying or a solo instrument. In *q*, the triad is retarded by a chord of the major seventh which expresses a descending appoggiatura on the second above the bass. We have already seen several such examples. This retardation is only occasionally good, but bad taste makes constant use of it.

Figure 405

Andante

9. Other appoggiaturas, in addition to those on the second, call for consideration. In the examples of Figure 406 the chord of the seventh is retarded by this ornament. In *a,* the appoggiatura may be included in the accompaniment as indicated by the figures above the staff, which refer to the bass notes. But the setting that follows may also be used. This accompaniment, which holds the diminished fifth and third throughout the bar, provides the principal part with freedom to perform its appoggiatura with the appropriate affect.

The same remarks apply to *aa.* In *b,* $\frac{6}{4}$ may be taken over the first bass note and $\frac{7}{3}$ over the second, or the appoggiatura and release may be omitted and, if necessary, only 4 3 played. The two-part appoggiaturas of *c* are accompanied as illustrated. In a delicate setting the appoggiaturas are replaced by a quarter rest and $\frac{7}{5}\flat$ is played afterwards. Examples *d* and *dd* are alike, the difference between them being only that *dd* contains a two-part appoggiatura. The accompaniments to both are almost identical. Rests are not used in the accompaniment to *dd,* because the notes of the original are slow and legato; but in the more rapid tempo of *d* they are effective. Example *e* and its accompaniment are identical.

10. In the examples of Figure 407 the chord of the second is retarded by appoggiaturas. In *a* the $\frac{4}{3}$ is played over the eighth rest

Figure 406

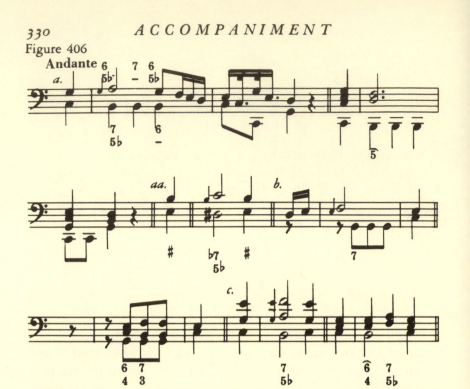

and followed by the major triad on *e*. In *b*, $\overset{6}{\underset{2}{5}}$ is taken over the second *f*, after which the fifth moves to the augmented fourth while the sixth and second remain stationary. In *c*, $\overset{4}{3}$ is played, after which the third moves to a second while the other tones are held. In *d*, $\overset{7}{\underset{2}{4}}$ is played, followed by a sixth over the held fourth and second. If the seventh lies in an inner part, the appoggiatura must be replaced by a quarter rest. In *e* only the seventh and fifth are taken and succeeded by the chord of the second. To indicate omission of the third, a slur can be placed over $\overset{7}{5}$. In *f*, the preceding $\overset{6}{5}$ is retained and followed by a chord of the second. In *g*, the major sixth is omitted because of the preceding minor sixth, thus leaving only the fifth and second ($\overset{\frown}{\overset{5}{2}}$). The fifth succeeds to the augmented fourth. In *h*, it is best to double the third of the first chord and lead the lower third to the fourth of the succeeding $\overset{4}{3}$. In *i* the common chord or triad in three parts is played because of the preceding three-part setting. Example *j* might very well be accompanied in four parts by playing the appoggiatura; but in a delicate accompaniment, the principal part must not be hampered at a *fermata* from resolving the ornament freely, according to the affect. Furthermore, the accompanist in playing the ornament exposes himself to the risk of performing the release before or after the principal part. We have already seen in the first part of this Essay that the affect at *fermate* calls for great liberty of execution and that, consequently, appoggiaturas are often shortened through the introduction of elaborations and decorations or lengthened and held without further manipulation. In both events the accompanist, as a precautionary measure, should limit himself to a three-part accompaniment or strike the bass note alone and play the chord of the second afterwards. In *k*, where the same example appears with two-part appoggiaturas, the bass alone is taken and followed by a slow upward arpeggiation of the chord of the second. In *l*, the example and its accompaniment are identical, but $\overset{6}{5}$ may be taken as an accompaniment to the appoggiatura.

11. In the examples of Figure 408 the chord of the sixth is retarded by appoggiaturas. In *a*, a four-part realization may duplicate

Figure 407

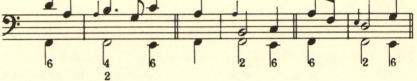

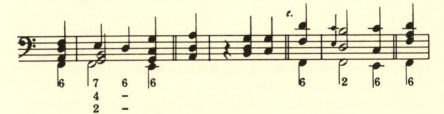

the bass of the triad over *e* or, better, double its third. In a three-part setting only the fifth and third are taken; but if only one part is played by the right hand it should be the third, subsequently held. In *aa* with its allegretto and piano indications, the accompanist may employ either of the illustrated settings. If the passage is to be played loudly, the appoggiatura and its release may be included in the first accompaniment. In *b* only three parts at most should be employed, for the undecorated chords require no more. If the accompaniment must be soft the bass should be accompanied by thirds alone; but the register of the upper part must be watched carefully in order to prevent the fourths which it forms against the principal part from becoming fifths. As indicated in Example *c* and its illustrated accompaniment, it is a matter of opinion whether a minimum of three parts or four are to be employed. Three parts are correct for *d*; but if a delicate accompaniment is decided upon for reasons similar to those addressed to Example *j*, Figure 407, the third alone, subsequently held, should be realized over *g*-sharp. The accompaniments to *e* and *f* are identical with the originals. A very loud accompaniment must be required before a fourth part is taken. In *g* the illustrated accompaniment may be taken if the accompanist decides against $\overset{4}{3}$ as discussed in Paragraph 5.

Figure 408

12. In the examples of Figure 409 the triad is retarded by appoggiaturas. In *a*, $^7_4$ is taken above *c* and succeeded by the triad. But in *b* only $^7_2$ is realized, followed by $^8_3$. Either of the illustrated accompaniments to *c* may be realized. Both have been discussed with their signatures in Chapter V.[5] There are five accompaniments to *d*, of which the last two are the most delicate. They have been purposely assembled here, even though each one has already appeared separately. Nothing should be struck against the chromatic appoggiatura of Example *e;* hence the right hand, its parts replaced by a quarter rest, does not play.

Figure 409

[5] Cf. sections on $^9_4$ and $^5_4$ chords.

13. In the examples of Figure 410 the six-five chord is retarded by appoggiaturas. In *a*, the ornament may be played or only the

Figure 410

sixth taken according to circumstances. The appoggiatura in *b* is best replaced by a rest. In *c* selection of an accompaniment is dictated by the required loudness or softness of the setting. The first of the illustrated accompaniments is best in the notated distribution of tones. The accompaniment to *d* is identical with the example itself.

14. In the examples of Figure 411 the chord of the major seventh is retarded by appoggiaturas. A desire for orderliness has brought about the reappearance of certain examples. In *a* $\frac{8}{4}$ is realized and followed by the seventh while the fourth and second are retained. If it is decided not to play the appoggiatura (since it

Figure 411

forms an empty octave), $\frac{4}{2}$, but nothing less, must be taken. In *b*, $\frac{7}{4}$ alone may be played and held; but if the ornament is included it must lie on top. A three- or four-part accompaniment may be taken in *c*. If the latter is chosen, the notated distribution of tones is best. The most appropriate accompaniment to all of the examples under *d* is the appended one with its quarter rest.

15.   In the examples of Figure 412 the six-four chord is retarded by appoggiaturas. In *a* the accompanist may play the fourth and fifth together or the fifth and the sixth and, in the latter case, resolve the fifth by stepwise descent. If he takes the fourth and fifth the fifth must lie on top. The fourth alone is realized in a soft accompaniment. Example *b* and its accompaniment are identical. If the chromatic appoggiatura in *c* is played, it can be supported quite well by the fourth. Example *d* and its accompaniment are identical. In *e* a triad accompanies the appoggiatura and is succeeded by a chord of the sixth. The same accompaniment is applied to the two-part appoggiaturas of *ee*. In *f* a complete chord of the seventh may be played against the appoggiatura; also $\frac{7}{3}$ or even the seventh alone. Considerations of execution and affect should govern the choice of a complete or incomplete setting. When this example appears with two-part appoggiaturas (*ff*), the realization should be similar to the example itself or to the appended accompaniment. Examples *g* and *h* are similar to *f* and *ff*.

Figure 412

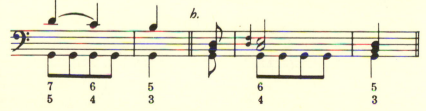

16. The examples of Figure 413, excepting the last, illustrate
the four-three chord retarded by appoggiaturas. In *a* the accompanist may choose three or four parts. In the first of the illustrated
accompaniments, the notated distribution of tones is best. The six-
five chord should be retained in *b*, after which the fifth succeeds
to the fourth. But the appoggiatura may be omitted as illustrated
in the slightly varied example (*bb*). In *c* the chord of the seventh
is taken and its third held while the seventh and fifth descend to
the sixth and raised fourth. In *d*, the accompanist may select the required realization from those illustrated in four, three, and two
parts. A nine-four chord is retarded by an appoggiatura in *e*. Since
the ornament disagrees completely with the figures it is replaced
by a rest.

Figure 413

17.   When the principal part of solos or other pieces requiring a delicate accompaniment has many appoggiaturas in a slow tempo, the accompanist, in order to avoid an obscuring of the melody, should not play all of the ornaments. Those that cannot be readily omitted should be modified by the introduction of partial rests as a means of differentiating the accompaniment from the solo. A momentary withholding of the accompaniment gives the soloist an opportunity to introduce the appoggiaturas alone. This modification, brought about by rests, is increased in effectiveness when the bass maintains a uniform pattern throughout the passage. The beauty and charm of appoggiaturas are most clearly perceptible when performed in this manner. Composers are well aware of the effectiveness of such an execution and often place rests in the bass at the entrance of appoggiaturas. But even when they do not appear

in the left hand they may be interpolated in the right. Rests are good in Figure 414.

Figure 414

18. In the examples under *a* (Figure 415), which are met occasionally, the first of each pair of eighth notes in the bass should be lengthened by the addition of a dot, as shown in the illustrations which follow each passage. A literal performance of the appoggiaturas would prove that the example is wrong, its errors being caused by ignorance or absent-mindedness on the part of the composer. If the ornaments were written out in their correct values, such errors would never arise. Performed as notated, the ornaments clash intolerably with the bass and in so doing lose their essential charm. Even rests for the duration of the appoggiatura are in the main not very helpful, for the right hand must re-enter on the dissonant release, since both appoggiatura and release disagree with the moving bass. The examples suggest no middle parts or, at most, no natural or good middle parts. This is an unmistakable sign of a poor or poorly conceived piece. Those who wish to think correctly about composition must give simultaneous consideration to melody and harmony. It would be difficult to find examples that present so many ready opportunities to write fifths. However, the addition of dots to the bass makes the signatures and the accompaniment natural and simple. In those cases where only one acceptable accompaniment can be realized it has been appended, but it must never lie above the principal part. At times the accompanist will find himself in a situation where nothing may be altered. If in such a situation he finds it impossible to fashion an accompaniment, he must resort to *tasto solo*. In *b*, if an accompaniment were realized from the figures, which unfortunately are found far too often, it would sound exceedingly ugly. In the appended accompaniment the correct figures are given. In the bass of *c* the first eighth note of each bar can be easily replaced by a rest as a means of avoiding the miserable accented fifths.[6] Passages like this can be found in light, present-day Italian works. Experienced accompanists who can and dare make minor extemporaneous corrections in a composition should receive full credit for their deeds, but this should not lessen the composer's responsibility for such blemishes. In our example it is advisable that both hands pause for the duration of the appoggiatura. In *d* the accompaniment is similar to the original. The dissonances are passing and the right hand should be an exact duplication of the motion

[6] Perhaps Bach's own direct fifths of similar type are misprints! Cf. Prussian Sonatas, no. 1, last movt., bars 25–28, 73–76 (Nagels Archiv no. 6).

of the principal part. A composer could only be made unhappy by a strict resolution of the dissonances or the slightest alteration of the sonority or motion of the parts. The last two bass notes carry four parts. In *e* the original may be duplicated or the right hand may rest. In *f* and *ff* the accompaniment must not cross the principal part.

Figure 415

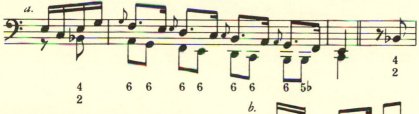

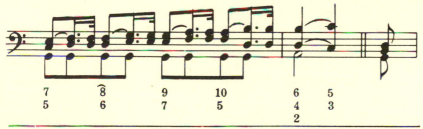

19. The short, invariable appoggiatura is not realized. In fact it calls for no modification of the accompaniment. However, a few examples (Figure 416) in a slow tempo are illustrated here which call for certain precautions.[7] In *a* over the second *g*-sharp only the diminished fifth and third may be played, not the seven-five chord nor the chord of the sixth. In *b* and *c* rests are good. They bring about a rhythmic modification and help to clarify the appoggiatura in *b*. In *c* they are required as a means of avoiding ugly accented fifths between the third above the bass and the principal part. In *d* also, the rests lessen the harshness of the chords which result from the successive appoggiaturas. In *dd*, with its two-part appoggiaturas, the right hand should not play at all, for it is better to omit chords

[7] Note that none of these is written in small notation.

Figure 416

than to strike disagreeable ones. Rests are needed in *e* for the reasons stated in *b*.

20.   Unless an appoggiatura in the bass is set with its own signature, it is accompanied by the chord which belongs to the release.

SYNCOPATED NOTES [1]

1.   Chordal tones are either anticipated or retarded by syncopations.[2]

2.   Slow syncopations which anticipate chordal tones require no modification in the accompaniment. The accompanist strikes the indicated chord over its proper bass note (Figure 417, Example *a*). But when a chordal tone is retarded by syncopation the accompaniment is fashioned in the manner discussed in connection with appoggiaturas. The retarding tone may be played or omitted, the harmony may be reduced to those figures which agree with the retarding and retarded tones (*b*), rests may be inserted (*c*), or the syncopations may be played in their entirety (*d*). In *c* the right hand must leave the keys immediately on the entrance of *d*-sharp in the principal part. If Example *d* is slow and supported by thirds (*dd*) the three-part accompaniment is identical with *dd*. But in other than a slow or, at most, moderate tempo it is accompanied *tasto*

---

[1] Cf. Arnold, *op. cit.,* pp. 431 ff.

[2] *Die Rückungen.* The term has no unequivocal English parallel. *Syncopations* is satisfactory provided that the term is stripped of the narrow meaning that it derives from its use in strict counterpoint, and understood only in the sense of rhythmically shifted notes. Arnold's translation, "Driving Notes," is an old English term. Cf. Arnold, *op. cit.,* pp. 127 ff., Note 2.

solo. Example *d* in a rapid tempo without the supporting thirds is accompanied as illustrated in *e.*

Figure 417

3. Rapid syncopations are never played as such by the accompanist but are supported by chords containing anticipations or retardations according to the nature of the manipulation. Regardless

of whether they lie in the principal part or in the bass, the accompanist plays in an even rhythm as, for example, in Figure 418, where each of his chords has the value of a quarter note. Thus when the bass is syncopated the right hand holds to the rhythm of the bar (*a*).

Figure 418

4.   The accompaniment to chromatic syncopations must be delicate in order to bring them into relief and avoid ugly clashes. In Figure 419, Example *a*, the triad without the octave duplication is taken. In *b* the accompaniment consists of a nice imitation of the chromatic tones (*bb*). Should a fuller setting be required, the intervals of the principal part may be included as indicated in the signatures of *bb*. All of these examples presuppose a slow or, at most, a moderate tempo.

Figure 419

THE DOTTED COMPOUND APPOGGIATURA [1]

1.   This section cannot be read profitably unless the reader is familiar with the earlier discussion which appears in Part I of this Essay.[2] If he is not, much of the present treatment will be incomprehensible and most of it incorrectly understood. Once the nature of the ornament is known it can be seen that it has an important bearing on harmony.

2.   The dotted compound appoggiatura appears only in pieces that are dependent on taste and affect, in which the accompaniment must be especially delicate. The proper chord of a bass note is more retarded by this ornament than by the appoggiatura, for in execution the principal tone of the principal part does not enter until the last short note of the ornament has been played. With respect to loudness and softness, the performance of our embellishment is the same as that of the simple appoggiatura; the retarded principal tone is played softly and the retarding tone loudly. It would seem that these factors would certainly lead to an exact figuring of this originally vocal embellishment. But unfortunately the same complaint must be raised here as in the case of the appoggiatura. Up to now, figurists have not treated the ornament with due care.

3.   In accompanying a bass note over which a dotted compound appoggiatura appears, the same expedients are necessary as were illustrated in connection with the appoggiatura. The indicated harmony may be changed, reduced, or at times even omitted. When the ornament appears in succession with only a few chords, rests are not always good except in the slowest tempo, for the numerous divided beats of the right hand can easily disturb the sustained melody.

4.   Chords that are struck on divided beats usually enter on the second half of the bass note. But if the latter is of great length, its second half is subdivided and the delayed chord enters on the last quarter of its total length.

5.   In the examples of Figure 420 a second above the bass is retarded by our ornament. Again in this section the usual figures which appear with each example have been computed without reference to the ornament; but the correct signatures appear in the illustrations of the accompaniments. In *a* the right hand pauses on

[1] Cf. Arnold, *op. cit.*, pp. 433 ff.
[2] Cf. Ch. II, "The Compound Appoggiatura," ¶ 7 ff.

the first quarter over *b*, and the six-five chord enters later. The correct division of the ornament can be seen in *a* and its usual notation in *x*. Example *b* has the same accompaniment. In *c* the seventh alone is played on the entrance of *b* in the bass, and the third comes in later. In *d* the seventh and diminished fifth are played first and the six-five chord is taken afterwards. In *e*, if a thin accompaniment is called for, the seventh alone is played first and the third afterwards. But if a fuller chord is required, the second is struck with the seventh. These remarks apply to all similar cases. In *f*, the diminished fifth is played alone, the second being included if necessary; the sixth is omitted. In *g* the right hand pauses and then plays the chord of the sixth. In *h* the sixth is played and, if necessary, the second. In *i* the chord of the ninth and *ii* the nine-four chord are struck and followed by their usual resolutions. In a light accompaniment both chords may be omitted and triads played on the second quarter. In *j* and *k* the fifth, alone or in company with the second, may be taken. In addition, *k* may be accompanied by a passing chord of the second followed by a triad in three or four parts, whichever is appropriate (*x*). In *l*, after an eighth rest, the fifth enters alone followed by the third. In *m* there are three possible accompaniments: The seventh may be played alone and succeeded by the augmented sixth and the third; or the second may be struck with the seventh; or $\overset{6}{3}$ may be taken after an eighth rest. All three are good depending on the required volume of the performance and the affect. In *n* it is best to pause and then play $\overset{6}{3}$. In *o* the sixth and the augmented fourth are taken and the third is omitted. In *p* rests in the upper part clarify the ornament. The seventh may enter immediately. In *q* the fifth, alone or with the third, may be struck, depending on circumstances. In *r* the seventh and fourth are played and succeeded by their resolutions.

Figure 420

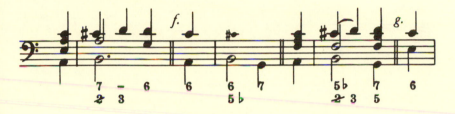

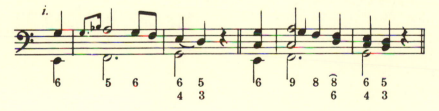

6.   There are other retardations in addition to those on the second. In the examples of Figure 421 the chord of the seventh is delayed by our ornament. Either one of the two accompaniments under *a* may be selected. The first may be realized in four parts. Example *aa*, which consists of rapid notes and does not portray any affect, may be accompanied in four parts. In Example *b* the opening tone of the ornament increases the harshness of a simultaneously realized diminished seventh. Hence, it is better to introduce an eighth rest and strike ♭7 5♭ afterwards in three parts. In *c* the illustrated accompaniment may be used or, in its place, an eighth rest followed by 7 5♭ without the third. The last two examples under *d* sound ugly, although they will be encountered. Our ornament, here, defeats its purpose, which is to provide a pleasant, caressing quality. The passage sounds better without it, and if there is need for an embellishment at all it should be the rapid compound appoggiatura. It is best to accompany our ornament with an eighth rest followed by ♭7 5♭ in three parts. As for the first example (*d*), the triad may also be played in three parts. Example *e* is not good, for the ornament makes the passage sound like a dull succession of sixths and almost obliterates the seventh from which the progression gains its attractiveness. The third should be taken on the entrance of the ornament, and succeeded by the sixth and third on the last quarter. Example *f*, with its preceding diminished fifth, is better. A three-part five-three chord is played on the first quarter and followed by the six-five chord. Either one of the accompani-

Figure 421

ments to g may be used; or as an alternative, pause on the first eighth and on the second take $\overset{7}{5}$ or $\overset{7}{3}$ in three parts. The reason for the omission of an interval from the chord of the seventh is the light manner in which the last note of the ornament and the principal tone are performed.

7.   In Figure 422, Example a, the chord of the second is retarded by our ornament, which owing to its length makes the passage rather unattractive. A shorter compound appoggiatura would be better. The triad is taken on the f and followed by the chord of the second, both preferably in three parts. In b, c, and d the chord of the sixth is retarded. In b the triad is played and followed by the chord of the sixth. Or the third alone may be taken over f, followed by the sixth. In c if the accompanist does not wish to use an eighth rest, he may play either of the illustrated accompaniments. The accompaniment to d is like that to b. The examples under dd, in which a three-part eight-six chord is retarded, are all accompanied in the manner of the appended illustration. In the remaining examples the triad is retarded. In e the accompaniment may be $\overset{7\ 8}{2\ 3}$ in three parts, or an eighth rest followed by a triad. In f the accompanist takes $\overset{7\ 8}{4\ 3}$ in three parts, or pauses for an eighth before playing the triad. In g the chord of the ninth and its resolution are played. But in h the nine-four chord is required, followed by its resolution. In i, $\overset{7}{5}$ and then $\overset{\frown{5}}{3}$ are played.

Figure 422

8.   In Figure 423, Examples *a* and *b,* the six-five chord is retarded
by our ornament. Any of the appended accompaniments to each
example may be used. In the remaining examples the chord of the
major seventh is retarded. The rapid compound appoggiatura is
better than our dotted kind in *c.* The latter sounds empty because
of the long retardation on the octave. It is up to the accompaniment (either of the appended ones may be used) to restore the in-

Figure 423

tended relationships. The accompaniments to *d* and *e* are identical: they may be in three or four parts. In *f* the four-part chord of the major seventh is taken on the entrance of the ornament. In order to separate the sixth from the seventh, the principal part must lie above the accompaniment. In *g* and *h* the rapid compound appoggiatura would be better than our dotted kind. In *g* the ear demands a chord directly on the entrance of the ornament, but in *h* a quarter rest is in order.

9.   In the examples of Figure 424 the six-four chord is retarded by our ornament. In *a* the accompanist may choose any of three accompaniments. The first two may be realized in three or four parts, but the third, which is the lightest, should be left in two. The first cannot be used readily in any but the illustrated disposition. If an

Figure 424

eighth rest over the second *c* of Example *b* is not used, the appended accompaniment should be taken. The rest is required in *c*. The accompaniment to *d* must remain in the notated disposition; otherwise, an eighth rest accompanies the entrance of the ornament. A rest is required in *e* and *f*. But if in *d*, *e*, and *f* the triad on *c* replaces the initial chord on *f*-sharp, the illustrated accompaniments are to be retained.

10.   In Figure 425, Examples *a* and *b*, the five-four chord is retarded. Example *a* is not good, for our long ornament destroys the beauty of the intended dissonance. A short compound appoggiatura would be better. The accompaniment must remain in the notated disposition; otherwise an eighth rest must be introduced over *g*, followed by a complete five-four chord. In *b* the accompaniment is optional; over the note *c*, 4 or $\overset{9}{4}$ may be taken. The same applies to *c*. In *b* and *c* the nine-four chord and in *d* the nine-seven are retarded. The accompaniment to the final example may be in three or four parts. An eighth rest is introduced with the ornament, and succeeded by nine-seven.

Figure 425

THE DOTTED SLIDE [1]

1. All that has been said in the first two paragraphs of the preceding section about prior knowledge of the dotted compound appoggiatura as discussed in the first part of this Essay,[2] the important bearing that the ornament has on harmony, and the consequent need for a clear indication of its presence, applies equally to the dotted slide.

2. Although the dotted slide does not appear as often as the two ornaments that have already been discussed, chords are sometimes more retarded by it than by the others. The affect with which the slide is sometimes performed requires that the initial tone be held beyond its usual duration, with the result that the entrance of the succeeding chord must be delayed by half its notated length and the preceding chord correspondingly prolonged. In Figure 161 there are several examples that have various executions. In the following examples, the bearing of these variants on the accompaniment will be illustrated.

3. In the following cases the accompanist realizes the prescribed signatures, even though they are computed without reference to the ornament. But certain executions of the ornament require slight changes in the accompaniment. These have been noted in the examples. In Figure 426, Example *a,* the accompaniment is not changed regardless of the length of the slide. But in *b* the accompaniment which is appended to each example should be followed if the first note of the ornament is held through part of the succeeding bass note. Although $b(x)$ will be encountered occasionally, the prolonged fourth in the slide does not sound well. If ornament and principal tone together have a value no greater than a quarter note, or if the dotted *d* is retained over the last bass note in the bar, the effect may be acceptable. But it is not good when the division is such that the *f* in the bass and principal part are played simultaneously. The empty octave after an insipid fourth makes an awkward progression. Regardless of the execution of this example, the accompanist takes the sixth and third in three parts or the fourth and third similarly, as illustrated. To do justice to $b(y)$ the empty octave should not be held too long; but if it is, and the *f* enters over *c* in the bass, 4 3 is played instead of the triad.

1 Cf. Ch. VI, "The Dotted Compound Appoggiatura," Note 1.
2 Cf. Ch. II, "The Slide," ¶¶ 10 ff.

Figure 426

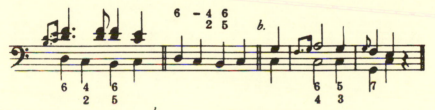

4. In the examples of Figure 427 the accompaniment would sound ugly if it were constructed in agreement with the usual signatures; hence the figures must be changed as indicated in the illustrations appended to each example. The usual signatures appear with the examples. Additional modifications, which are made necessary by an extraordinarily slow performance of the ornament, are shown in the last of each series of illustrations. In *b* the slide mollifies the harshness of a simultaneously realized seventh. Even though this tone appears in the preceding chord, it is well to omit it from the accompaniment to the ornament and to play only the diminished fifth and the third throughout the bar. The examples under *c* have identical accompaniments. In *d* the triad cannot be

played, because of the sixth on which the slide commences. But, since only the triad and no other chord fits the bass, the accompanist must take the one interval, aside from the octave, which the chord of the sixth and the triad have in common, namely, the third; or he may play the bass alone. When a piece begins in this manner, it is best not to play the bass to the ornament. If the slide in *e* is of normal length, that is, if *g* in the principal part enters on the last *b* in the bass, the complete six-five chord should be repeated on the last quarter. But if the initial tone of the ornament is retained over this *b*, the accompaniment must be fashioned in the manner of the appended illustration. Both examples under *f* take the accompaniment which has been placed between them. In *g* the six-four chord must enter on the second quarter of both examples. In *h*, the four-three chord is played and in *i*, a three-part $\overset{\frown}{6}\ 4\ 3$. If, in this last example, the first note of the slide is held beyond its normal length, the third should be played on the last eighth and the sixth repeated at the same point. This is shown in the final illustration.

Figure 427

PERFORMANCE

1. It is wrong to believe that the rules of good performance pertain only to the playing of solos.[1] The material on performance which is contained in the first part of this Essay (to which the reader is referred) must also be observed in certain respects in fashioning

[1] *Handsachen.* Cf. Pt. I, Foreword, Note 2.

an accompaniment. This latter has more elements which are concerned with the rules of good performance than solos have, for an accompanist is responsible for more than a correct realization of a bass; he must make intelligent adjustments with respect to the volume and register of chords. As stated in Paragraph 19 of the Introduction to Part Two, it is required of the accompanist that he fit to each piece a correct performance of its harmony in the proper volume and with a suitable distribution of tones.

2.   The fewer the parts in a piece, the finer must be its accompaniment. Hence, a solo or an aria provides the best opportunity to judge an accompanist. He must take great pains to catch in his accompaniment all of the nuances of the principal part. Indeed, it is difficult to say whether accompanist or soloist deserves greater credit. The latter may have taken a long time to prepare his piece, which, after the present fashion, he himself must compose. Nevertheless, he cannot count on the applause of his audience, for it is only through a good accompaniment that his performance will be brought to life. On the other hand, the accompanist is usually given much less time; he is allowed only a cursory examination of the piece, but must nevertheless support and enhance extemporaneously all the beauty on which so much time and care have been expended by the principal performer. Yet the soloist takes all bravos to himself and gives no credit to his accompanist. But he is right, for he knows that ignorant custom directs these bravos to him alone.[2]

3.   Gratuitous passage work and bustling noise do not constitute the beauties of accompaniment. In fact, they can easily do harm to the principal part by robbing it of its freedom to introduce variations into repetitions and elsewhere. The accompanist will achieve eminence and attract the attention of intelligent listeners by letting them hear an unadorned steadiness and noble simplicity in a flowing accompaniment which does not interfere with the brilliance

---

[2] Francois Couperin in *L'Art de toucher le clavecin* (pp. 44–45) expresses himself just as bitterly: "If it were a question of choosing to bring to perfection either the playing of pieces or accompaniments, I suspect that vanity would lead me to prefer pieces. I admit that nothing is more diverting by itself, nor brings us more into the company of others than to be a good accompanist. But what injustice! We are the last to be praised at concerts. On such occasions the accompanist is regarded merely as the foundation of an edifice which, although it supports everything, is almost never mentioned. On the other hand, those who excel in pieces revel in the attention and applause of the audience."

of the principal part. He need feel no anxiety over his being forgotten if he is not constantly joining in the tumult. No! An understanding listener does not easily miss anything. In his soul's perception melody and harmony are inseparable. Yet, should the opportunity arise and the nature of a piece permit it, when the principal part pauses or performs plain notes the accompanist may open the draft on his damped fire. But this demands great ability and an understanding of the true content of a piece. In truth, it suffices to realize an accompaniment which does nothing more than meet the requirements, whether expressly called for or not, of Paragraph 19 of the Introduction to Part II. To this end we shall proceed to relate these precepts, along with questions of pure style, to the construction of a fine accompaniment.

4.   It is sometimes necessary and not really improper for the accompanist to discuss a piece with the performer of the principal part before its performance and let him decide on the liberties that are to be taken in the accompaniment. Some want the accompanist to be greatly restricted; others not. Since opinion varies so greatly and it is up to the principal part to decide, the safest procedure is to seek a preliminary understanding.

5.   We shall open the subject of performance by discussing volume. Of all the instruments that are used in the playing of thorough bass the single-manual harpsichord is the most perplexing with regard to forte and piano.[3] To make amends for the imperfection of the instrument in this respect the number of parts must be increased or reduced. But care must be exercised to include all necessary tones and avoid incorrect doublings. Some resort to a highly detached touch in order to express a piano, but the performance suffers tremendously by this; and even the most detached staccato performance requires pressure. It is better to reduce the volume by using the right hand less frequently over passing tones. The fine invention of our celebrated Holefeld [4] which makes it possible to increase or decrease the registration by means of pedals, while playing, has made the harpsichord, particularly the single-manual kind, a much-improved instrument, and, fortunately,

[3] Marpurg (*Der Critischer Musicus an der Spree,* 26 August, 1749) writes, "Clever artists . . . know how to deceive the ear at the harpsichord in such a manner that we believe that we hear soft and loud tones, although the quills deliver all with almost equal force."

[4] *Sic* for Hohlfeld. Cf. Part II, Introduction, ¶ 2 and Note 1.

eliminated all difficulties connected with the performance of a piano. If only all harpsichords were similarly constructed as a tribute to good taste!

6. But aside from this invention, the clavichord and pianoforte enjoy great advantages over the harpsichord and organ because of the many ways in which their volume can be gradually changed. The pedal on the last-named instrument does commendable service when the bass is not too rapid; and it can be made more penetrating by means of a sixteen-foot registration. However, rather than mutilate the melody of the bass, the pedal should be omitted when not all of its notes can be played by the feet, and the lowest part played solely by the left hand.

7. There are certain general rules that govern the performance of forte and piano on the organ and the two-manual harpsichord: fortissimo and forte are played on the louder manual. Fortissimo may be attained by duplicating in the left hand all tones of consonant chords, and the consonant tones of dissonant chords when the nature of the bass makes it possible to do so. The low register must be avoided, the doubled tones being placed close to the right hand in such a manner that the notes of both hands adjoin, leaving no intervening space. Otherwise, the rumbling low notes will create a miserable blur. A simple octave doubling of the bass by the left hand also has a penetrating effect; it is indispensable when the notes are not very rapid and are easily played, but yet express a well-defined theme with a fairly wide range. These octave doublings are very good for imitations which are to be loudly performed or for the entrance of fugal subjects. But when a subject or any passage of significance contains lively figuration which cannot be easily executed by one hand in octaves, at least the principal tones should be doubled and the others played simply (Figure 428). The right hand continues with its chords, which cannot be readily omitted from contrapuntal works. In a mezzo forte the left hand may play the bass as written on the louder manual while the right accompanies on the softer. In a piano both hands use the softer manual. A pianissimo can be expressed on this manual, but with reduced parts. In order to practice these precepts the ear must provide constant assistance, for indications are not always exact; moreover, matters of tonal volume depend on the desires of the performer of the principal part.

Figure 428
Allegro

8.   An accompanist must be careful to observe whether the high and low registers of the singer and instrumentalist whom he accompanies are equally loud, and whether his tones are just as clear from a distance as near by. If they are not, he must modify his playing in order not to cover the weak tones with a loud accompaniment. For example, it is common knowledge that the upper tones of the transverse flute are brilliant, but the lower tones not, although otherwise its tones are uniform.

9.   A forte in a tutti passage is to be differentiated from a forte that accompanies a soloist. The latter must be accurately proportioned to the strength of the principal part, but the former can, of course, be much louder.

10.   Modulatory changes are announced by a reinforced accompaniment. Thus, for example, in a fortissimo, a full chord is taken by both hands and arpeggiated rapidly upwards, the bass with its octave and the tones in the right hand being retained (Figure 429, Example *a*). When certain passages are repeated in transposition, double only the principal bass notes in the interests of greater clarity (*b*). But if such passages are so fashioned that they can be played throughout in octaves, differentiate the principal notes through the use of reinforced chords, played, perhaps, by both hands. The notes referred to are those in *c* over which a stroke has been placed. Aside from these cases, chords struck during short rests achieve a distinct weight and greatly assist the other performers, for it is generally acknowledged that, except for the keyboard, such rests present considerable difficulties (*d*). This last suggestion applies to all passages in which short rests appear.

11.   The first note after a *fermata* or general pause is struck loudly. Even if the note is marked piano, a certain weight is given to it by means of a moderately strong attack. Such liberty is especially needed when the bass alone breaks the silence. It is better

Figure 429

to play one note somewhat louder than indicated and thereby retain order in the ensemble, than to observe all indications with exaggerated exactness and fail to give an indispensable signal to the others. There is a possibility that the resultant confusion might ruin a considerable part of a composition, into which the composer may have introduced especially beautiful effects. In such places the instrument that first resumes is the leader, even if it should be the viola.

12.   Notes that introduce closing cadences are played loudly regardless of whether they carry express indications. By this means the principal part is informed that an elaborated cadence is expected, for which the accompanist will halt. This signal is especially necessary in allegros, for elaborated cadences are more usual in adagios. In the latter the principal part often plays the note before the cadence with a retarded forte so that the accompanist may know that the cadence is going to be elaborated.

13.   When the principal part has a long held note which, according to the rules of good performance, should commence pianissimo, grow by degrees to a fortissimo, and return similarly to a pianissimo,[5] the accompanist must follow with the greatest exactness. Every means available to him must be employed to attain a forte

_____
[5] A nuance that was generally called *messa di voce.*

and piano. His increase and decrease must coincide with that of the principal part; nothing more, nothing less.

14. With regard to staccato and legato, it should be observed that in playing chords over a bass which is not marked staccato, it is not obligatory to use a fresh attack on every note. Tones that already lie in a preceding chord and can be carried over to a following one are held. Such an execution, when associated with flowing progressions in the best distribution, gives the accompaniment a singing effect. It is indispensable with legato notes. For these good reasons, most of the examples in the present book should be taught in this manner, so that the student will be introduced early to a sustained delivery and be preserved from the hacked thorough bass which is as frequent as it is ugly. If the tempo is very slow and the instrument so unusually poor that held notes do not last long enough, a fresh attack is, of course, in order. But this expedient does not apply to the organ.

15. The sixteenths in the examples of Figure 430 sound insipid in an adagio if dots are not placed between them. It is advisable to correct this fault in performance. Because proper exactness is often lacking in the notation of dotted notes, a general rule of performance has been established which, however, suffers many exceptions. According to this rule, the notes which follow the dots are to be played in the most rapid manner; and often they should be. But sometimes notes in other parts, with which these must enter, are so divided that a modification of the rule is required. Again, a suave affect, which will not survive the essentially defiant character of dotted notes, obliges the performer slightly to shorten the dotted note. Hence, if only one kind of execution is adopted as the basic principle of performance, the other kinds will be lost.

Figure 430

16. Among the signatures not yet in use are dots.[6] There are just as many grounds for placing them between figures as there are for

[6] Dots in signatures were used much earlier by Johann Staden (*Kurzer und einfältiger Bericht*, 1626). Their use is described in Arnold, *op. cit.* . . . , p. 105. Neither Staden's nor Bach's practice was widely followed.

placing them between notes. It is strange that they have been over-looked despite the fact that our present elegant taste must make the need for them quite obvious. How much unevenness in resolutions can be caused by their absence! And how the performance and character of pieces suffer! How ceaselessly attentive must be the ear that will permit no error! Figure 431 will illustrate my meaning.

Figure 431

17.   When many repeated slurred notes appear in a slow tempo and the lower octave is to be taken with them, the doubling should occur on only the first and third notes, or, in a triplet, on only the first. Furthermore, these tones in the lower octave should be held (Figure 432, Example *a*). But if such repeated notes are to be played

Figure 432

staccato and rapidly so that they sound loudly (*b*), the execution in *c* may be employed However, the passage must not last long, for if it does the wrists will grow stiff and exhausted. Such being the case, it is better to play the notes in the manner of other drum basses as described in the Introduction to Part I, Paragraph 9*a*.[7]

18.   In a concerto or any heavily scored piece, when the bass and ripieno parts hold a tone while the principal part continues with its own motion, even varying it at times with syncopations, it is wise for the accompanist to maintain the beat and guide the other performers by playing a chord with the right hand on the divisions of the bar even though the harmony does not change. If the bass alone has the held note, the accompanist may repeat solely the bass note just as it dies out. But this must not be done "against the beat," as the expression goes. In a duple bar the repetitions may occur at the beginning and in the middle, according to its divisions and the pace In a triple bar only the downbeat is played. But if in the course of a passage a forte appears after a piano, the accompanist should give up the prescribed division and, observing closely, play the bass in the left hand and the chord in the right directly on the entrance of the forte in a fortissimo both hands take a full chord. Here again, because of a lack of signs, the entrance of loud and soft cannot be accurately indicated in the bass or the figures.

19.   When the bass and several other parts perform their notes pizzicato, the accompanist pauses, leaving the passage to the cellos and double basses. But if only the bass is pizzicato the accompanist plays staccato, employing his left hand alone, unless the composer has with good reason placed figures over the notes, in which case the right hand adds its chords, which are also played staccato. When pizzicato and *coll'arco* are interchanged after but a few notes, the one must be sharply distinguished from the other, regardless of whether this is achieved by way of a pause, a detached *tasto solo* or *unisoni,* or a staccato performance of the chords. If during this required detaching the principal part has appoggiaturas, which under normal conditions would be played in the accompaniment, they should be omitted and only the remaining appropriate figures

---

[7] See also Arnold. *op. cit* pp 774 ff., where Heinichen's views are stated and Saint Lambert s mentioned. The latter's opinions appear on p. 196 of that book. Bach is in agreement with both

realized. A legato appoggiatura and release do not go well in a staccato passage.

20.   In slow or moderate tempos, caesurae are usually extended beyond their normal length, especially when the rests and notes in the bass are the same as those in the other parts, or in the principal part in the case of a solo. Great pains must be taken to achieve a uniform performance and prevent anyone's coming in before or after the others. This applies to *fermate,* cadences, etc., as well as caesurae. It is customary to drag a bit and depart somewhat from a strict observance of the bar, for the note before the rest as well as the rest itself is extended beyond its notated length. Aside from the uniformity which this manner of execution achieves, the passage acquires an impressiveness which places it in relief (Figure 433).

Figure 433

21.   Closing trills are often extended, regardless of the tempo. But if a piece has reprises, the extension of trill and accompanying bass note takes place only at the end of the final repetition. By this means weight is added to the conclusion and the audience is made to feel that the piece is about over. This kind of close, however, despite its good uses, cannot be introduced into all contexts. Hence the accompanist must be extremely watchful, especially because some closing trills must be played strictly in tempo due to either the brilliant or the reflective character of a passage (Figure 434, Example *a*). It is understood, moreover, that the accompanist does not hold back when the trill appears over a moving bass (*b*). But if

the last of these bass notes is the fifth of the key, it should be held until it is observed that the principal part or the òther executants are ready to conclude their trill (*c*). The same procedure is to be followed when solely the fifth of the key is repeated in the upper or lower octave after the entrance of the trill (*d*). But if a piece ends without a closing trill, it should be played in tempo without holding back (*e*).

Figure 434

22.[8] When the principal part moves in tenths with a middle part, the accompanist plays thirds in the lower register rather than tenths. This octave doubling of the principal part is better than a similar doubling of the middle part [9] (Figure 435).

[8] From the ed. of 1797.
[9] Which would happen if the thirds were played in the higher octave.

Figure 435[10]

23. In accompanying a solo on a low instrument (i.e. a bassoon, cello, etc.), or an aria for a low voice (i.e., a tenor or bass), close attention must be given to the range of the melody so that the chords will not be placed too high above the principal part. Ordinarily the right hand should not venture above the one-lined octave. If it is necessary to take the chords quite low, they should be reduced, for full chords played low lose their clarity.

24. If a piece for a low principal part has ripieno parts, their range must be carefully observed and the keyboard accompaniment placed in the same register. The melody of the principal part must not be obscured by middle parts which lie above it. Hence composers occasionally place the middle parts first in the low register in the interests of a good setting and variation from the norm, and later, in the ritornello, restore them tellingly to their usual upper register. The accompaniment must be fashioned in conformity with such a procedure. In a following section of this Essay attention will be directed to those cases where different registers are exploited in the interests of refinement.[11] At present it will suffice to remind the accompanist of a point which we have stressed repeatedly, namely, that care must be taken to construct a good melody in the upper part. And in connection with this, the best distributions are to be taken at all possible times. Should it become necessary to ascend above the principal part, tones must be placed in the upper part which move in thirds or sixths with lower middle parts (a), the principal part (b), or the bass (c) (Figure 436).

25. Although it is poor constantly to duplicate the melody of the principal part in the accompaniment, there are times at the beginning of rapid pieces when it is necessary and hence permissible,[12]

10 From the ed. of 1797.

11 Cf. Ch. VI. "Some Refinements of Accompaniment," ¶¶ 9, 10.

12 Cf. J. S. Bach's correction of a figured bass accompaniment by N. Gerber in Philipp Spitta, *J. S. Bach*, Vol. III, Appendix, beginning of second and third movements. However, the beginning of the last movement, allegro, which is similarly constructed, has a four-part chord.

Figure 436

especially when they are in two parts. Both hands thereby pick up the tempo in the same manner,[13] and the audience will not miss any part of the beginning, for it will be uniform and orderly. This is an expedient which may be employed by weak musicians, whether accompanists or leaders, at any point in a composition as a means of retrieving a uniform beat, once it has been lost.

26.   If, as a result of many downward-resolving dissonances, the right hand descends too low, the accompanist must make use of all of the means which have been described in this Essay in order to return gradually to a high register. They are to be employed especially over long bass notes, on the appearance of consonant chords and repetitions of them, over passing tones in the bass, etc. Sometimes, when the principal part is not notated in the continuo part, this procedure is a requirement of good planning, for principal parts and others too, but not the continuo, may leap abruptly from the low to a high register. It can be seen from these cases and others (which, although they defy description, are soon discovered) that the accompanist must practice diligently in order finally to achieve mastery of the registers. I mean here more than the mere ability to realize intervals forthwith in any register; I refer to the artistry with which chords can be used in order to reach a required register, be it what it may. In this connection, a few situations await illustration which expedite a change of register. For example, when the

---

[13] Presumably they play in unison.

bass of a consonant chord leaps an octave the register may be more safely changed through opposite motion than in other leaps (Figure 437, Example *a*). Further, progressions which contain dissonances on divided beats and unprepared dissonances are also convenient, for they leave the accompanist free to select the register (*b*).

Figure 437

27.   In accompaniments, just as much as in solos, a constant playing on the surface of the keys must be avoided; rather they should be depressed with definite force. This will not occur unless the hands are raised somewhat. Provided this is not done in the manner of a woodchopper, the raised hands are not only not wrong, but necessary and good, in that they provide a simple way of indicating the tempo to the other performers and make it possible to strike the keys with proper weight so that the tones will sound clear, in accord with the rules of good performance.

CLOSING CADENCES [1]

1.   My readers will have learned from Part I of this Essay that closing cadences appear both with and without elaborations.[2] In

[1] Quantz furnishes a historical note on the cadenza (*Versuch einer Anweisung die Flöte traversiere zu spielen*, Ch. XV, ¶ 2): "The best information that can be given on the origin of the cadenza is that some years before the close of the last century [the 17th] and during the first ten years of this one, the performer would add a short passage over a moving bass, and append a good trill, at the conclusion of a concertizing part. But between roughly the years 1710 and 1716 the present type of cadenza, during which the bass pauses, became fashionable. The *fermata* or retard *ad libitum* in the middle of a piece may well be of earlier origin." To this it should be added that the cadenza, as discussed both by Bach and by Quantz, is different from the later Mozartean type in that it is not compounded of the thematic material of the main body of the movement which it graces.

[2] Cf. Ch. II, "The Elaboration of *Fermate*."

the present section we shall instruct the accompanist in the treatment of both kinds.

2. On the entrance of an elaborated cadence, the accompanist, regardless of whether a *fermata* appears over the bass, holds the six-four chord for a while and then pauses until the principal part, at the end of its cadenza, plays a trill or some other figure which requires resolution of the chord. At this point the triad is struck at the keyboard, the seventh being taken as a fifth part. From adagio molto to andante the six-four chord and the succeeding triad are arpeggiated upward either slowly or rather rapidly according to the requirements of tempo and affect.

3. When the bass of a piece in more than two parts has a rest after the beginning of an elaborated cadence, the accompanist strikes the triad on the dominant at the conclusion of the cadenza, regardless of whether it is announced by a trill, or lacking this, some other figure, or a pianissimo, and then pauses again if other rests follow.

4. At times the bass enters immediately after the conclusion of a cadenza or a cadence prolonged simply by means of an extended trill. The entrance must be made with firmness and an assured resumption of the tempo as soon as it is observed that the trill in the principal part has been sufficiently extended and if continued may grow weak. The tones which the bass plays must be performed strongly and loudly, even in the absence of an indication, so that the other performers will grasp the restoration of the normal tempo. If such bass notes are marked piano (a case which arises only rarely) at least the first of the tones which precede the approaching bar should be struck loudly, or some motion of the body should be made as a means of indicating the division of the bar (Figure 438).

Figure 438

5. Occasionally the principal performer feels disinclined to elaborate a cadence, despite the presence of a *fermata* over the bass. Such being the case, he motions with his head or body to inform his accompanist. The latter, having observed this, substitutes for

the long, sustained bass note a series of short notes similar to the previous ones, as a means of maintaining good order and letting the other performers hear the uninterrupted continuation of the tempo (Figure 439).

Figure 439

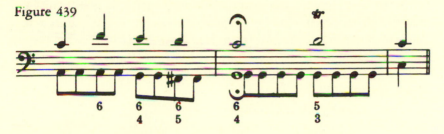

6. When, as in Figure 440, a composer, unmindful of elaborations, allows his bass to continue its motion through a closing cadence, the accompanist holds the first *g* and repeats it on the trill, after which he begins the following bar. This case, which often occurs in allegros, requires an attentive ear.[3]

Figure 440

7. In an andantino and allegretto, the six-four chord and its succeeding triad are arpeggiated upward quickly and held. In allegros, however, the six-four chord and its bass are often quitted abruptly before the cadenza. The principal performer is thus granted the freedom in fiery pieces to begin his elaborations after a very short hold and to introduce many rapid and other notes that are somewhat related to the preceding chord. This need not always be the case, although the six-four chord should be kept as much in mind as possible at the beginning of elaborations. If too narrow limits were placed on the elaborated cadence, the abuse would be more unbearable than it is already, for even now we must patiently endure much that cannot be remedied. Aside from this case, in

---

[3] This is the earlier type of cadenza described by Quantz (*op. cit.*, Note 1). Bach's suggested modification is a means of bringing it up to date.

which the principal performer commences his elaborations immediately after the six-four chord, he usually holds the *fermata* for a while in order not to be too greatly restricted by the reverberating six-four chord, and begins his cadenza only after the sound of the keyboard has almost expired. This execution is good, further, because the listener will be properly prepared, the preceding six-four chord having been well impressed upon his ears.

8.   It is more custom than musical law that leads the concluding trill of cadenzas to be played on the fifth above the bass, or on the sixth, occasionally, in the minor mode. Because the accompanist awaits this trill and strikes his triad directly on its entrance, he must be extremely careful, in the case of cadenzas that are fashioned out of a series of trills, to avoid coming in with his chord on the entrance of a long trill on the third. Such a trill is usually a clear sign that the cadenza is not at all ended, and if he plays the triad prematurely there is a danger that many subsequent tones will appear that disagree with it. A competent principal performer will make every effort in such a situation to shorten and conclude his part so that no one will hear ugly sounds. But accompanists should not provoke such a change. Should it be a performer's pleasure to conclude his cadenza with a trill on the third, it must also be his pleasure to wait for an accompanist who does not play his triad immediately, but listens to the trill for a moment to make certain that the cadenza is going to be ended by it. Some principal performers take satisfaction out of playing a long trill on the fifth, leading the accompanist to enter with his resolution of the six-four chord, after which they continue with elaborations which very often do not harmonize with the resolution. The accompanist should contain himself in the face of so bold a stroke, in the assurance that no justifiable criticism can be directed at him. And he should gainsay his leader neither his pleasure nor the credit for an effective variant.

9.   In the examples of Figure 441, which are found at times, the triad, in a rapid tempo, is struck over the first note and retained until the last appears, at which point the hold occurs. The intermediate notes are played without any change in the right hand, despite the signatures (*a*). In a slow tempo the signatures are modified as indicated in *b* and the hold starts over *d*.[4]

⁴ The reason for the modification is that the first *b* in each example is extended

Figure 441

10. Half cadences, in which there appears over the next to last note of a piece 7 6, or 7 6♯, are no longer as frequent as they used to be. The chord of the seventh is held until the principal performer plays the resolution, which is usually a long trill on the sixth or third over the bass, often in the wake of a few embellishments. The accompanist then plays and sustains a chord of the sixth which may be arpeggiated in a slow tempo (Figure 442).

Figure 442

11. When an aria or other piece in the major mode changes to minor in the second section and a *da capo* follows, the final chord of

Figure 443

beyond its written length and thereby delays the entrance of *a* until the last quarter of the bar. Further, since this is a closing cadence, the *a* is trilled beyond its written length, hence the hold starts on the last quarter. Cf. Arnold, *op. cit.*, pp. 289 and 293, where this deviation is related to eighteenth-century practice.

the second section after the cadenza must be major even in the absence of an indication. Similarly, care must be exercised in pieces in the major mode, for composers sometimes approach the cadenza by way of the minor of the original tonality. Although the major sixth and seventh become minor,[5] the last chord, following the cadenza, must be major (Figure 443).

12.   In Figure 444 the signatures have been constructed without regard to an extended cadence. The accompanist does not play the prescribed progression, but realizes $\overset{6\ 5}{4\ 3}$ over *g* instead of 4 3, once he has observed that the principal part will be prolonged, whether with or without elaborations. All similar cases should be realized in this manner, regardless of their signatures.

Figure 444

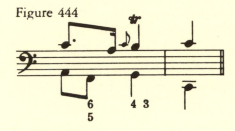

THE FERMATA [1]

1.   We know from Part I of this Essay that *fermate* are performed in various ways.[2] Nothing remains here but to show how the accompaniments are constructed.

2.   The principal part may approach a *fermata* through a leap or an appoggiatura. In both cases the accompanist strikes the held bass note with his left hand alone and, at the end of the *fermata*, repeats it, arpeggiating the appropriate harmony above it. The principal part is thereby granted all possible freedom to execute the hold in any desired manner. Thus, in Example *a*, Figure 445, an artistic increase and decrease in the volume of the trills or held notes will not be obscured by the sound of a chord, and in *b* there will be no interference with the execution of the appoggiatura. If

---

[5] I.e., the six-four chord and the seventh of the chord of the seventh on *f*-sharp.

[1] This is the "retard *ad libitum*" mentioned by Quantz (cf. Ch. VI, "Closing Cadences," Note 1). The present section treats cadenzas that occur in the course of a piece and is thereby distinguished from the preceding section, which discusses only final cadenzas.

[2] Cf. Ch. II, "The Elaboration of Fermate."

other embellishments are introduced, *tasto solo* becomes indispensable. If a forte appears at *a* under the held bass, the right hand may strike its chord, sharply detached or very rapidly arpeggiated, against the bass note.

Figure 445

3. When the principal part broadens before entering a *fermata,* the accompanist must do likewise. The notes in question are marked with crosses in Figure 446. Should the principal performer hold the *a* and then introduce embellishments, the accompanist continues up to the *f*-sharp and remains on it and its respective chord until he observes that the appoggiatura over the following bass note has appeared, whereupon he plays *g* with the left hand alone and at the conclusion of the embellishments repeats it under its arpeggiated triad.

Figure 446

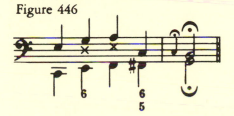

4. With regard to holding and continuing in tempo at *fermate,* the accompanist must follow exactly the precepts that have been stated in Part I of this Essay.[3] The primary concern is that the plain notes as well as the embellishments of the principal part, which precede the *fermata,* harmonize properly and enter simultaneously with the bass and its chords.

5. *Fermate* without appoggiaturas or elaborations, and passages in which the hold is placed over a succeeding rest, are realized forthwith and plainly.

6. Figure 447, similar to Figure 433, is sometimes performed in the manner of a *fermata,* even though none is indicated. For

[3] Cf. Note 2 above.

reasons of affect, the principal part, deviating from a strict beat, moves quite slowly from the appoggiatura *c* into *b*. This note is held, the sixteenth rest is extended, and only thereafter is the tempo resumed. The accompanist must follow this closely and, above all else, avoid a premature resolution of the fifth over the third *f*, for this interval is the same as the appoggiatura. The resolution appears on the divided beat as part of a slowly arpeggiated chord of the second, immediately after the principal part has taken *b*.

Figure 447

SOME REFINEMENTS OF ACCOMPANIMENT [1]

1.   It is worth repeating that the refinements of accompaniment need not consist of inappropriate rapid figuration and embellishments, with which some accompanists distort the melody of the bass. We have already shown quite different ways by which the accompanist may win acclaim, and we shall continue here in a similar vein.

2.   Much will appear here of which the accompanist should not avail himself until his insight has progressed to the point where he knows precisely when and where refinements may be introduced. He should not ascend higher than his wings will carry him.

3.   The most usual expression that is used to describe a good accompanist is, "He accompanies with discretion." Such praise has an inclusive meaning; it amounts to saying that the accompanist can discriminate and hence fashion his setting according to the nature of a piece, the number of its parts, the other performers, especially the principal performer, the instruments, voices, place, audience, etc. With extreme modesty he tries to assist those whom

---

[1] *Von gewissen Zierlichkeiten des Accompagnements.* Much valuable supplementary material is contained in Ch. IV of Arnold, *op. cit.* In addition to generous excerpts from Bach, Arnold includes material from Heinichen (with whom Bach disagrees in certain respects), Geminiani, and Mattheson, and a reference to Saint Lambert as probably the first to discuss such matters as are here treated.

he accompanies to win coveted honors, even though his powers may at times outstrip theirs. He exhibits this modesty especially toward amateur performers. Far from overshadowing them, he allows them to predominate. Moreover, he always puts himself in agreement with the aims of performer and composer; and he seeks to advance and support these aims. He employs every possible nuance of performance and accompaniment, provided it is required by the content of a piece. But in using these nuances he takes every precaution to see that no one will be hampered by them. With this in mind he is not lavish with his artistry, but indulges it sparingly and only when it creates a good effect. He is never afflicted with overbearing wisdom, and he never forgets that he is an accompanist, not a soloist. He knows that a good accompaniment brings a piece to life; that, on the other hand, the best performer suffers immeasurably from an inept accompaniment, for all of his nuances will be ruined by it and, even worse, his appropriate disposition will be destroyed. In short, a discreet accompanist must have a fine musical soul, which comprises great understanding and good will.

4.   To accompany with discretion means also to make adjustments to others' errors and to give way before them. This may occur out of politeness or necessity, as, for example, in the usual performance of a large piece whose numerous players are not of uniform ability. The best leader must give way in such a situation, and so must the accompanist.

5.   To accompany with discretion means moreover to make modifications in accord with certain liberties that are taken at times by the principal performer, who, without its being actually required, may depart somewhat from the written notes in introducing embellishments and variants. A knowing principal performer will do this when he knows that he has an able accompanist, and thus abandon himself with complete freedom to the affect of a piece. Such liberties spring not from faltering uncertainty but from a rational sovereignty and pertain only to details which exact from the accompanist nothing but attentiveness. In Figure 448, Example *a,* the principal performer in introducing embellishments sometimes substitutes one of the illustrated series of signatures for the other. The accompanist must modify his harmony accordingly. In addition to such substitutions, the accompanist must be attentive and give way when embellishments, introduced into the prin-

cipal part, lead to a later entrance of chords than actually denoted
by the signatures (*b*):

Figure 448

6.   Outstanding among the refinements of accompaniment is
parallel motion in thirds with the bass.[2] The right hand here never
restricts itself to a uniformly full setting. A consistent four-part
accompaniment is rare, occurring only in connection with slow
notes (Figure 449, Example *a*), for thirds in a four-part setting cannot be clearly brought out at a rapid tempo. Preferable are three-
part and, in most cases, two-part accompaniments, the latter consisting simply of a bass part duplicated in the third above. From the
examples of Figure 449, it can be seen that a stepwise bass and one
that leaps in thirds are most convenient for this kind of setting. The
accompanist often plays thirds in order to avoid a bad progression.
Some transitional passages can also be accompanied by thirds alone
(*b*). The second accompaniment under *b* must be changed when it
appears in the minor mode (*c*):

Figure 449

[2] This paragraph and those that follow, through ¶ 8, treat in detail a kind of
refinement which is discussed in a textbook used by J. S. Bach, F. E. Niedt's *Musicalische Handleitung*, 1700 (cf. Arnold, *op. cit.*, pp. 213 ff., especially pp. 229-230).
J. S. Bach's copy of the work is reprinted in *The Bach Reader*, W. W. Norton and
Co., 1945. Examples of thirds used in imitative passages appear in Figure 458 here.

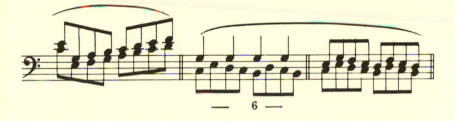

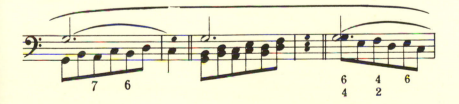

7. When the bass of a two-part piece is so constructed that it might be accompanied in thirds by the right hand, but the principal part has these thirds or some other interval which moves in the same rhythm as the bass, the chords should be played simply and the thirds abandoned. In the first case the accompaniment would duplicate the notes of the principal part, and in the second case the melody of both principal part and bass would be obscured by an interpolated new motion. Consequently, parallel thirds in the right

Figure 450

hand against the bass are best when the principal part has a held
note (Figure 450, Example *a*), a repeated note (*b*), slower notes (*c*),
or notes which are at least again as fast as those in the bass (*d*). In the
last case the precautions which are always followed where thirds
are used must be doubled in order to avoid an ugly clash (*e*) or forbidden progressions (*f*).

8. Sometimes sixths may intersperse with successions of thirds
(Figure 451, Example *a*). Many errors can be eliminated by such an
interchanging of the tones of the middle voice with those of a pass
ing bass (*b*). In *c* with its presto, the first note should not be weighted
down with a full chord; rather the accompaniment should be constructed in the manner of the illustration that succeeds the example.
It is easy to perform, and its speed makes it sound fuller than it
really is. The same applies to *d*. In *e*, where the bass leaps down a
third from a note with the signature 6, and then back again, all
three bass notes may be set with thirds, or the third over the first
note may be held and 6 3 6 taken in the middle part. The illustrations under *f* are noteworthy in that various rhythms, suspensions,
and held notes appear in the principal part. In *g*, a uniform four-
part setting over the rapid bass would be difficult to perform; consequently the setting should agree with the succeeding illustration,
which, moreover, can be conquered by average fingers. It can be
seen from this illustration how easy such rapid basses can be made
by the use of thirds and sixths and, above all, held tones. These latter are good for several reasons; they connect chords, promote the
singing style and, at the same time, are easier and less of a risk than
repeated attacks, which, in a four-part setting at a rapid pace, are almost impossible and ineffective. Example *h* illustrates the use of
thirds in a series of chords of the seventh. Since the accompaniment
is in four parts, the tempo must not be very rapid. In *i* the contrary
motion of the middle part circumvents octaves; hence it is unnecessary to leap to the fifth of the second chord. In *j*, thirds may be played
on every bass note. Because of the chromatic change, motion in
thirds cannot be used in *k;* hence, plain chords are played or use is
made of opposite motion to the bass, starting from the first third.
Under *l* and *m* a series of illustrations appear in which the right
hand moves in a graceful relationship with the bass. Several other
examples can be deduced from those cited in *n*, in which the right
hand plays lower thirds or sixths throughout, as illustrated. This

accompaniment occurs only in two-part pieces in which the principal part is notated in the figured-bass part. Uniform volume in the performance of principal part as well as accompaniment is presupposed.

Figure 451

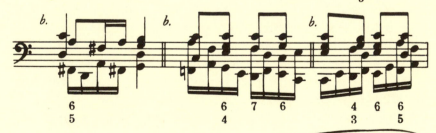

9.   An elegant accompaniment that is not restricted to a uniform number of parts may express certain leaps at times in the right hand. These often provide variety. The most frequent opportunities to indulge this liberty occur in passages which allow for imitation (Figure 452, Example *a*) or which contain held notes (*b*) or repeated figuration with (*c*) and without transposition (*d*). In the case of these last two examples, the justifiable demand of the ear for variation, which is caused by the excessive uniformity of the figuration, can be met very easily and with great freedom by an understanding accompanist. It can be observed generally that those passages which contain only slight changes in themselves are most adaptable to variation in the realization of the chords. But even though pieces which contain such passages can be aided by an elegant, free accompaniment, caution must be exercised to avoid excessive and untimely employment of such nuances.

Figure 452

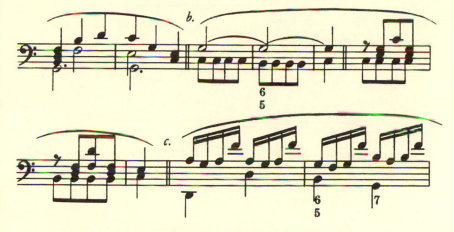

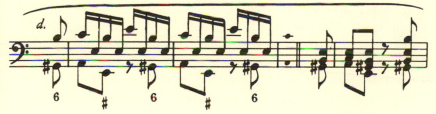

10.   Divided accompaniment, which can be mastered by playing good keyboard music, is often one of the best refinements. In the preceding chapter attention was directed to the occasional necessity of using it. Aside from such cases, it is well known that open harmony is often extremely effective as a contrast to close harmony. For instance, we can see in Figure 453, Example *a*, that the usual construction of the chords sounds disagreeable because of the excessive uniformity of the passage, and, hence, that it is better to use another distribution of the chord of the second, but best to take it in a divided accompaniment (*b*). A repeated passage can be made attractive by the alternation of undivided and divided accompaniments (*c*). In *d* the sixths in the right hand come through better and the melodic progression is made clearer when the lower middle part, which expresses no melody but simply completes the setting, is played by the left hand in a rhythm similar to that of the bass.

Figure 453

11. The filling out of slow notes is one of the refinements of accompaniment. When the tempo is slow, turns may be inserted over the dots in Figure 454, Example *a*. Were this ornament played in the bass also, the effect would be unclear. Because the tone of a harpsichord does not always last long enough, and slow or sustained notes usually sound a bit empty, an accompaniment that fills out

the dotted notes may be chosen for *b* in a slow tempo. This example illustrates a connecting passage during which the principal part pauses, thus requiring the accompanist to find something that will prevent a feeling of emptiness. But when the principal part leads into the following section, playing thirds or such against the bass, the accompaniment should remain simple. Aside from this, how-

Figure 454

ever, transitional passages provide enticing challenges to an accompanist's inventiveness. But his invention must be in accord with the affect and content of a piece. So much the better if part of a preceding phrase can be reintroduced, even if this requires a modification of the bass and a revision of the transition. Rational [8] sovereignty must be granted to the accompanist in this case, so long as the principal part is not thereby hampered. In *c* either of the appended accompaniments may be employed to fill out, but the tempo of the second must be slower than that of the first. The principal part may have a held note or a rest. Should it be desired to let the principal part stand out in *d* (whence the accompanist would avoid a duplication of the tones which enter after the bass), the accompaniment may be either of the settings under 1. But if the principal performer varies this example by holding the third above the bass throughout the bar (2), with or without a trill, the accompaniment under 3 should be chosen.

12. In conclusion, we shall examine some signatures that are used for purposes of instruction in refinements (Figure 455). They are found singly and at times in combination. They are realized after the entrance of the bass or on passing tones and illustrate a decorative progression of one or more parts. The passing dissonances that are created by them do not require resolution. The remaining tones of the preceding chord are held. All of the following examples take a four-part accompaniment except the last four, which are realized in three parts. The signatures that are based on the decorative progressions appear below the notes; the usual signatures have been placed above. Great care must be taken in the use of these harmonic nuances in order to avoid a hampering or obscuring of the principal part.

Figure 455

[8] This sentence appeared in the first ed. as a footnote.

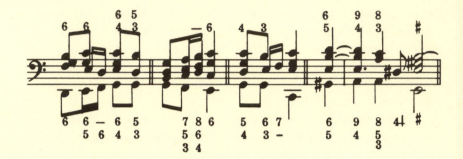

IMITATION

1. Imitation is often used in passages which are varied on their repetition. The accompanist must participate in the variation so

that his imitation will remain clear and lose none of its attractiveness. The accompaniment must be patterned as closely as possible after the leading part (Figure 456).

Figure 456

2.　In these imitations leader and follower must stand in close rapport and be familiar with each other's powers and inventiveness. Otherwise much can be spoiled in performance. Especially important is this to an accompanist who must lead an imitation, for he must know how dependable his follower is in the ways of variation. If he lacks full confidence in the ability of the latter

Figure 457

he must deny himself the delights of variation and play the notes simply. In Figure 457 the bass leads the imitation.

3. If the accompanist has an incompetent leader who precedes him with inept or even wrong variations, he must choose the safest way out and, again, play the notes only as written. He thus frees himself of complicity, knowing well that it suffices to hear a poor variation but once.

4. But if the fellow-performer is sufficiently able and intelligent, the accompanist may rouse him, as always by a good accompaniment, but especially by his varied imitations. And his inventive leading or correct imitating may spark the fire that puts the other in a disposition which he may have lacked previously. However, the accompanist who leads in a variation must allow his follower sufficient freedom afterwards to imitate correctly. The brilliant and the plain must be judiciously alternated, the procedure being in general as indicated in the last paragraph of Part I of this Essay. The accompanist who leads an imitation must pay close attention to the kind of notes, if any, that appear simultaneously in the principal part, so that he may fashion a variation which is sufficiently different from it. And at the conclusion of his variation he must return to a simple accompaniment, so that the principal part's imitation, especially if it is made of many notes, will be distinct. It is just as wrong for both to be noisy at the same time as it is for both to fall asleep. Hence, they should not play out of either ignorance or malice. In the first case they will ruin each other's part unintentionally; in the second, intentionally.

5. The keyboardist who plays in an ensemble with duplicating bass instruments must withhold his varying if he is uncertain that the others will follow him.

6.[1] In some passages which may be accompanied in thirds, it is possible to have the middle part participate in a varied imitation while it moves in thirds with the bass (Figure 458, Example *a*). When the principal performer abandons the simple setting of *b*

---

[1] Note that the preceding paragraphs have dealt exclusively with an imitation specified by the composer, the point of the discussion being the ways in which accompanist and soloist can work hand in hand to vary the prescribed relationships. In ¶¶ 6–7, however, the discussion centers on the ways in which middle and upper parts may be constructed so that they form voluntary imitations of the principal part. Figure 452 provides an additional example. Heinichen's discussion and illustration of such techniques appear in Arnold, *op. cit.*, pp. 383 ff.

in favor of *c*, neither the bass nor the inner part can imitate exactly. It suffices in such a case to contrive an imitation whose figuration is rhythmically the same as that of the leading part while the bass retains its original, or slightly varied, tones.

Figure 458

7. Those who have a good knowledge of voice leading may also substitute for the usual accompaniment a middle part in decorative imitation of the principal part. Passages which express successive chords of the seventh or six-five chords over a leaping bass lend themselves best to this purpose. The tempo, however, must not be very rapid, for if it is there will be a loss of clarity (Figure 459).

Figure 459[2]

SOME PRECAUTIONS OF ACCOMPANIMENT

1. Because most of this subject matter has already been treated in various appropriate places, there remain only a few additional observations on certain cases which call for caution on the part of the accompanist.

[2] The meaning of these examples is not immediately apparent. Note that each long slur encloses three identical bass parts, but that each upper part is different from the others. The first two bars under each slur represent a bass and principal part as written. The next two show the soloist's variation, and the last two the accompanist's imitative accompaniment. In the last two bars under each slur, the first *f* in the upper part is the cued-in initial tone of the soloist. Hence it is not to be played by the accompanist. The figure was apparently misunderstood by Arnold (cf. Arnold, *op. cit.*, p. 387).

2.   When the principal part in Figure 460, Example *a*, lies above
the accompaniment, 7 6 should be taken over *b* instead of 6 alone
in order to avoid fifths. In *b* omit the sixth above *e* and play instead
$\overset{3}{9}$ followed by $\overset{3}{8}$ over the dot. In *c* the sixth over *a* is also omitted, a
$\overset{3}{}$ $\overset{6}{}$
doubled third and fifth being taken in its place. In both examples,
b and *c*, fifths would be created if the accompaniment as distributed
in the example followed the signatures.[1] A similar example appears
in Figure 380. All progressions that contain successive fourths are
dangerous when the distribution of tones is changed. Of course,
the best and safest distribution should be taken whenever possible;
but at times this cannot be done. Such being the case, the accompanist should try to remove the danger and reach another distribution. This may be done by doubling a consonant tone in order to
create a fifth part, or by repeating the chord if the bass note is long
or comprises one or more passing tones. But if none of these expedients can be employed, the signature that causes the trouble must
be omitted. In *d* it is easy to repeat and change the disposition of
the chord over the figuration of the bass, if required, as a means
of averting an error. In *e* the second accompaniment is preferable
to the first when the tones of the principal part are not duplicated
in the upper part. If the first accompaniment lies above the principal part, with which it moves in parallel motion, there will be
fifths.[2] In *f*, where dissonances are resolved by the broken bass, the
accompaniment must be modified in order to avoid ugly octaves on
the divided beats. Hence the dissonances in the signature may be
omitted without scruple. In *g* the extension is omitted which is
often found in the bass at the end of pieces after a prolonged clos-

[1] It is to be gathered from this statement that the context of these examples is
such that the accompanist finds himself obliged to play the opening chords in the
notated distribution. The *Bibliothek der schönen Wissenschaften* . . . (1763), unwilling to make this assumption, writes of example *b:* "Would not this example be
just as melodic if the octave of the first bass note were played by the right hand in
the uppermost part, to be followed by *c*, the sixth of the bass *e*, and then *b* over *g?*
The other two parts which are the upper parts of the example would retain their
places as middle parts. The harmony would be fuller and more agreeable without
an unnecessary doubling of the third [over *e*]." In fact the same holds true when the
first note in the top part is *f*. Obviously, Bach knew this.

[2] There will also be fifths if the second accompaniment lies above the principal
part, for they are caused by the accompanying part that moves from *b* to *a*, present
in both illustrations. In any event, J. S. Bach was not quite so fastidious as his son
in the matter of superficial fifths. See, for example, the fifths between bass and soprano
in the chorale, *Jesu, der du selbst so wohl*, bar 15, caused by the action of a changing
note in the bass.

ing trill. The accompanist therefore ceases at the same time as the principal performer.[3]

Figure 460

3. Resolution of a dissonance can be disregarded when *unisonus* is prescribed, since the unison must be played by both hands.

[3] This refers to the arpeggio in sixteenth notes. It is to be assumed that the reason for this abridgment is the omission of the customary trill or other elaboration in the principal part.

A practiced ear will replace the suppressed resolution with an imaginary one.

4. It is rather usual, though not exactly necessary, that the beginnings of pieces should sound confused. In the interests of orderliness and a precise start, it is customary for even the most experienced performers to show one another the kind of notes each has in the opening bars of a piece. But because there is often no opportunity to examine parts for this purpose, and because a single piece may contain many kinds of tempo, it would be good to notate at least the beginning of the principal part in small notes over the bass. This precaution might also be extended to passages which succeed general rests and *fermate,* especially when the bass does not resume simultaneously with the principal part.

THE NEED FOR FIGURED BASSES [1]

1. We learned in the Introduction to Part II that even when a bass is figured as it should be, a good accompaniment comprises many additional factors. This alone exposes the ridiculousness of the demand that accompaniments be realized from unfigured basses, and makes evident the impossibility of fashioning even a passable accompaniment. In recent times there has been a marked tendency to notate short, essential ornaments and signs that pertain to good performance. If only there were a corresponding decrease in unfigured basses! If only keyboardists were less willing to do everything demanded of them! Other ripienists can complain when they are given an incorrectly written part; but accompanists must be satisfied with a part that is either unfigured or so sparsely figured that the signatures appear only over those notes whose chords are self-evident. In short: It is unjust to expect an accompanist to learn thorough bass both with and without figures.

---

[1] This section expresses strong disagreement with attempts by many theorists to formulate rules for the reading of unfigured basses. Many of these writings were superficial, transitory affairs that were forgotten almost as soon as they appeared, but others came from the principal theorists of the thorough-bass period, starting with Viadana and continuing later with Francesco Gasparini (*L'Armonico pratico al cimbalo,* 1708), Rameau (*Traité de l'harmonie reduite à ses principes naturels,* 1722), and Heinichen (*Der General Bass,* 1728). These are discussed by Arnold in his *Art of Accompaniment from a Thorough-Bass,* pp. 65 ff. and 265 ff. To the list may be added the dissident Bach on his own admission (¶ 2 here) and reluctant promise (Ch. IV, "Intervals and their Signatures," ¶¶ 2–3), largely unfulfilled. Marpurg (*op. cit.,* April 29, 1749) reached conclusions similar to Bach's in answering an inquiry from a young lady.

2. Some have gone to great trouble to systematize the realization of unfigured basses, and I cannot deny that I have undertaken similar experiments. But the more I have thought about it, the richer have I found harmonic usages. And these are increasing to such an extent, what with the fineness of our tastes, that it is impossible to formulate hard and fast rules which will at once shackle free creations and enable one to surmise the optional twists of a composer to whom bountiful nature has granted a glimpse of the inexhaustibility of the art. Even granting that some formulating is possible, are we to rack our memories in learning rules which by their nature must be numerous and not always valid? And having finally learned the given rules, are we then to squander endless time and energy on the mastering of exceptions? Even if we did all of this, the results would be of only small value, for the ablest musician can err when presented with only one alternative, let alone several.

3. And so it remains irrefutable that a correctly figured bass is an indispensable adjunct to the good performance of a piece. The composer who wants his works to be played as well as possible must take every step to reach this end. His notation must explain everything with such clarity that each detail will be understood. This is the very least that can be demanded, for we have stated repeatedly that exact indication of an accompaniment includes something more than signatures. We have even shown that there is still a lack of signs for certain situations. Here we have clear proof that an accompaniment made from no indications at all can only be poor. We already have signatures; let us use them and torture neither ourselves in the formulation of inadequate rules, nor our students in the learning of them. Those who are too indolent or ignorant to figure their basses as required for a good effect should let an able accompanist do it for them.

4. Of course signatures are not needed for every smallest detail, and a figured bass should not be made into a solo. Nevertheless, nothing that is necessary and essential should be overlooked. Many are too sparing in their use of figures because they want to avoid an overtaxing of the accompanist's eyes. But an experienced accompanist can easily scan basses which contain more indications than are usually given, for, long before his study of accompaniment, he had to read in two staves containing many notes, accidentals, and

other superimposed characters. Which is easier to read, this latter with its web of attendant difficulties, or three and, at the most, four figures, one over the other, which he must learn anyway in studying thorough bass, which arise constantly in active accompanying, and which, consequently, cannot be as fearful as many an indolent accompanist seems to believe?

PASSING TONES [1]

1.   It is as necessary to indicate passing tones in most cases as it is to indicate figures. But since figurists do not proceed with adequate care, the accompanist must learn to pick out passing tones (Figure 461, Example *a*) through constant practice and attentive listening. They can be surmised at times from a preceding chord which contains the bass notes that follow it (*b*), and from a required preparation and resolution (*a* and *c*).

Figure 461

2.   Indeed, there are rules for the recognition of passing tones, but they are not always dependable. Because these rules do not provide a solid foundation, because passing tones cannot always be surmised, and, finally, because it is generally acknowledged that there are far more poor than good accompanists, it would be safest to provide exact indications; in fact, too many rather than too few. A good accompanist is not confused by an additional dash, and beginners are much helped by it. It is a tribute to the French to assert that they designate passing tones with great diligence. Usually, they employ a diagonal stroke (Figure 462).

Figure 462

[1] *Von durchgehenden Noten.* Cf. Ch. IV, "Intervals and their Signatures," ¶¶ 69 ff. and Note 9. An exhaustive study of the accompaniment to passing tones in the bass appears in Arnold, *op. cit.,* Chs. XVIII and XIX. Ch. XVIII is concerned especially with Heinichen's rules to which Bach is alluding at the beginning of ¶ 2 here.

3.   Passing tones appear in stepwise and leaping contexts, and are often rather rapid. When they occur singly they are not indicated. Of the stepwise and leaping notes in Example *a*, Figure 463, those on the divided beats are passing. This rule is acceptable: Stepwise passing tones may not be followed by a leap,[2] and the octave of a disjunct passing tone must lie previously in the right hand.[3] Thus, each note in *b* is accompanied, for these conditions are not present. When a bass note, instead of moving down a second (*c*), leaps to the seventh above (*d*), the following tone may be passing, even though its octave is not previously played.[4] Leaps of an octave are not regarded here as leaps but as repetitions. When passing tones appear in succession, the use of a dash is just as necessary as when slow notes pass (*e*).

Figure 463

4.   The following bass notes usually take a chord apiece; half notes in an *alla breve* and a fast three-two whose most rapid notes are eighth; quarter notes in a slow three-two, in the so-called simple meters from allegretto (with nothing faster than thirty-seconds) to

[2] The term "passing tone," in the general sense in which it is used here, includes the neighboring note, complete and incomplete. The incomplete neighbor (échappée) or the incomplete double neighbor would require an extension of the rule here stated, for it is precisely a "passing tone" that is followed by leap. Examples from Heinichen are quoted by Arnold in the reference given in Note 1 here. For the rest, it is of interest to note that the neighbor appears only once in the present section (Figure 464, example *c*) without its being mentioned in the text. However, it is clear that Bach included this element among his "passing tones." For an example see Figure 280, first illustration, and the accompanying text.

[3] In other words, the leap must be to a tone in the prevailing chord.

[4] Bach included this clause because he had just stated that the octave of a disjunct passing tone must lie previously in the right hand. The case under discussion here is, of course, not to be regarded as a type of disjunct passing tone, but as a special kind of conjunct passing tone.

presto, and in three-four and six-four meters in rapid tempos; eighth notes in a four-four meter from adagio to allegretto, and in a slow three-eight, six-eight, nine-eight, twelve-eight, three-four, and six-four. When these latter meters appear in a rapid tempo every group of three eighth or quarter notes has its own accompaniment.

5. Notes that seem to take an accompaniment, but are in fact passing, must, of all notes, carry a dash. Notes that look like passing tones, but are in fact accompanied, must be figured. An incorrect indication of the former is a much greater risk than the latter.

6. The use of thirds alone to accompany passing tones has been discussed in the section "Some Refinements of Accompaniment." [5]

7. Various additional remarks remain to be made on the accompaniment to repeated tones. These remarks will be based on tempos as they are performed here,[6] where adagio is far slower and allegro far faster than is customary elsewhere.

8. From the slowest tempo to largo, quarter notes and greater are played by both hands and held fully. Eighth notes are played similarly but held for only half of their length. All sixteenths are played by the left hand and, in the absence of a staccato sign, are fully held. The right hand accompanies these sixteenths and faster notes with eighths which are held for half of their length, provided that the expression does not require a different execution. When the bass has a continual flow or, at least, great numbers of thirty-seconds or faster notes, the left hand may omit one or more notes, provided that there is an accompanying bass instrument.[7] If there is none, the keyboardist alone must submit to the tortures of this trembling motion. The right hand comes in on only the first note of every triplet of one or two beams. The same procedure holds for each group of three eighth notes or the equivalent in three-eight, six-eight, nine-eight, and twelve-eight.

9. From larghetto and andante to allegro the right hand plays fully held quarters when the bass expresses quarters, eighths, faster notes, and triplets. Longer notes are fully held by both hands.

10. In a siciliana, be it fast or slow, quarter notes and longer are played and held by both hands. The single eighths which follow the quarters are also accompanied by the right hand. In all

[5] In ¶¶ 6–8.
[6] I.e., in Berlin.
[7] As discussed at length in Pt. I, Introduction, ¶ 9a.

other cases, regardless of the construction of the bass, the right hand plays only once for each group of three eighth notes or the equivalent.

11.   From allegro assai to prestissimo the right hand plays either fully held half bars or half-held quarters to an eighth-note bass. Quarters are struck by both hands and held for half their length, and longer notes are fully held. For the rest, I refer the reader to Paragraph 9a of the Introduction to Part I.

12.   These remarks hold only in so far as a change is not called for by signatures or signs of performance.

13.   When transitional passages cannot be accompanied by thirds or other ornamental relationships, as discussed in the section "Some Refinements of Accompaniment," they should be allowed to pass. Extensions at the end of a piece are to be treated similarly.

14.   The examples of Figure 464 will serve to conclude this section. In *a,* an unusual kind of expression (which may be revealed by the content of a piece or the construction of the ripieno parts) sometimes requires a chord on each note instead of the usual omission of a separate chord from the short notes. This occurs frequently in accompanied recitatives. In *b,* the composer who wants a chord to be struck on the note *e* because of the expression, must place the signature 6 over it. In *c,* the passing tones must be accompanied in order to avoid errors. One part may interchange its tones with those of the bass, or the entire chord may be repeated. In *d,* preparation of the seventh above *f*-sharp requires an accompaniment to the passing *e* in the form of a redistributed chord. In *e,* the second chord of the bar is repeated over the passing bass as a means of avoiding too great a descent and averting fifths. The repetition in *f* accomplishes several ends: it avoids fifths when the third of the preceding *a* is doubled; it avoids octaves when $\frac{6}{3}$ is taken over this *a;* [8] and it helps to retain the preceding register. In *g,* where it is presupposed that the notated doubling of the sixth, or a doubled third, is required over the first *f,* the chord of the sixth must be repeated, undoubled, over the passing tones. This enables the *g*-sharp to be accompanied without an impure or awkward progression, and without descending to a lower distribution. In Italian *bel canto,* singers

[8] The octaves would come from the strong beat progression, *a* to *g,* bass and middle voice.

announce the end of a hold by rising and then falling a half or whole step according to the situation, without any slightest trace of an indication. Example *h* illustrates the notation, and *i* the execution of such a hold, although the latter is occasionally written out. This refinement is unaccompanied, the chord being struck but once in order to preserve the clarity of the principal part's rise and fall. Two such cases are illustrated in *j* with their accompaniments. The figuring of these examples, as in *k,* is incorrect. The most experienced accompanist is liable to err if the composer does not figure with sufficient accuracy; especially when he fails to indicate passing tones in passages which seem to contain a resolution (*l*); and similarly, when he fails to figure those notes which look like passing tones but require their own chords (*m*). The accompanist in such cases will be free from blame if, in addition, the principal part is not notated over the bass part. This was stated earlier in Paragraph 5. A good precautionary use of figures over passing tones is illustrated in *n*. The average accompanist is thereby led unmistakably to recognize the necessity of altering his doubling in order to avoid errors. In *o,* a dash is needed as a means of informing the accompanist that instead of repeating the foregoing chord he must play the triad of the following tone on the rest.

Figure 464

CHORDS THAT PRECEDE THEIR BASS NOTES [1]

1.   It is often necessary to strike chords over short rests in advance of their bass notes, as a means of retaining order and winning variety.

2.   Some figurists follow the commendable practice of indicating such chords by placing over the rest the signature or dash that pertains to the following bass note. It would be excellent if everyone adopted such an exact means of indication, for it would lighten the tasks of many accompanists.

3.   In the absence of proper signs, two observations can be made: first, the rests discussed in this section are not greater than a sixteenth rest in an allegretto; second, parts that enter on the rest must agree with the tones of the anticipated chord. The examples that follow will clarify my meaning.

4.   In order to catch the beat with certainty, a beginner is allowed to strike the C major triad over the rest in Figure 465, Example *a*, but an experienced accompanist will let the rest and the first *c* pass, and wait until *e* appears before playing a chord of the sixth in the right hand. In *b*, there is no alternative to taking a chord over the rest, unless half the bar is allowed to pass unaccompanied. In a fast tempo this means of establishing the beat is as much needed by the principal part as by the accompanist. The right hand may enter after the rest only when the tempo is no faster than andante, for otherwise confusion of beats might be caused by it. In *c*, regardless of the tempo, the chord may not be struck before the entrance of the first bass note, since the *f* in the principal part does not harmonize with it. In *d*, the chords must be played in an eighth-note rhythm, even in a slow tempo, in view of the stationary principal part and the syncopated bass. But the first eighth of the bar may be allowed to pass in order not to obscure the usual soft beginning of held notes. In *e*, a chord over the rest is indispensable, especially when this example appears in a piece for a large, heavily doubled orchestra in which all instruments enter on the rapid notes. This situation is commonly found in operas, where it occurs in dramatic, accompanied recitatives, with singers who, because of the constant, vigorous action, may be declaiming upstage, downstage, at the sides, or in the center, with additional

[1] *Von dem Vorschlagen mit der rechten Hand.*

noises to boot. Here the accompanist must take the lead and, on the short rest, give his cue with as heavy an attack as possible. In *f*, where the notes which follow the rest are not as rapid as those in the previous example (although again all parts enter in unison following a general pause), the chord is not played. In *g* with its dotted notes the accompanist again does not play his chord in advance, for there is an appoggiatura in the principal part which resolves only after the first short note in the bass has been played. Anticipatory chords are not employed over bombastic basses in the French manner, for their use would rob the passage of its resolute nature (*h*). Example *i* illustrates a case in which the composer has placed a certain stress on the principal part, and consequently wishes to have this part alone introduce each harmonic change. The accompaniment is appended to the example. In *j* the appoggiatura will not suffer a triad on the rest; hence, it is best to withhold the chord until the second eighth of the bar appears. In *k*, chords are played over the dots and tied notes.

Figure 465

THE RECITATIVE

1.   Not so long ago, recitatives used to be crammed with endless chords, resolutions, and enharmonic changes. A special kind of beauty was sought in these harmonic extravagances, without there being the slightest excuse for their employment. Natural harmonic

progressions were considered too plain.[1] But today, thanks to our intelligent taste, exceptional harmonies are introduced into the recitative only rarely, and then with sufficient motivation. In setting his chords to this present kind, the accompanist need no longer sweat so profusely. Nevertheless, an exact figuring is still required, even when the principal part is notated over the bass.

2. Some recitatives, in which the bass and perhaps other instruments express a definite theme or a continuous motion which does not participate in the singer's pauses, must be performed strictly in time for the sake of good order. Others are declaimed now slowly, now rapidly according to the content, regardless of the meter, even though their notation be barred. In both cases, especially the latter, an accompanist must be watchful. He must listen constantly to the principal performer, and when there is action, watch him as well, so that his accompaniment will always be ready; he must never desert the singer.

3. When the declamation is rapid, the chords must be ready instantly, especially at pauses in the principal part where the chord precedes a following entrance. At the termination of a chord, its successor must be struck with dispatch. Thus the singer will not be hampered in his affects or their requisite fast execution, for he will always know in good time the course and construction of the harmony. Were it necessary to choose between two evils, it would be preferable to hasten rather than to delay. Indeed, the better is always better. Arpeggiation must always be withheld from rapid declamation, especially when there are frequent chordal changes. For one thing, there is no time for it, and even if there were, it might very easily lead accompanist, singer, and audience into confusion. Furthermore, arpeggiation is not required here, for it finds its natural employment in quite different situations, in slow recitatives and sustained chords. In such cases it serves to remind the singer that he is to remain in a given chord, and prevents him from losing the pitch because of the length of the chord, or from assuming that the chord has changed. These fiery recitatives often occur in operas where the orchestra has a wide range with basses playing *divisi,* while the singer declaims upstage, far removed from his ac-

---

[1] This refers to the type of recitative which is discussed in Heinichen, *op. cit.,* Pt. II, Ch. III, pp. 769 ff. He writes: "It is generally known that the recitative, unlike all other styles, has no regular key, but rather casts its tones quite irregularly, moving abruptly and without order forwards and backwards to the most remote keys."

companiment. Such being the case, the first harpsichordist, when there are two, does not await the termination of the singer's cadences, but strikes on the final syllable the chord which should rightly be played later. This is done so that the remaining basses or other instruments will be prepared to enter on time.

4.   The pace with which a chord is arpeggiated depends on the tempo and content of a recitative. The slower and more affettuoso the latter is, the slower the arpeggiation. Recitatives with sustained accompanying instruments are well adapted to arpeggiation. But as soon as the accompaniment shifts from sustained to short, detached notes, the accompanist must play detached, resolute chords, unarpeggiated, and fully grasped by both hands. Even if the score expresses tied white notes, the sharply detached execution is retained. A heavy attack is most necessary in the theater with its memorized recitatives, because of distance. Of course, the accompanist must also play quite softly at times in the theater, but more so in the church or the salon, where noisy, furious recitatives are not quite at home. In recitatives, as much as elsewhere, chords must be expressed in proper volume.

5.   In recitatives with sustained accompanying instruments, the organ holds only the bass, the chords being quitted soon after they are struck. Organs are seldom purely tuned, with the result that held chords, which are often chromatic in such recitatives, would sound ugly and disagree with the other accompanying instruments. It is often difficult in such a case to make an orchestra—which need not be the most wretched—sound in pitch. Arpeggiation is not employed at the organ. Other keyboard instruments do not use ornaments or refinements, aside from arpeggiation, in the accompaniments to recitatives.

6.   In intermezzos and comic operas with much noisy action, and in other works for the theater where the action often occurs backstage, constant or frequent arpeggiation must be resorted to, so that the singer and accompanist will hear each other clearly at all times. When the sense of the words or an intervening action delays the entrance of the singer after the preparatory chord has been played, the accompanist must repeat the chord, broken slowly upward, until he observes that the declaiming has resumed. Unless it is urgently required, neither too little nor too much unfilled space should be allowed in the accompaniment. When recitatives are ac-

companied in detached fashion by instruments other than those that perform the bass part, incidental harmonic modifications, such as 8 ♭7 or 6 ♭5, must be played softly or omitted by the keyboardist when they are indicated solely over the bass part and, as is often the case, appear in succession. Thus, the principal part will not be overaccompanied and the other instrumentalists will hear the singer more clearly, with the result that they will be able to direct attention to their subsequent entrance. The harpsichord, which sounds loud to those close to it, especially when it has a penetrating tone, can easily disrupt orderliness. And sometimes this suppression of tones on the part of the keyboardist adds to the impressiveness of words that the composer wishes the singer to recite while the instruments, for good reasons, remain silent. When there is vigorous action upstage, this precaution is even more essential, for the singer's tones will often pass unheard over the orchestra pit, which is rightly constructed on a lower level than the parterre.

7. When a singer departs from the written notes, it is better to strike a full chord repeatedly than to play isolated tones. In recitatives, correct harmony is the primary factor; hence singers should not be expected to sing only the written notes and no others, especially in indifferent passages. It suffices if they declaim within the confines of the proper chord. Of course, a single tone may be struck in the case of a remote modulation. If the singer is of sufficient ability, there is no need for alarm when he chooses to sing Example *a* of Figure 466 in the manner of Example 1 or 2. Causes for such changes may be a desire to find a convenient register, or

Figure 466

simply forgetfulness. In memorizing their parts, singers often confuse the many similar patterns of recitatives, for they are more impressed by the underlying harmony than by the melody. I would be less apt to forgive an accompanist who hesitated over a modification of *a,* than I would one who was startled by *b,* a case that arises occasionally, where signatures might be lacking, the tempo might be rapid, and half of the passage, perhaps directly after the beginning, might be written on a new stave.

8.   On the last arpeggiation of a preparatory chord it is wise to place in the upper part the singer's initial tone. Thus placed it will be most clearly heard and thereby ease the singer's task. Rather than abandon such an expedient, it would be better to tolerate certain irregularities when they cannot be avoided, such as disrupting the preparation of a dissonance, or placing its resolution in the wrong part, the aim being simply to reach the required distribution quickly. However, it is often easy to do this by means of a rapid arpeggio without indulging in such liberties.

9.   When, in a recitative with accompanying instruments, the bass enters ahead of the other performers after a cadence or pause, the keyboardist must strike his chord and bass note strictly on time, with a sure, full attack, especially when the orchestra is large (Figure 467, Example *a*). However, if all the instruments attack simultaneously, the keyboardist does not anticipate, but signals with his head or body in good time so that all will enter together (*b*). In Example *c,* a six-four chord is required over the first bass note,

Figure 467

preferably with the octave on top. At the rest, the seventh and fifth of the same bass note are played. Finally, I refer my reader to Figure 465, Example *e*, and the accompanying text. Many similar examples can be deduced from this one.[2]

CHANGING NOTES [1]

1. The meaning of changing notes or irregular passing tones has been stated in Chapter IV, Paragraphs 73 to 78. Their indication is most essential, for beginners in thorough bass cannot easily surmise their presence.

2. Some figurists place signatures over the note against which the chord is struck; others over the following note. The first procedure is not bad, especially when the signatures are familiar ones (Figure 468, Example *a*), and ambiguity can be thereby avoided (*b*). But aside from these considerations changing notes that are identified by means of an oblique stroke make for simpler signatures, and the accompanist is spared his hesitancy over the unusual successions which are often expressed by the other method of indication. Nevertheless, it is advisable that the student of thorough bass become completely familiar with the figures, for both methods of indication are still in use.

Figure 468

instead of

3. Irregular passing tones are to be regarded as appoggiaturas that have been written out and given an exact length. Against these appoggiaturas the right hand plays the chord that pertains to the following bass note. Hence if a tone that is normally consonant forms a dissonance against the changing note with which it is struck, it retains its original freedom and character. It may be doubled (Figure 469, Example *a*), and it requires neither preparation nor resolution (*b*). Similarly, dissonances do not forsake their basic ways when they are momentarily made into consonances by the action of a changing note in the bass (*c*).

[2] Cf., par ex., J. S. Bach's *Werke*, 11.2, pp. 164 ff.
[1] See Ch. VI, "Passing Notes," Note 1.

Figure 469

4. In the presence of changing notes a triad cannot be denoted by the absence of a signature; at least one of its figures must be posted (Figure 470, Example *a*). When an oblique stroke is succeeded by chords which require doubling (*b*), or may be taken in more than one way (*c*), the accompanist must make provisions in advance for correct construction, especially when there is the possibility of committing an error (*d*).

Figure 470

BASS THEMES

1. Good bass themes, evolving naturally, are among the master touches of composition. The famous *Kapellmeister* Telemann and Graun,[1] along with my deceased father, have given us many excel-

[1] Of the three Graun brothers, two, Johann Gottlieb and Carl Heinrich, were active at the court of Frederick the Great. The former was *Konzertmeister* and the

lent examples of such themes which may well serve as perfect
models. Such a theme should have a manly bearing which on occasion may express tones from other parts of its proper chords, by
breaking to them or by other means of melodic elaboration; but
without sacrifice of its essential nature. Its lineaments must not be
extravagant. Cadences and caesurae must be basslike; at least, the
chords of the latter should sound natural. Appoggiaturas should be
introduced into such a bass with great caution, in order not to disturb the flow of the harmony. Moreover, these and other melodic
complements are better left to the principal part, for this latter
would be entirely too much restricted, if the bass were made to
share equally in all garnishments. Rather, the bass should be accompanied by chords that express numerous, effective suspensions
which allow for the construction of a singing principal part. Especially recommended are progressions which permit the use of many
seventh, five-four, six-five, and ninth chords, as illustrated by the
plain basses of Figure 471.

Figure 471

latter, to whom Bach is referring, *Kapellmeister*. Since Bach refers to him as still
alive, or at least since his death in 1759 is not mentioned, it would seem that the
present section was written before this year.

2. Composers commit two kinds of errors in constructing bass themes. At times they want a shower of beautiful song, although it is inappropriate; they proceed to write a fine melody, which, however, is high and lacking in bass progressions, and which itself allows for the addition of a good bass. An experienced accompanist, instead of seeking an upper melody to this kind, might find it easier to give the theme to the right hand and, in the left, improvise a bass that provides the proper harmonization. The other kind of error concerns themes which are too dry. Here, the composer wishes to avoid the faults mentioned above and to provide every opportunity for the elaboration of the principal part; consequently he writes a good, forthright, simple, but inexpressive bass. However, this latter kind has in its favor the fact that it permits an adroit accompaniment, whereas the former very often defies the superimposition of chords.

3. Bass themes are performed either in unison by all instruments or by bass instruments alone. In the first case the accompanist omits chords and plays the written notes in octaves with both hands. But should the composer place signatures over the bass advisedly, they must be realized. The reason is that the suspensions which may be thereby introduced need to be heard, for they will not only not obscure the theme but make it more lucid. Some themes are so constructed that an understanding listener is only half satisfied in the absence of an accompaniment, for in his inner comprehension the harmony is inseparable from the tones that he hears. In such a case the organ provides the best accompaniment, not only because of the suspensions but also because of its penetrating volume. The second case mentioned above, which is found in vocal and instrumental pieces, requires a chordal accompaniment.

4. There are two accompaniments to bass themes, and they provide an able accompanist with excellent opportunities to display his skill. Those who possess an adequate knowledge of composition and whose propitious inventive faculties are tempered by good judgment may fashion an additional melody to be played by the right hand instead of the usual accompaniment when the principal part pauses or performs plain, sustained notes. This melody must agree with the content and affect of a piece and never hamper the principal part.

5. But those who lack the ability to do this should adhere to the

prescribed harmony and perform it in keeping with the rules of good performance, their attention being directed to the selection of the best progressions and distributions and the construction of a singing upper part.

CHAPTER SEVEN

IMPROVISATION

THE FREE FANTASIA [1]

1

A FANTASIA is said to be free when it is unmeasured and moves through more keys than is customary in other pieces, which are composed or improvised in meter.

2. These latter require a comprehensive knowledge of composition, whereas the former requires only a thorough understanding of harmony and acquaintance with a few rules of construction. Both call for natural talent, especially the ability to improvise. It is quite possible for a person to have studied composition with good success and to have turned his pen to fine ends without his having any gift for improvisation. But, on the other hand, a good future in composition can be assuredly predicted for anyone who can improvise, provided that he writes profusely and does not start too late.

3. A free fantasia consists of varied harmonic progressions which can be expressed in all manner of figuration and motives. A key in which to begin and end must be established. Although no bar lines are employed, the ear demands a definite relationship in the succession and duration of the chords themselves, as we shall see later, and the eye, a relationship in the lengths of notes so that the piece may be notated. Therefore, it is usually assumed that such fantasias are in a four-four meter; and the tempo is indicated by the words which are placed above the beginning. We have already learned of the fine effect created by fantasias in Chapter III of Part I of this Essay, to which I refer my reader.[2]

4. Especial care must be exercised in improvising at the harpsi-

[1] A detailed study of this chapter and an analysis of the appended Fantasia (Figure 480) appear in Heinrich Schenker's *Das Meisterwerk in der Musik*, Drei Masken Verlag, München 1925, Vol. I, p. 11 ff.

[2] In ¶ 15.

chord and the organ; at the former, in order to avoid playing in a single color; at the latter in order to sustain constantly and hold chromatic progressions in check. At least, they should not be introduced sequentially, for the tuning of the organ is very rarely tempered. The best instruments for our purpose are the clavichord and pianoforte. Both can and must be well tuned. The undamped register of the pianoforte is the most pleasing and, once the performer learns to observe the necessary precautions in the face of its reverberations, the most delightful for improvisation.

5.   There are occasions when an accompanist must extemporize before the beginning of a piece. Because such an improvisation is to be regarded as a prelude which prepares the listener for the content of the piece that follows, it is more restricted than the fantasia, from which nothing more is required than a display of the keyboardist's skill. The construction of the former is determined by the nature of the piece which it prefaces; and the content or affect of this piece becomes the material out of which the prelude is fashioned. But in a fantasia the performer is completely free, there being no attendant restrictions.

6.   When only little time is available for the display of craftsmanship, the performer should not wander into too remote keys, for the performance must soon come to an end. Moreover, the principal key must not be left too quickly at the beginning nor regained too late at the end. At the start the principal key must prevail for some time so that the listener will be unmistakably oriented. And again before the close it must be well prolonged as a means of preparing the listener for the end of the fantasia and impressing the tonality upon his memory.

7.   Following are the briefest and most natural means of which a keyboardist, particularly one of limited ability, may avail himself in extemporizing: With due caution he fashions his bass out of the ascending and descending scale of the prescribed key, with a variety of figured bass signatures (Figure 472, Example *a*); [8] he may interpolate a few half steps (*b*), arrange the scale in or out of its normal sequence (*c*), and perform the resultant progressions in broken or

[8] The upper signatures of the first ascending and descending scales in major and minor agree with the older *Regola dell' Ottava*, which was used by 17th- and 18th-century theorists to instruct beginners in the proper chord for each step. It was adopted with minor variants by Rameau, Heinichen, and Mattheson, among others. It formed the first step of instruction in the reading of unfigured basses, and was

sustained style at a suitable pace. A tonic organ point is convenient for establishing the tonality at the beginning and end (*d*). The dominant organ point can also be introduced effectively before the close (*e*).

Figure 472

---

recommended by Heinichen as the basis of improvised preludes. The great variety of Bach's other signatures and his failure to mention the *Regola*, which he must have known, indicate that he placed little weight on it. Cf. E. Borrel, *Tribune de St. Gervais*, XXI, p. 175.

8.   When the performer is allowed adequate time to have attention directed to his work, he may modulate to remoter keys. But formal closing cadences are not always required; they are employed at the end and once in the middle. It suffices if the leading tone (*semitonium modi*) of the various keys lies in the bass or some other part, for this tone is the pivot and token of all natural modulation. When it lies in the bass, the seventh chord, the chord of the sixth, or the six-five chord is taken above it (Figure 473, Example *a*); it may also be found in chords which are inversions of these [4] (*b*). It is one of the beauties of improvisation to feign modulation to a new key through a formal cadence and then move off in another direction. This and other rational deceptions make a fantasia attractive; but they must not be excessively used, or natural relationships will become hopelessly buried beneath them.

Figure 473

9.   In a free fantasia modulation may be made to closely related, remote, and all other keys. Strange and profuse modulations are not recommended in pieces performed in strict measure, but a fantasia with excursions to only the next related keys would sound too plain. From a major key the acknowledged closely related keys are on the fifth degree with a major third and on the sixth with a minor third. And from minor keys modulation is made chiefly to the third degree with a major third, and the fifth with a minor third. But the remote keys in major are on the second and third degrees, both containing minor triads, and on the fourth with a major triad. The

---

[4] *Die Verkehrung jener Accorde.* Inversion here has a looser meaning than it had in Rameau's systematic use of the term.

remaining keys are the most distant; any of them may be included
in a free fantasia even though they stand in varying distances from
the tonal center. This may be seen from an examination of the well-
known Circle of Keys.[5] But in a free fantasia, the performer should

Figure 474

[5] The Circle of Keys was invented by Heinichen, on his own testimony, after hearing from Kuhnau about Kircher's method of moving through keys by fourths or

feel no further obligation to the circle, for it would be wrong in this kind of piece to make a cyclic excursion through all twenty-four keys. I shall leave it to the private study of my reader to practice modulation to the closely related keys by means of a skillful attaining of their leading tones, and shall illustrate here, in the interests of brevity, a few particular ways to approach these keys gradually (Figure 474). We own immediately to the possibility of there being many other ways to accomplish these ends; after the initial bass note, any other may be taken be it what it may. We are stopped from attempting a clear proof of this statement by the threat of diffuseness.

10. The examples of Figure 475 illustrate slightly circuitous ways of modulating from a major key to the distant keys which were mentioned in the preceding paragraph. The close relationship of A minor to C major relieves us of the repetitious task of furnishing similar examples for the minor mode. When it is desired to reach distant keys conclusively instead of simply passing through them, it is not sufficient merely to reach for the leading tone in the belief that once it is found the goal will have been attained and that further ends may then be sought immediately. The ear, in order not to be disagreeably startled, must be prepared for the new key by means of intermediate harmonic progressions. There are keyboardists who understand chromaticism and can explain their progressions, but few who know how to employ it agreeably, relieved of its

Figure 475

fifths. Mattheson was scornful of Heinichen's Circle and offered an improved construction. Both are reproduced in Arnold, *op. cit.*, pp. 268 and 277.

crudeness. It should be observed generally, but particularly in the following examples, that the progressions which introduce remote modulations from an established key must be played more broadly than those of other modulations. By transposing these and the preceding examples, and combining them, a facility in modulation will eventually be attained.

11.   As a means of reaching the most distant keys more quickly and with agreeable suddenness no chord is more convenient and fruitful than the seventh chord with a diminished seventh and fifth, for by inverting it and changing it enharmonically, a great many chordal transformations can be attained. And when there is added to this all the harmonic artistry and rare progressions of the preceding chapters, what an endless vista of harmonic variety unfolds before us! Does it still seem difficult to move wherever we will? Hardly, for we need only decide how circuitous or direct our route must be. There are only three of these chords of the diminished seventh with their three superimposed minor thirds, for the fourth chord is a repetition of the first, as illustrated in Example *a*, Figure 476. It would take too long to demonstrate all of the opportunities afforded by this chord to guide harmony in any conceivable direction. The possibilities of experimentation which are suggested under *b* must suffice for the present. We repeat that such chromatic progressions are to be played only occasionally, with artistry, and broadly.

Figure 476

12.   The beauty of variety is made evident in the fantasia. A diversified figuration and all attributes of good performance must be employed. The ear tires of unrelieved passage work, sustained

chords, or broken chords. By themselves they neither stir nor still the passions; and it is for these purposes that the fantasia is exceptionally well suited. Broken chords must not progress too rapidly or unevenly (Figure 477, Example *a*). Occasional exceptions to this precept may be introduced with good effect into chromatic progressions. The performer must not break his chords constantly in a single color.[6] Both hands may progress from the low to the high register, or the left hand may do this alone while the right remains in its own register. This kind of execution is good on the harpsichord, for out of it there comes an agreeable alternation of devised forte and piano. Those who are capable will do well when they depart from a too natural use of harmony to introduce an occasional deception; but if their attainments are insufficient for the purpose, they must enhance by means of a varied and fine execution of all manner of figuration those harmonies which sound plain when performed in the usual style. Most dissonances may be doubled in the left hand. The ear will accept the resultant octaves in full harmony; fifths, however, must be avoided. The fourth, when it appears in company with the fifth and ninth, and the ninth at all times are not doubled.

Figure 477

13. All chords may be broken in many ways and expressed in rapid or slow figuration. Broken chords in which principal as well as certain neighboring tones are repeated (Figure 478, Example *a*) are especially attractive, for they are more varied than a simple arpeggio where the tones are played successively just as they lie under the hands. In the interests of elegance the major (*b*) or minor (*c*) second may be struck and quitted below each tone of a broken triad or a relationship based on a triad. This is called "breaking with *acciaccature*." In runs, the normal tones of chords are filled in. These runs may pursue a direct course through one or more octaves upward and downward. But an agreeable variety arises out of repetitions (*d*) and the insertion of foreign tones (*e*). Runs which contain

[6] I.e., at a fixed dynamic level.

many half steps require a moderate speed. All manner of groupings
may be alternated in the course of runs (*f*). The triad and its inversions may be expressed by the same run, and also the seventh
chord and its inversions. At times the augmented second is avoided
in chords which contain that interval (*g*); but in certain figurations
it is acceptable (*h*). Imitations in parallel and contrary motion can
be very well introduced into various parts (*i*). The chromatic chords
which were discussed in Paragraph 11 are best fitted to slow figuration and the expression of profound feeling, as we can see in the final
movement of the last Lesson in Part I of this Essay.[7]

14. In order to provide my reader, through continuous ex-

Figure 478

7 Sonata VI, third movement. Cf. Pt. I, Introduction, Note 17.

amples of all kinds, with a clear and useful conception of the construction of a free fantasia,[8] I refer him to the Lesson mentioned in
the preceding paragraph, and Figure 480. Both are free fantasias;
the first is interspersed with much chromaticism, while the second
consists largely of natural and usual relationships. The framework

[8] This paragraph will serve to illustrate Bach's views on musical analysis as described in a letter to a friend, dated from Hamburg, Oct. 15, 1777 (cf. Bitter, *Carl
Philipp Emanuel Bach und Wilhelm Friedemann Bach, und deren Brüder*, Vol. I, p.
348): "In my opinion, in instructing amateurs, several things could be omitted that
many musicians do not, indeed, need not know. A most important element, analysis,
is lacking. True masterpieces should be taken from all styles of composition, and the
amateur should be shown the beauty, daring, and novelty in them. Also, he should
be shown how insignificant the piece would be if these things were lacking. Further,
he should be shown how errors, pitfalls, have been avoided, and especially how far a
work departs from ordinary ways, how venturesome it can be, etc."

of the latter, in the form of a figured bass, may be found in Figure 479. The note values have been written as accurately as can be expected. In performance each chord is arpeggiated twice. When the second arpeggio is to be taken in a different register by either the right or the left hand, the change is indicated in the fantasia. The tones of the slow, fully gripped chords, which are played as arpeggios, are all of equal duration, even though restrictions of space have necessitated the superposing of white and black notes in the interests of greater legibility. At the beginning and end (1) of the sketch (Figure 479) we find long extensions on the tonic harmony. At 2 there is a modulation to the fifth on which the performer remains for some time until at x he moves toward E minor. The three tones at 3, joined by a slur, elucidate the transition to the repetition of the chord of the second which is regained by means of an interchange of chordal tones. This transition is performed in slow figuration, the bass being purposely omitted from the piece as performed. The change from the seventh chord on b to the following chord of the second on b-flat is an ellipsis, for normally the six-four chord on b or the triad on c would precede the chord of the second. The chord at 4 seems to point toward D minor, but the minor triad is omitted and instead the chord of the second (5) with an augmented fourth is played on c as if the plan were to move on to the G major chord. Instead, the G minor chord is played at 6, to be followed largely by dissonant relationships leading back to the principal tonality, on which the fantasia ends over an organ point.

Figure 479

(6.)   (1.)

Figure 480

Allegro

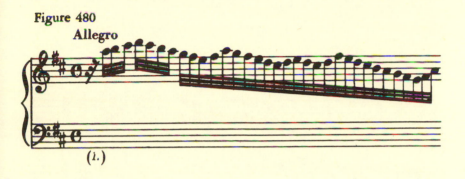

(1.)

BIBLIOGRAPHY

Aldrich, Putnam. *The Principal Agréments of the Seventeenth and Eighteenth Centuries,* Diss. unpublished, Harvard University, 1942.

Allgemeine musikalische Zeitung, Leipzig, 1798–1848. Numerous articles and notices pertaining to C. P. E. Bach, especially in the early volumes.

"Anmerkungen über einige der besten musikalischen Schriften von der Ausführungskunst insonderheit Hrn. C. P. E. Bachs Versuch über die wahre Art, das Clavier zu spielen," in *Bibliothek der schönen Wissenschaften und der freyen Künste,* Vol. 10, Pts. 1 and 2, Leipzig, 1763–64.

Arnold, F. T. *The Art of Accompaniment from a Thorough-Bass,* London, 1931.

Bach, C. P. E. "Einfall einen doppelten Contrapunct in der Octave von sechs Tacten zu machen ohne die Regeln davon zu wissen," in *Historisch-Kritische Beyträge,* F. W. Marpurg, ed., Vol. III, Pt. I, pp. 167 ff.

Bitter, C. H. *Carl Philipp Emanuel und Wilhelm Friedemann Bach, und deren Brüder,* 2 vols., Berlin, 1868.

Burney, Charles. *A General History of Music,* Vol. IV, London, 1789.

Burney, C. *The Present State of Music in Germany, The Netherlands and United Provinces,* London, 1773.

Cherbuliez, A. E. "C. P. E. Bach," in *Allgemeine Musikgesellschaft in Zürich, Neujahr Blatt,* 1940.

Chrysander, F. "Eine Klavierphantasie von Karl Philipp Emanuel Bach," in *Vierteljahrschrift für Musikwissenschaft,* No. 7, 1891.

Clercx, S. "La forme du Rondo chez Carl Philipp Emanuel Bach," in *Revue de musicologie,* Vol. XVI, pp. 148 ff., Paris, 1935.

Cramer, C. F. See *Magazin der Musik.*

Cramer, H. "Die Violoncell Kompositionen P. E. Bachs," in *Allgemeine Musik Zeitung,* Jahrg. 57, pp. 316 ff., Berlin, 1930.

Cramer, H. "Einiges zu P. E. Bachs Kammermusik," in *Allgemeine Musik Zeitung,* Jahrg. 57, pp. 519 f., Berlin, 1930.

Daffner, H. "Die Entwickelung des Klavierkonzerts bis Mozart," in *Publikationen der Internationalen Musikgesellschaft, Beihefte,* zweite Folge, Heft IV, pp. 24 ff., Leipzig, 1906.

Dannreuther, E. *Musical Ornamentation,* London [n.d.]

Daymond, E. R. "Carl Philipp Emanuel Bach," in *Proceedings of the Musical Association, 33rd Session,* London, 1907.

Dolmetsch, A. *The Interpretation of the Music of the XVIIth and XVIIIth Centuries,* London [n.d.]

Essner, W. "Über die Kunst Carl Philipp Emanuel Bachs," in *Zeitschrift für Musik,* No. 103, pp. 922 ff., 1936.

European Magazine, London, October 1784. (Contains a sharp attack on Bach and his music.)

Flueler, M. *Die norddeutsche Sinfonie zur Zeit Friedrichs des Grossen,* Berlin, 1908.

Hamburger unpartheiischer Correspondent, Hamburg. (Contains articles and notices pertaining to C. P. E. Bach during the period of his Hamburg residence, 1767–88. Cf. No. 7, January 11, 1773.)

Hase, H. von, "Carl Philipp Emanuel Bach und Joh. Gottl. Im. Breitkopf," in *Bach Jahrbuch,* 1911.

Hoffmann, H. *Die Norddeutsche Triosonate des Kreises um J. G. Graun und C. Ph. E. Bach,* Kiel, 1927.

Jalowetz, H. "Beethovens Jugendwerke in Ihrem melodischen Beziehungen zu Mozart, Haydn, und Ph. E. Bach," in *Sammelbände der internationalen Musikgesellschaft,* Jahrg. 12, 1910–11, pp. 417 ff.

Kaswiner, Salomon. *Die Unterrichts-Praxis für Tasteninstrumente, 1450–1750,* Diss. Vienna, 1930.

Kothe, W. *Friedrich der Grosse als Musiker,* Braunsberg, 1869.

Magazin der Musik, ed. C. F. Cramer, Jg. 1–2, Hamburg, 1783–87; Jg. 3, Copenhagen, 1789. Numerous references to Bach.

Mersmann, H. "Ein Programmtrio K. P. E. Bachs," in *Bach Jahrbuch,* 1917.

Miesner, H. "Aus der Umwelt Ph. E. Bachs," in *Bach Jahrbuch,* 1937.

Miesner, H. "Ungedruckte Briefe von Philipp Emanuel Bach," in *Zeitschrift für Musikwissenschaft,* XIV, pp. 224 ff.

Miesner, H. *P. E. Bach in Hamburg* Leipzig, 1929.

Miesner, H. "Ph. E. Bachs musikalischer Nachlass," in *Bach Jahrbuch,* 1938, 1939, to be cont.

Monthly Musical Record, Vol. 12, No. 142, pp. 222 ff., London, 1882.

Monthly Musical Record, Vol. 20, No. 239, pp. 242 ff., London, 1890.

Müller, F. "Carl Philipp Emanuel Bach," in *Zeitschrift für Musik,* No. 105, pp. 1323 ff., 1938.

Nohl, L. *Letters of Distinguished Musicians,* London, 1867. Translation by Lady Wallace of *Musiker Briefe,* Leipzig, 1867.

Opel, R. "Über Beziehungen Beethovens zu Mozart und zu Ph. Em. Bach," in *Zeitschrift für Musikwissenschaft,* V, 1922–23, pp. 30 ff.

Reichardt, J. F. *Briefe eines aufmerksamen Reisenden die Musik betreffend,* Pt. 1, Frankfurt and Leipzig, 1774, Pt. II, Frankfurt and Breslau, 1776.

Reichardt, J. F. [?]. *Musikalischer Almanach (Alethinopel)* [n.p.], 1782.

Reichardt, J. F. *Musikalischer Almanach,* Berlin, 1796.

Reichardt, J. F. *Musikalisches Kunstmagazin,* Berlin, 1782, 1791.

Riemann, Hugo. "Die Söhne Bachs," in *Präludien und Studien,* Vol. III, Leipzig, 1901.

Rochlitz, F. "Karl Philipp Emanuel Bach," in *Für Freunde der Tonkunst,* Vol. IV, pp. 177 ff., 3rd ed., Leipzig, 1868.

Rolland, R. *A Musical Tour through the Land of the Past,* New York, 1922.

Salzer, F. "Über die Bedeutung der Ornamente in Philipp Emanuel Bachs Klavierwerke," in *Zeitschrift für Musikwissenschaft,* XII, 1929–30.

Schenker, H. *Ein Beitrag zur Ornamentik,* Universal Edition No. 812, Vienna, 1908.

Schenker, H. "Die Kunst der Improvisation," in *Das Meisterwerk in der Musik,* Vol. I, Munich, 1925.

Schering, A. "Carl Philipp Emanuel Bach und das 'redende Prinzip' in der Musik," in *Jahrbuch der Musikbibliothek Peters,* Vol. 45, 1938.

Schmid, E. F. *C. P. E. Bach und seine Kammermusik,* Kassel, 1931.

Schmid, E. F. *Die Vorfahren Haydns*, Wien, 1932.

Schmid, E. F. "Haydn und Ph. Em. Bach," in *Zeitschrift für Musikwissenschaft*, XIV, pp. 299 ff., 1931–32.

Schneider, M. "Bach-Urkunden," in *Veröffentlichungen der neuen Bachgesellschaft, Jahrg. 17, Heft 3*, Leipzig, 1917[?].

Sincero, D. "La Sonata di F. E. Bach," in *Rivista musicale*, Vol. 5, pp. 677 ff., 1898.

Steglich, R. "K. P. E. Bach und der Dresdener Kreuzkantor Gottfried August Homilius im Musikleben ihrer Zeit," in *Bach Jahrbuch*, 1915.

Stilz, Ernst. *Die Berliner Klavier Sonaten zur Zeit Friedrichs des Grossen*, Diss. Berlin, 1930.

Terry, C. S. *Origin of the Family of Bach Musicians*, Oxford, 1929.

Thouret, G. *Friedrich der Grosse als Musikfreund und Musiker*, Leipzig, 1898.

Thouret, G. *Friedrichs des Grossen Verhältnis zur Musik*, Berlin, 1895.

Torrefranco, Fausto. *Le origini italiane del romanticismo musicale*, Turin, 1930. Pp. 388–433, *La fortuna di P. E. Bach*, appear also in *Rivista musicale*, Vol. 25, Nos. 3–4.

Uldall, H. *Das Klavierkonzert der Berliner Schule*, Leipzig, 1928.

Vrieslander, O. *Carl Philipp Emanuel Bach*, Munich, 1923.

Vrieslander, O. "*Carl Philipp Emanuel Bach als Theoretiker*," in *Von neuer Musik*, Cologne, 1925.

Wien-Claudi, Hertha. *Zum Liedschaffen C. P. E. Bach*, Reichenberg, 1928.

Wotquenne, Alfred. *Catalogue thématique des oeuvres de Charles Philippe Emmanuel Bach*, Leipzig, 1905.

Zelter, Karl Friedrich. *Karl Friedrich Christian Fasch*, Berlin, 1801.

Books that Live

The Norton imprint on a book means that in the publisher's estimation it is a book not for a single season but for the years.

W·W·NORTON & CO·INC·